T0331039

'Kukard does two astonishing things with this book: first, she takes something we hate (stuckness) and makes it our generative friend, and second, she tells us how to move through stuckness to fluidity. The combination will help anyone who has ever tried to get themselves or someone else unstuck. A groundbreaking and helpful book!'
Dr Jennifer Garvey Berger, CEO Cultivating Leadership, author *Unlocking Leadership Mindtraps*

'A useful process-based book, which will help practitioners and coaches to rethink their own, as well as their clients and colleagues, historical mental models, old ways of being and the resulting behaviours. It encourages readers to practically adapt for contextual relevance, and facilitate more authentic enactment(s) in the world.'
Prof Kurt April, Allan Gray Chair, University of Cape Town

'The Cycle of Stuckness is a cycle of loss and healing, rupture and repair. Loss and grief are natural companions as we grapple to merge our past into the creation of our new lives. Kukard describes how we coaches can flow with these cycles whilst supporting our clients to do so as well. It is a manual for the cycles of life and a must-read for all coaches.'
Dr Helena Dolny, author of *Before Forever After*, leadership coach, co-founder of LoveLegacyDignity (NPO encouraging life-affirming conversations about mortality)

'Leaders get stuck in outdated ways of responding to the world. As a result, they make decisions that do not create the outcomes their organisations need. Leadership 'stuckness' has become an epidemic with severe negative impact for the future of human life on earth. This excellent book helps those who support leaders, their coaches. It describes coaching practices that unlock stuckness in leaders and help them to be more agile and responsive to an increasingly complex context.'
Prof Richard Calland, sustainability strategist, governance professor, political commentator, author

The Art and Joy of Stuckness for Coaches and their Clients

This book offers an existential understanding of the process of stuckness, exploring how we can soften stuckness and become more fluid in our work and world.

We can't avoid getting stuck, it's a vital part of learning and healing, but we can develop the skills to get stuck less painfully and recover quicker. When we do this, stuckness can enable us to process our pasts and incubate our futures. Illustrated by relatable, global case studies, this book will help readers and coaches understand and work with stuckness in their own and their clients' lives.

Based on the author's doctoral research and extensive experience as a coach and coach trainer globally, this book is valuable to coaches, therapists, and human development practitioners.

Dr Julia Kukard is a well-seasoned leadership coach and existential psycho-therapist from Cape Town, South Africa, working with leaders across the world. She has a doctorate in existential psychotherapy, an MBA, MA, and BA Hons. Her passion for exploring stuckness grew from personal experience, as well as through partnering with leaders grappling with complex, volatile, and sometimes inhumane corporate and institutional worlds.

The Art and Joy of Stuckness for Coaches and their Clients

Julia Kukard

Routledge
Taylor & Francis Group

LONDON AND NEW YORK

Designed cover image: 'Where inner and outer worlds meet', Oil on canvas, 2019 by Peter van Straten

First published 2025
by Routledge
4 Park Square, Milton Park, Abingdon, Oxon OX14 4RN

and by Routledge
605 Third Avenue, New York, NY 10158

Routledge is an imprint of the Taylor & Francis Group, an informa business

British Library Cataloguing-in-Publication Data
A catalogue record for this book is available from the British Library

Library of Congress Cataloging-in-Publication Data
Names: Kukard, Julia, author.
Title: The art and joy of stuckness for coaches and their clients / Julia Kukard.
Description: Abingdon, Oxon ; New York : Routledge, 2025. | Includes bibliographical references and index. |
Identifiers: LCCN 2024035907 (print) | LCCN 2024035908 (ebook) | ISBN 9781032881195 (hbk) | ISBN 9781032881171 (pbk) | ISBN 9781003536253 (ebk)
Subjects: LCSH: Personal coaching. | Leadership.
Classification: LCC BF637.P36 K85 2025 (print) | LCC BF637.P36 (ebook) | DDC 658.3/124--dc23/eng/20241024
LC record available at https://lccn.loc.gov/2024035907
LC ebook record available at https://lccn.loc.gov/2024035908

ISBN: 978-1-032-88119-5 (hbk)
ISBN: 978-1-032-88117-1 (pbk)
ISBN: 978-1-003-53625-3 (ebk)

DOI: 10.4324/9781003536253

Typeset in Times New Roman
by SPi Technologies India Pvt Ltd (Straive)

Contents

Acknowledgements	*viii*
Preface	*ix*

1 The world of stuckness and fluidity   1

2 Understanding stuckness and fluidity from a human
and a coach perspective   8

3 Understanding stuckness and fluidity from a context perspective   24

4 An incomplete wound finds a salient context and hope blossoms   33

5 Losing *self* and sedimentation   39

6 Experiencing contextual shifts (or not)   57

7 Losing *others* and isolation   62

8 Losing *meaning* and falling into the void   79

9 Experiencing stuckness   93

10 Growing *self*   101

11 Growing relationships with *others*   124

12 Growing *meaning*   136

13 Experiencing fluidity   146

14 Growing in spite of our *self*   153

Index   *161*

Acknowledgements

It takes a village to write a book, here is my village.

This book is for my dad, Richard Frank Paul Kukard, believer of dreams and creator of adventure. May I stand proud in at least one of your shoes. It is also in memory and appreciation of my beloved friends, Chantel Christiansen, Val Tapela, Nina Goldschmit, Dawn Gotkins, and Alison Nortje, lovers of life and love.

Thank you to the generous participants in my doctoral study, I can't say your names but you know who you are.

Thank you Simon Kettleborough, who nudged me when my feet dragged, my heart sank, and my lip hit the floor. Sometimes I was too timid to act or take myself seriously. Without you, this book would be dead in the water, a floppy drive on a dusty shelf. Thank you for backing this project and me.

Thank you to the brilliant brains of Aephoria Partners which I have been picking for the past 14 years, most notably Lucille Greeff, Christo van Staden, Ntyatyambo Sibanda, Cherise Nortje, Makgathi Mokwena, Kate Clayton, and so many others who came to my conversations on stuckness early on and helped me think through ideas in a practical way.

I thank my readers, Ntyatyambo Sibanda, Kate Johns, Lindy Ackerman, Cheryl Frank, Chantelle Wyley, Roland Cox, Melanie Dugmore, and my sister Nicola Smith for their encouragement and guidance. Nicola in particular, who found the wherewithal to read and comment encouragingly on a very early and very bad draft.

Thank you Russel Brownlee, my writing coach, who gave me pure encouragement and enthusiasm. I desperately needed this to get through the early days of writing this.

Thank you Dr Jennifer Garvey Berger, Prof Kurt April, Prof Richard Calland, and Dr Helena Dolny for endorsing this book, I experience great joy from knowing this work is backed by such great thinkers and humans.

For my darling Oli, wise and strong beyond his years, thank you. And to Justin Cooke who has been calm and helpful during tricky times, thank you too.

Lastly, Joanne Wilson, I thank you for the high jinks and low jinks, may we always have the jinks.

Julia

Preface

We may as well drop our pretences right now and just get down to business. You know that I know that you get stuck sometimes, otherwise you would not be eyeballing this preface. I know that you know that I do as well, otherwise I would not have written this book.

What you may not know is that getting stuck is a normal pursuit for humans and can and should be joyful and life-affirming. It is nothing to be ashamed of, it is not an indictment of your character, but rather a reminder to be ambitious about your life. There are very few reasons to foreclose on living life fully, and getting stuck is not one of them.

It took me eight years of graft to realise this. My road was winding, tangential, with many moments of apparently terminal impasse that ironically enough gave this exploration more life. I was not in control, stuckness had a mind of its own. It would not go to bed after I completed my doctorate in existential psychotherapy (in stuckness). It would not go to bed after I had applied the learning in my day job (coaching, coach training, and supervision, leadership development). I doubt it will go to bed now or maybe ever. It is a joyful meta-narrative that keeps on giving.

Like all healing and learning cycles, the Cycle of Stuckness describes how we move into new ways of being, grow and learn, peak and plateau, get stuck and exasperated, and then learn into, around, and beyond our stuckness. We never complete the cycle fully, just find a good enough place to hang out for a bit before we start all over again. This is the nature of things, and we should not fixate on trying to be fluid all the time, this is just another version of stuckness.

Working with stuckness is paradoxical, the more you go one way on a continuum the more you find yourself at the other pole. We need both parental poles to birth a new us. So, when all that you can see is dead ends, don't forget to listen for the accompanying sound of life waiting to burst forth and enlarge your world. This is the gift of stuckness.

Chapter 1

The world of stuckness and fluidity

It took me a very long time to understand how I was the biggest obstacle and danger to living the life I wanted. In fact, I had to do a doctorate on stuckness to understand just how systematic I was at skulking in a holding pattern, squandering my gifts, and spoiling my opportunities. I had (and still have) too many historical ideas and assumptions interfering in my reading of and response to the world. For me, there was (and can still be) too much living in the world as I am in it and too little living in the world as it is. This is the heady and unctuous recipe for stuckness.

I am wondering if you are the same? Are you filled with compulsions and behaviours informed by past lives that don't get you anywhere, or that threaten to alienate you from those whom you love most. Compulsions that distract you from the important things in life like loving people, raising children, doing good work, and having a meaningful existence. Compulsions like winning arguments or being the best, or saying *fuck you* to the world, or even yourself. If you have even the slightest inkling that you may suffer these same conditions, even just temporarily, then you are in the right place, and I would love you to settle into these words.

This book is for coaches and their clients. Generally, each chapter covers humans or clients first, thereafter focusing specifically on how the issue in discussion lives in coaching.

My existential orientation?

In this book I use an existential frame for coaching. This is a philosophical approach drawing on the work of existential thinkers ranging from Kierkegaard in the early 1800s to more contemporary writers such as van Deurzen, Yalom, Spinelli, Fanon, Biko, Vos, Mbembe, and more. The existential house is large and inclusive, making space for philosophers, traditional healers, body workers, liberation theorists, theologians, and others.

There are, however, some commonalities across this variegated field. These include the honouring of individuality, authenticity, and a focus on individual agency, freedom, and responsibility. An existential orientation normalises

DOI: 10.4324/9781003536253-1

some types of anxiety and acknowledges the importance of *others* and *meaning*. It also has a deep appreciation for the paradoxical and absurd aspects of our humanity.

Taking our freedom is a central focus within this orientation and in this book as well. In fact any study of stuckness is always a study of freedom. This is a book about inner freedom; yours, mine, and ours. Outer freedom is a different issue, referring to political, social, and economic freedoms. Outer freedom is not enough on its own. Without the agency and direction enabled by inner freedom, we will struggle to act in the space opened by outer freedom; we remain just as trapped as before. We need both, as both are key to changing the world outside. Both types of freedom are a personal and political act.

What is stuckness and fluidity?

Simply put, stuckness is a developmental impasse where we live in a holding pattern. This holding pattern does not relate to our current context, thus our actions have no traction. We can feel defective, isolated, and meaningless.

Fluidity is a state where are present in our current context. We can see the world as it is and adapt to it. Our actions have traction and we feel relevant, useful, and meaningful. It is not a mad state of wild flip flopping. Rather it is a more thoughtful state of moving fluidly and responsively within a context, and working with it to sculpt the life you desire.

Stuckness occurs on many levels: individually, in pairs, small groups, and bigger groups. Stuck people, pairs, and groups are like black holes in a solar system; they suck energy in and this impacts on the performance of the whole system. Stuck humans (individuals, pairs, groups) slow down and stabilise change on a systems level, as well as preserve a level of continuity. So on a systems level, there is a value to stuckness.

What causes stuckness and fluidity in humans?

The developmental impasse that causes stuckness is precipitated by an historical wound requiring completion. It finds a salient environment in which to do this. While we are living in our historical wound we disengage from the world, our broader *self*, *others*, and *meaning*.[1] We develop a host of unproductive behaviours that reinforce our stuckness. As a result we become frozen, unable to move forward.

We are going to get very detailed and technical about this in the next chapters, so don't worry if it sounds confusing here.

For us to live in a more fluid connection with the world, we have to deal with the incomplete wounding. This happens as we work directly with our wounding and reconnect to our *self*, *others*, and what is meaningful for us. Working with our grief and shame precipitates the change towards fluidity.

What are the burdens and benefits of being stuck?

I don't need to get technical when reminding you what the problem of being stuck is. We have all experienced times in our lives when we feel stuck, frustrated, lost, and in pain. When we get stuck, our actions have little traction, people can leave us, and we wonder what the *meaning* of our life is. We can get stuck for a long time and this can become very demoralising. We can get stuck in addictions, grieving, shame, ways of doing our job, ways of being in our relationships, and more.

When we are stuck, we stop reading the world as it is, and read it instead as we are in it. We confuse what is being looked at with what is doing the looking.[2] This means we are acting on the wrong information, hence we become disconnected from the world and our *self*.

Stuckness is like stress, good for you in the short term, but bad for you if it lingers, when the medication becomes the disease. Stuckness only lingers as long as it takes to deliver its message of redemption, digestion, or vision. Thus the sooner we get this message, the sooner we can move into a more fluid state of existence.

Getting stuck is part of being human and, as I will show you, can be very helpful in kickstarting our lives, if we know how to work with it. We all want to live lives where we love people, feel loved, accomplish things, and feel satisfied – stuckness can enable this. It is our opportunity for redemption, the digestion of our pasts, and the incubation of our futures. This is what this book is about, how to live your life more fully and contribute to the world in a way that is uniquely yours.

What causes stuckness in coaches?

All coaches get stuck from time to time and we do this in many ways. We can get stuck in our own lives and in our coaching practice, as well as more temporarily in sessions. Sometimes, quite often, stuckness in a coach's own life bleeds over into their practice.

Coaches get stuck the same way other people do. However, there are additional ways that relate to our professional practice, including projecting our *self* onto our client. We get stuck when we are not connected to our *self*, *others*, and *meaning*. We will explore this more deeply in the following chapters.

What are the burdens and benefits of stuckness for coaches?

When coaches get stuck, we can lose our relationship with clients and generate less effective outcomes. Sessions can become characterised by an unsatisfying lack of movement and cycling around a stalemate. The coach may also start to doubt their own skills, feel less satisfied with their work, and even wonder if this really is the career for them.

Stuckness can help coaches kickstart their learning and growth, get us out of bad habits, and enable better outcomes for clients. Stuckness brings the gift of more life to our work, something we all want.

The cycle of stuckness

Stuckness occurs as a cycle through which we tumble many times over the course of our lives and careers. The aim of this cycle is to complete the healing of our inner worlds so that we can see our context better and respond more adaptively to it. It begins with an initial wounding that interacting with a context leads to the loss of *self*, *others*, and *meaning*. When we experience these losses, we become rigid and inflexible, stuck in an outdated way of being. The context is a critical player in this drama and it changes all the time, demanding that we respond accordingly. When we can't do this, because we are disconnected from our *self*, *others*, and *meaning*, we become stuck. To move towards fluidity and inner freedom, we need to explore the original wounding/patterning and rebuild our *self*, *others*, and *meaning*. This is true for both people and coaches.

The diagram below provides a description of this cycle. You will be referred to this diagram many times in this book, so don't bother to memorise it at this point, just notice that it's a cycle and that we are always tumbling in it.

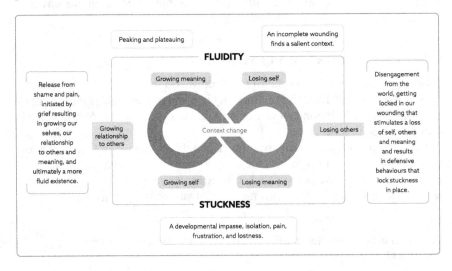

This is a coaching book for coaches who work with a client group that tends to be relatively healthy. However, as we know, this is not always true. The Cycle of Stuckness could be useful with clients suffering from addiction and other mental illnesses, but these may require different kinds of interventions.

My sense is that the model can be used to understand broader mental health issues, but that coaches tend not to work in this area.

What can this book do for you?

This book won't save you from getting stuck in your life – and anyway, staying fluid all the time is also a form of stuckness. This book also won't stop you from getting stuck in your coaching practice.

What this book can offer us is new ways to think about our life, help us identify where we tend to get stuck, and remind us that it is always the right time to work on our *self*. Lastly, this book can help us to have less pronounced peaks and troughs of stuckness, and increased fluidity in our own lives and coaching practice. In this way, it can help us weather our life and work more easily and more productively.

My now-to-be-revealed secret objectives for this book are to remind you and me to be our *self*, that our value to the world is derived from being our full *self*. It is also to remind us to be in the world more, engage with *others* and the dynamics of the world, and allow these forces to pull us towards growth. And lastly, that part of being our *self* is to remember that we are human and that our own humanity is a source of all humanity and thus vital to our survival as a species. You see, I cannot be human without you being human too.

How to read this book?

Inner freedom and stuckness can be rather serious topics, but it does not have to be that way. I would be most pleased if you took the freedom to actively choose your learning style and to read this book as you desire. Start at the back, middle, or front – it's all fine by me. And please don't settle into reading in a fixated, disciplined, and focused kind of way. Do it more like drifting in and out, in between this world and your inner world. If you relate to having ADD, or have been stoned or anaesthetised, feel free to draw on this experience as a way in. The idea is that a part of you sees and reads the words in this book, while another part of you wanders in and out of your own memories or fridge, garden, subway, or office block There is absolutely no requirement for focus or your full attention. It may, however, be useful to aggregate all parts of yourself at some point, but it doesn't matter whether it's in your memories, this book, or the fridge. Also, please feel free to rail against my words, force your interpretation in where you see fit, or mutter, 'WHAT THE FUCK', from time to time.

I have used some theory, hopefully not too much, as well as case studies, some of which are cautionary in nature while others offer more positive learning. These case studies are simplified versions of what happens to stuck people and I am hoping you can see this simplification. Human transformation is more complicated in real life. I am also hoping that you can see yourself in the case studies and apply the learning to your life and work.

My credentials

This book comes from my personal experiences with stuckness, my practice as a coach and psychotherapist, and my doctoral research.[3] Over the years I have become quite an expert in stuckness, both personally and professionally.

My academic research provides a rigorous backbone for this book. My own experience as a stuck person and a coach allows me to describe the lived experience of stuckness.

Many of the ideas in this book do not come from me. I have in fact pilfered plenty of ideas from multiple illustrious authors, chewed them up, mixed them together, and presented them in the stream of my words. The endnotes indicate their origin and also where you can find more information.

Lastly, it would be useful to know my methodological framework so you can see where I am coming from in this book. I have received training in integral, ontological, gestalt, developmental, and somatic coaching; however, my primary orientation and first love is existential coaching. I am also trained as an existential psychotherapist.

Unusually, for an existential helper, I have worked with the Enneagram for 30 years and a maturity typology for 15 years (Adult Development/Leadership Maturity framework/Vertical Development/Identity Maturation framework). I am hugely influenced by the coaching literature on adult development and developmental coaching, in particular the work of Jennifer Garvey Berger.[4]

This link is unusual because an existential approach assumes a completely idiosyncratic approach to personality and maturation. Typological approaches premised on groups of people doing things in the same way do not always fit in easily within the existential frame that values individuality. I am naming this because it has deeply influenced the kind of coaching that I do and where my views may differ from other existential coaches.

Questions to ask your *self*

I am going to end each chapter with a set of questions that you can ask your *self*. The questions are intended to support you to apply the learning of the chapter to your life as a human and as a coach. You can use these with your clients as well. Here are some things to think about with regards to the first chapter.

- Can you read and apply the learning from this book to your own life at the same time? Can you process two things at once? I am hoping that you already do a bit of this parallel processing in your sessions; thinking about or listening to your client and processing your reactions to the client all at the same time. This book is another opportunity to hone these skills.
- What kind of information do you have the easiest connection with? Is it information about emotions, theory, philosophy, visual maps, information

that relates to you as a human, or information that relates to you as a coach? When you know your organic reading orientation, you can play with it and linger a little longer on less accessible types of information, or not.
- Do you get an intuitive sense of what stuckness and fluidity look and feel like in your life? For a deeper experience go to the fridge, laptop, remote control, booze cabinet, or cleaning products, and experience some of your own stuck behaviours more deeply.

Notes

1 I italicise 'self', 'others', and 'meaning' in this book when I refer to them in the context of stuckness. I also prefer using the term 'self' rather than 'selves'. I am hoping that this will help the readers see their *self* more objectively and reduce confusion.
2 Languaging borrowed from Dr Khaled ElSherbini (June 2024). Enneagram in action: Systems thinking for thriving in a complex world. Presentation at the European Enneagram. Conference, Amsterdam.
3 Kukard, J. (2021). *Bewitched, amputated or dead: An existential study of leadership stuckness*. DProf thesis Middlesex University/New School of Psychotherapy and Counselling (NSPC) Psychology.
4 Garvey Berger, J. (2011). *Changing on the job: Developing leaders for a complex world* (1st ed.). Stanford University Press; Garvey Berger, J. (2019). *Unlocking leadership mindtraps: How to thrive in complexity* (1st ed.). Stanford University Press.

Bibliography

ElSherbini, K. (June 2024). Enneagram in action: Systems thinking for thriving in a complex world. *Presentation at the European Enneagram. Conference*, Amsterdam.

Garvey Berger, J. (2011). *Changing on the job: Developing leaders for a complex world* (1st ed.). Stanford University Press.

Garvey Berger, J. (2019). *Unlocking leadership mindtraps: How to thrive in complexity* (1st ed.). Stanford University Press.

Kukard, J. (2021). *Bewitched, amputated or dead: An existential study of leadership stuckness*. DProf thesis Middlesex University/New School of Psychotherapy and Counselling (NSPC) Psychology.

Chapter 2

Understanding stuckness and fluidity from a human and a coach perspective

The objective of this chapter is to give us a deeper understanding of what stuckness is from a human and a coach perspective. To achieve this, we will start with an existential understanding of what a human is.

What is a human?

Now we know already that this is a rather large question and so to make it smaller I am going to pull in my ideological hand rails and focus on my existential interpretation of this vast question. This approach will cut out all sorts of other physiological, scientific, psychological, and spiritual accounts of what a human is. Perhaps this is too much simplification for you, but it will suffice for the purposes of understanding stuckness from the existential philosophical position embedded in this book.

The existential view is that the defining quality of a human is our capacity to *self*-reflect, change, and adapt. Humans can emerge from one thing and grow into another, and we do this through *self*-reflection and choice. Objects do not have the same capacity for transformation, thus a rock is a rock even when it is a rockstar's rock ashtray.[1]

Self-reflection is the process of reflecting on how we are doing, both inside and outside our *self*. This is, of course, intrinsically challenging because the thing doing the reflecting is also the thing being reflected upon. Furthermore, if our capacity for *self*-reflection is weak and under-developed, then we may also have problems noticing what is, in fact, happening inside our *self*. When this happens, we don't have the critical information that can and should inform our growth.

Choice is the other ingredient that enables this human quality of growth and emergence. We can choose to respond, and even when we don't actively choose, we are choosing. This is because no choice is a choice after all. Choice is directional, that is, it takes us somewhere, hopefully somewhere we want to go.

The bit I really want us to know, is that it is the choice-based, adaptive, and emergent nature of our *self* that makes us human. Furthermore, this capacity

DOI: 10.4324/9781003536253-2

can be enabled or disabled by our ability for *self*-reflection and active choice. If we want to hang on to our humanity, then this is the one quality we need to protect at all costs. Let us look now at how humans do life.

How do humans do life?

The goal of philosophy is to help us to live well, and this means helping us understand what we are doing on this planet and how we should do life. The existential view is that humans are thrown into a specific context[2] where we are befuddled and beset by four existential givens. These include freedom, death, isolation, and meaninglessness.[3] To live well, we have to deal with all four of these elements but, as we will discover, they each come with caveats, ironies, and blessings.

Freedom refers to the very real freedom that exists for us to do what we want with our lives (even commit suicide). However, with this freedom comes responsibility and the resultant anxiety of uncertainty, not knowing, and choice.[4] This freedom is very scary because it also implies that there is no innate structure to our world, that we have to create it, and to create it we need to make choices. To take this freedom, we need a sense of *self* and what we want, we need *others*, and we need *meaning* to guide us towards how we will express this freedom. If we don't, we can become stuck and have no freedom. This is what this book is all about: gathering the necessary ingredients for freedom, real freedom, real inner freedom, painful though it may be.

The chapter on *self* covers what it means to have a *self* and how we lose it and experience it as bewitched, amputated, or dead. Death refers not just to our own death, but also to the death of other people, situations, events, and even objects. Death anxiety is a very big deal for humans and a critical part of living. This is because the fear of death is our biggest reminder to live.[5] If we did not know we were going to die, we could just float along fiddling about here and there because there is no apparent end or submission date. Who hands in an assignment if there is no submission date? Thus if we deny death then we somehow land up delaying or denying life.

Stuckness itself can feel like death, which is probably why we find it so very painful. I explore this later in the chapter on experiencing stuckness, but it is important to bring the link in here while we are talking about death.

Isolation is the next existential given, and this is fairly self-explanatory and well covered in the chapters on *others*, where we find that we really do need *others* to live. In the existential way of thinking, to be able to connect with *others*, we need to accept that we are, in fact, alone. The logic is that if we build relationships based on the fear of isolation alone, they will be panicky, superficial, and rickety.[6] Thus, in order to have truly rich relationships based on real love and compassion for our *self* and *others*, we need to get comfortable with our fundamental isolation. It is another one of those curious existential ironies that when we accept isolation, we can truly accept companionship and intimacy.

Meaninglessness is covered in the chapters on *meaning*. It is linked to having a *self*, because without a *self*, it is tricky for a *self* to find *meaning*. *Meaning* includes *meaning* related to *others*. Our most invigorating *meaning* comes through transcending our *self* and being connected with *others*. *Meaning* is also coupled to death because death plays such a critical role in how, where, with whom, and when we have *meaning*. A lack of meaning can throw us into an existential void where we have no direction or sense of our existence.[7] We can look forward to covering this in the chapters on *meaning*. This includes the idea that life is intrinsically meaningless and we have to work hard to create it.

So, what is it like to live as a human? Well, often not very pleasant: we are beset by slavery of all kinds, made anxious by death, bereft through isolation, and despairing through meaninglessness. But we are also energised by freedom, inspired by death, universal and transcendent through *others*, and *meaning*. Both aspects of our paradoxical human life have one and the same ingredients, it's really about how one chooses to bake the cake.

Now that I have provided a broad description of what a human is, I would like to linger a little longer on the subject of pain, shame, and grief.

Pain, shame, and grief?

Pain

Pain is an uncomfortable and unpleasant feeling that is caused by many things, including physical and emotional sources. There is very little neurological difference between physical and emotional pain, it is all the same and registers in the same part of the brain in the same way.[8]

Pain or discomfort can be very helpful feelings when used appropriately. It is an alarm bell telling us that something needs healing, completion, and discharging. A cut leg needs soreness to tell us that we have cut ourselves, that we need to look after the wound, and we should not run with scissors in the future. Emotional pain such as grief tells us that we have lost someone valuable to us. That we don't have that person in our life any more, and that we need to adapt and build a life beyond that relationship. Existential pain tells us that we need more *meaning* in our lives, and loneliness that we need *others* to thrive as a human.

Pain can also enrich our experience of life, even while threatening it. It reminds us of our humanity, frailty, fallibility, and humility. It acts as a foil against which pleasure can be juxtaposed and measured, thereby enhancing the experience of pleasure. Without pain, pleasure is a neutral experience. When we deny and exclude our pain, we can develop narrow and superficial identities that float above and not within life.

Pain also helps us to know where our boundaries, comfort zones, and limits are. This is useful if we want to stretch our *self* in life without getting injured too much.

Pain is part of all learning. This is because to learn we must accept that we don't know everything. We may also feel pain when we overstep our comfort zone, or because the actual process of learning is painful. If we turn back from learning because of the pain of it, it will be very hard for us to grow.

Pain is an important part of the process of stuckness, an elegant partner that warns us of the need to get moving in our lives.

Shame

Shame is a form of pain, one that is possibly less useful. Guilt tells us that we have done something wrong while shame tell us that we are wrong.[9] Guilt is far more helpful because it assumes we are not completely defective and in need of redemption. There are two kinds of shame.

Healthy shame can tell us where our limits are and keep us from harming *others*. It is a collectively orientated emotion that can tell us how to live in a particular community, for example, by helping us to understand that murdering *others* is not good. However, healthy shame exists alongside us knowing that we are essentially ok and worthy.

Toxic shame tells us that we are defective and need to be something else. We may come to believe that we need to achieve superhuman things to redeem this, or even develop a false *self*. This in turn can drive us to present an overly positive version of our *self* that we have to work hard to maintain. Conversely, we can present an overly negative *self*, one that has internalised and become complicit to the idea of being bad and defective.[10]

While shame is a form of stuckness in itself, it is also a precursor, companion, and enabler of other forms of stuckness. This is because it may lead us to escape from our unworthiness through stuckness-creating pursuits (material success, addiction, perfectionism, bullying, righteousness, blaming). Shame itself is correlated with various forms of stuckness, including addiction, bullying, depression, violence, eating disorders, and even suicide. Shame plays a critical role in enabling and sustaining stuckness.

Grief

Grief is a moment when we are confronting death and life at the same time.[11] We are present to the death of someone we love and to our own lives which keep on living. It is an exquisite existential moment bridging together the worlds of the living and the dead. It is also hellishly painful. However, if we cannot be fully present on this bridge, we can stay there forever in a state of ennui. Grief is both a way to relieve stuckness and when not discharged fully with, a cause of stuckness.[12]

Grief is both an existential moment and an energetic discharge that relieves and eases stuckness, allowing us to soften and mould our lives around loss. When we do this our losses become sources of new life rather than dead ends.

This is the way we begin to relearn our *self*, relearn *others*, and relearn *meaning*, the world, and our place in it.[13]

When we get stuck we need to grieve our existing lives, our unlived lives, and the loss of *others* and *meaning* that characterised our stuckness. We may also grieve the damage we have done and more.

Some writers on grief suggest that humans follow a uniform pattern or pathway of grief.[14] Other authors argue that grief is idiosyncratic, non-linear, non-rational, and refuses to fit in with any homogenous typology.[15] My sense is that stuckness grief falls into the latter camp and can often come way after the fact, maybe even years later.

Humans live in a body

Lastly, we live in a body. Our body does not just carry us around but it also helps us think, feel, and sense the world. We experience the world through our body; without a body there is no world.[16] We can't be a full person or enable our healing without connecting to our bodies.

Many of us do not have cooperative or safe relationships with our bodies. We can control them within an inch of their life, or we can ignore them completely using them only as a taxi to our heads. We can also perpetrate traumas on our bodies, thereby repeating the traumas rent on our *self*.

A sedentary body or over-exercised and over-controlled bodies can enable stuckness and are versions of stuckness in themselves. When we don't move about enough, our bodies become less flexible and sclerotic. When we obsessively control everything that our bodies consume, and we continuously push them to their limits, we are also tempting stuckness. What we need is something in between, something more relaxed and collegial where our head, heart, and body enter the conversation equally, and work together in a kind way. We need to learn how to be a good companion to our body, not an obsessive, over-protective fascist friend, but one that is kind and useful.

What is an existential coach?

In general, coaches use talking, somatic, and other interventions to help clients think, sense, and feel through their lives differently so that they can create a more satisfying way of being. They co-create conversations and felt experiences[17] that transform people's thinking and feeling and lives. This is the same for existential coaches.

Existential coaches tend to have an increased focus on our client's lived experience through phenomenological exploration. We value personal agency and work with the existential givens (freedom, death, isolation, and meaninglessness). We also spend a lot of time exploring how clients can be more authentic in life, even while their *self* is changing all the time.[18]

Existential coaching does not seek to fix clients or use labels to describe pathologies. Instead we focus on supporting clients to accept challenges and find choices within these to enable a more satisfying life.[19]

Existential coaching supports people in the workplace too. However, because the approach is rooted in philosophy and not positivism, it 'takes the focus away from purely practical or cognitive goals, and into the realm of meaning-making, psycho-education, and philosophical awareness of one's life'.[20] This form of coaching deals with each client as a human and not a tool of production. We explore clients' humanity through existential dilemmas and paradoxes, build *meaning*, and sense-making skills. An existential approach accepts that anxiety can be a normal outcome of stretching into life and de-pathologises failure and stuckness.

Van Deurzen-Smith describes the broad range of existential coaching orientations. These include:

- 'The Nietzschean coach who works with clients on owning their individuality, and courage to stand out from the herd
- The gentle, phenomenological coach, who uses imagery and dreamwork to foster greater understanding of our being-in-the-world
- The Sartrean coach who focuses on ownership of choice and freedom, and how we find ourselves in Bad Faith
- The coach who focuses on existential crisis, and how we use despair and change to become more ourselves.'[21]

We as existential coaches must make individual choices about the approach we wish to foreground. As van Deurzen, quoting Nietzsche, states:

'If you want to rise high, use your own legs! Do not let yourselves be carried up, do not sit on the backs and heads of strangers.'[22]

What this means is that each must do our own work, build our own philosophy of life and healing, rather than taking on a ready-made, shrink-wrapped approach with three steps.

Typically, most coaching focusses on the present and the future, and less so the past. This is allocated to therapists and psychotherapists. I don't feel attached to this idea, possibly because I am trained in both psychotherapy and coaching. Perhaps too because existential coaching is more likely to become archaeological than other coaching methodologies. There are definitely pasts that need to be referred to therapists but very often a mindful and trauma-informed coach can do a good enough job of raising early narratives and seeing how they are affecting the client in the present. This is what an existential coach can do.

How do humans get stuck?

Stuckness is generally a 'normal', unavoidable, and recurring state in which someone gets stuck in their relationship with their context. This is prompted by a wound requiring completion. Everyone gets stuck from time to time in their lives and this can be chronic and last for years. The existential goal of stuckness is to enable us to heal our pasts and create new futures that are more in line with who we are. Figure (in Chapter 1) shows a map of the components and process of stuckness.

I have included more detail on each aspect of the cycle below. I have also included very short and simplistic case studies of four people showing how each stage manifests in their lives. Hopefully, this will start to give you a feel for how the cycle flows. And, just so you know there are chapters that cover each of these stages in more detail.

Stage one: A relationship between an incomplete wound and a salient context

We are all wounded in some way or another, and it is our task as humans to move beyond these wounds to create a satisfying life. Wounds can include severe trauma, existential guilt, or even being irrelevant. For wounds to complete their process and discharge their unexpressed energy, we need to find a way to understand them. We must grieve their impacts, and then build a narrative that is empowering, rather than shaming. I go into this in more depth in the next chapter.

Incomplete wounds are always present, but can become even more so when we are feeling positive and competent in the world. They also become more visible when the contexts are reminiscent of the patterning of our wounding. We can then either respond as we did last time, or in a new way.

For example:

- Pete finds a street drug that makes him feel better, at least while he is stoned. He wonders if feeling good on the drug can help him face his life more fully.
- Jacob, a corporate executive grew up in a street gang where he learned how to be tough. He used this toughness to work his way into senior management on a goldmine.
- Adelia grew up in a family that required children to be very compliant, not express their emotions, or be their child-like *self*. She did well in banking because she knew how to be compliant.
- Thami grew up poor and black, surrounded by unemployed family. She completed high school and got a degree in journalism. She was hired by a white-owned local newspaper to attract young black readers.

Stage two: Disengagement from the world, three losses, and defensive behaviours

We are now in a salient context where our wounds have an opportunity to be worked with and complete. While we are here, reliving the wounding, we start losing aspects of our broader *self*, *others*, and *meaning*. We do this because we are living in the wound and not our current context. When we lose aspects of our *self*, *others*, and *meaning*, we lose our adaptive capacity and direction. Our *self* and our actions relate to the context of the wound and not the current situation. To maintain this way of being, we develop a raft of defensive behaviours that take us nowhere.

For example:

- As Pete gets deeper into addiction, he is re-traumatised but this time by the addiction. He loses aspects of his *self*, *others*, and *meaning*. His actions are dominated by an addiction that keeps him in a wound.
- The company where Jacob worked decided that they wanted to change the command and control leadership culture to something more visionary and human-centric. Jacob was told that he needed to change his leadership style because it was ineffective and not future fit.
- Adelia received feedback that she would never advance to higher levels because she was experienced as pedantic and robotic.
- Thami reported on everything of interest to young black readers. This included their lived experience of racism, and the hardships they faced by 'being black in an anti-black world'.[23] The white editor told her to tone it down a bit, she was not Malcolm X's girlfriend. Thami was furious, not just at his request to tone down black narratives, but also at the sexism implicit in the comment about Malcolm X. Her writing became more focussed on racism, and the editor rejected more of her copy.

Stage three: A developmental impasse, pain, frustration, and lostness

The three losses and defensive behaviours block our capacity to learn and we move into a developmental impasse. We are disconnected from our *self*, *others*, and *meaning*, and our actions have no traction. We become isolated, lost, and ineffective, and this causes us pain and frustration. It is this pain that pushes us towards resolution, without it we could remain stuck forever.

For example:

- Pete becomes stuck in a circular world of addiction. His actions are dominated by the need to feed his habit. These actions defend the wound but are unhelpful in getting Pete going in life. Pete loses his home and is forced to move in with friends whose lives are similar to his. Pete is angry at life and his addiction and does not know how to turn the situation around.

- Jacob's company hired a coach to help him change his leadership style. Jacob did not attend the coaching because he believed that goldmines could not be run by 'soft sissies'. He continued with his existing leadership style. Jacob's bullying style was interpreted as racist by someone from another race and he was asked to resign.
- Adelia could not see what she was doing wrong. She felt picked on and conspired against. She became more pedantic and robotic to control her life. Adelia failed to deliver on her projects because she was demoralised and did not have relationships within the organisation. She stole stationery and time to punish the organisation. Leadership believed that she was destructive to the culture and sidelined her, marking her as the first to go in the next retrenchment cycle.
- Thami was incensed and the situation felt hopeless. Others in the newspaper watched but did not help her and Thami became isolated. She decided that she would leave as soon as she could find other work, but she needed work.

Stage four: Pain and grief initiate change, we rebuild our self, our relationships with others, and meaning

We are now in a painful and frustrating place, living the long-term consequences of our incomplete wounding. To move from here, we must work with the shame of the wounding and becoming stuck in our lives. If we don't do this, we will remain stuck.

During this time we grieve: grieve the wound, grieve the life the wound created, and grieve the unlived lives resulting from the wound. Grieving creates a fluidity that allows us to reconnect with our *self*, *others*, and what is meaningful to us. When we understand our *self* better, we know how to direct our lives more meaningfully, and we start to be able to see *others* and the world more clearly. We start to see the world as it is rather than as we are in it. This enables us to adapt and have traction in the world.

For example:

- Pete gets into an addiction programme, works with his shame, mourns his lost life, and rebuilds his relationship to his *self*, *others*, and *meaning*.
- Jacob leaves the mining company angry. This anger persists for years and threatens to ruin his marriage. He can't get another job because everyone in the industry is aware of his reputation. He takes to fishing all day. Fishing allows him to process his pain and anger and he begins to grieve. This grieving softens him and he can reconnect to his *self* more, his wife, and look for *meaning* in his life.

- Adelia gets a sideways, slightly downwards 'promotion'. She becomes enraged at this and a coach is hired, ostensibly to help her be less aggressive. The coach enables her express her anger and grieve her situation. They then start to work on rebuilding her relationship to her *self, others*, and *meaning*.
- Thami could not find a job anywhere else, and so she had to deal with the situation at hand. She felt that her choices were: a) to continue the fight as she was doing; b) broaden the reporting of black experience away from a racism focus; c) be cunning and slip stories about racism in under the cover of other stories; or d) leave without a job to go to. She sensed that to be an effective advocate for black lives in this publication, she had to process her anger and grieve that once again she was at the mercy of the white world. She had to figure out how she could choose her freedom, as well as support *others'* freedom in this context. She decides to stay in the system, hoping to change it, and thus chooses b and c.

Stage five: Peaking and plateauing

At this stage, we have grieved our losses and rebuilt our *self*, relationships and *meaning*. We have traction in the world and an enhanced ability to direct our lives. This new pattern begins to settle in as our usual way of being, reinforced by the fluidity and a more satisfying life. We relax into this new way of being and then the context changes again. Finally a new wound, or maybe even the old one pops up for attention, and we re-enter the process.

For example:

- Pete gets a job, finds new friends who are not in addiction cycles and starts taking responsibility for and control of his life. He finds a girlfriend and this relationship activates his wounding again. He is terrified she will find him wanting and leave.
- Jacob is invited to fill in as a rugby coach at a local school. He does very well at this and they offer him a job. He finds this work meaningful. Although Jacob has softened somewhat, he is still fairly tough, and soon there are complaints from parents about this. Jacob accepts the feedback and resolves to work on his style and its origins, even though he is deeply worried that he will lose his job, as he did last time.
- Adelia loves the coaching so much that she decides to train as a coach and facilitator. She goes to therapy and does her work. She finds new softer parts of her *self* and integrates these. Over time Adelia becomes an internal coach within the organisation and HR congratulates her on 'turning herself around'. Adelia is irritated by the comment but doesn't know why, perhaps they are being patronising.

- Thami stays in the organisation and becomes a senior editor. She is able to bring in more staff from diverse backgrounds and affect editorial policy. She grows the young black readership base for the publication. Not all the advertisers are happy with this, many leave and Thami is left with a new problem to solve.

Stuckness is always a relationship issue

Stuckness is always a relationship issue: relationship with the context, our *self*, *others*, and what is meaningful to us.

Much of the literature on stuckness seems to suggest that it is only intrapsychic,[24] that is, a result of the person's inner world getting stuck all on its own, probably because the person was defective or lazy. This is not true, stuckness is an impasse creating an opportunity to heal and incubate a new *self*. It is also a relationship issue. If the world did not change, these inner worlds would remain relevant, in fact, they would be just fine and dandy running on their old recipes in their old original contexts. But the world does change, and so do the people in it; the critical bit here is the relationship between the inner world of the person and the world outside the person. Stuckness is about this relationship, and how both human and context interact (or don't). If the plug does not fit in the socket, then no electricity will flow.

Other learning and healing cycles

Although I built this theory from the data up, when I finally summited to the metanarrative I found that others had been there before. I want to bring these others in now, just in case you know them.

There are many learning cycles in the organisational and coaching literature. Some that you may know include the work of Lewin,[25] Argyris,[26] Schön,[27] Kolb,[28] Senge,[29] and Action Research.[30] There are many more that speak to cycles of action and then cycles of reflection at various levels of thinking. Notably, there is no end to these cycles as we can keep on learning.

For those with a more therapeutic bent there are more cycles to be found. If you were Freudian you would call it repetition compulsion[31] or for those of a Winnicott orientation, rupture and repair,[32] or maybe for the Jungians the transcendent function.[33] I am an existential psychotherapist so I might call it a hermeneutic circle[34] if I did not want to call it the Cycle of Stuckness. In these instances, the cycle is initiated by some kind of wounding or incompletion that needs healing. These are cycles of healing, are as in are like peeling layers of an onion but never quite completely healing, just healing to a 'good enough for now' position.

The processes for healing and learning may differ, but the metanarrative is that we humans do cycles, and we do cycles because they are developmental and help us survive and thrive. Furthermore, cycles do not ever totally complete; if they did, they would not be a cycle. This is the same with the Cycle of Stuckness.

How do coaches get stuck?

All coaches get stuck from time to time. We make the wrong interventions, our inner world overshadows that of the client. We can misunderstand our clients, judge them, and offer outdated metaphors that don't land. We can even try to tie things up neatly before they are ready to be tied. Often, we get stuck when we avoid confronting something that needs to be faced in the session, or when we herd clients down a particular vein of exploration that they don't want to go down. Stuckness could also be created by a mismatch of client and coach. There are many more things that we as coaches do that get us stuck. Getting stuck is not the problem, however, we can get stuck as often as we can or want to.

The problem with stuckness in coaching is the same as it is with stuckness in humans. It's not about how often or how deeply we get stuck, it's about if and how we use stuckness as a growth point in coaching rather than a dead end. And, the bit that is truly interesting in this, is that this stuckness is a relationship, a partnership dance created by both the coach and the client.

It always takes two to tango when it comes to stuckness in coaching. This means that we can't just hand responsibility to the client by saying that the stuckness in coaching is only a proxy for how the clients do relationships outside coaching. We as the coach have also contributed to the stuckness and, as such, it will take sophisticated, brave, and humble unpicking to find out how the dance was created. Furthermore, the way in which we handle the part we played in the stuckness will guide the client as to how they work with their role.

A stuck coach is one who blames the client for not achieving the coaching outcomes. A stuck coach is one who does not refresh their tools and metaphors, who is separate from life as experienced by the client. A stuck coach is one who thinks that they already have the recipe for life and coaching, and do not go to supervision or therapy. A stuck coach is one who is not deeply connected to their *self*, *others*, and *meaning*.

How to use the cycle while we are reading this book

The Cycle of Stuckness was initially developed in my doctoral research and later deepened in my coaching and psychotherapy practice. It has also been used by other coaches and organisational development professionals. We have found that everyone goes through broadly the same cycle, with the stages following in the same order. This means that there is a good chance that the cycle will be relevant to us and our stuckness, as well as that of our clients.

The cycle is accurate as a summarised map of the process of stuckness. However, in reality, human growth is messy, accretive, iterative, interactive, and idiosyncratic. It really is a lot of big dense words. Any diagram that includes the real complexity of human behaviour would be too idiosyncratic and complex to be useful. We humans tend to work better off simple maps. So, when we are looking where to find your *self* in the stuckness cycle, look for the big story and wind in the details later.

When we apply the cycle, know that we are always in it, we are always going in or coming out; it is the nature of human growth. We grow into a context, we find our *self* effective in an environment and our growth plateaus. Our behaviours then sediment and we stop adapting. This carries on for a bit until the pain of stuckness wakes us up and thrusts us back again into the cycle of growth and change. We are always in the cycle.

Broadly, people move forwards through the cycle, following the pathway laid out in the cycle. However, the elements of *self*, *others*, and *meaning* are interdependent. This means that despite us moving forwards in the cycle, we may have diversions backwards, or even leapfrogs forward. For example, we might find we have lost aspects of our *self* and through this we have lost aspects of *meaning* as well. Or, that when we rebuild relationships with *others*, we create more *meaning* in our life. Don't worry about this, it's normal, if sometimes confusing. When trying to find out where we are on the map, look for a centre of gravity.

We can apply the cycle to an aspect of our life, or to our whole life. We can be stuck in some areas and fluid in others. However, if we find stuckness in a critical part of our life such as our relationship with our intimate partner or job, then there is a good chance we will be stuck overall. This is because stuckness is highly infectious and can bleed all over our life.

A useful tip for using the cycle is to first decide the area that you want to explore; is it your life, your job, your relationship, or something else? Then wonder to yourself, at which stage am I in this relationship, and use the following cues to guide you.

- Are you in a stage of growth and newness? Then you are probably on the left and top side of the cycle (as you are facing it on the page) (gaining *self*, *others*, and *meaning*).
- Are you in a stage of consolidation where you are embedding the newness? Then you are probably on the top-right side of the cycle (losing *self*).
- Are you in a phase of plateau and coasting? Then you are probably on the right-top and middle of the cycle (losing *self* and *others*).
- Are you in a stage of getting a bit bored, isolated, and frustrated? Then you are probably on the middle-right and bottom of the lemniscate (losing *others* and *meaning*).
- Are you in a stage where you are feeling deeply frustrated, unsupported, and lost? Then you are probably on the bottom-right and middle of the cycle (losing *meaning* and being stuck).

Once you have a feel for where you are on the cycle, you can use this to direct your reading attention. For example, you could think, 'I am in a phase of coasting and resting on my laurels, how did I get here and where am I going with this mindset in play?' Then think about this as you read the book.

Questions to ask your *self*

- Do you like the existential idea that what most determines our humanity is our ability to grow? If so why?
- Where have you avoided making a choice and how has this landed up being a choice?
- Is there a pattern to how you get stuck with clients? Can you think and feel through why this pattern repeats itself, and what the underlying drivers could be?

Notes

1 These ideas, of course, come from Jean-Paul Sartre and Martin Heidegger. Sartre, J. P. (1943). *Being and nothingness: An essay on phenomenological ontology* (2003 ed.). Routledge.
2 The idea of being thrown into the world comes from Heidegger (1927). *Being and time* (2018 ed.). Harper.
3 Yalom, I. D. (1980). Meaninglessness. In *Existential psychotherapy* (pp. 419–460). Yalom, I. D. (2008). *Staring at the sun: overcoming the terror of death*. Jossey-Bass.
4 Sartre, J.-P. (1943). *Being and Nothingness: An essay on phenomenological ontology* (2003 ed.). Routledge.
5 Yalom, I. D. (2008). *Staring at the sun: Overcoming the terror of death*. Jossey-Bass.
6 Yalom, I. D. (2001). *The gift of therapy: An open letter to a new generation of therapists and their patients*. Piatkus Books.
7 van Deurzen, E. et al. (2009). *Everyday mysteries: A handbook of existential psychotherapy* (2nd ed.). Routledge.
8 Fogel, A. (2012). *Emotional and physical pain activate similar brain regions, psychology today*. Available at: https://www.psychologytoday.com/za/blog/body-sense/201204/emotional-and-physical-pain-activate-similar-brain-regions (Accessed: 21 January 2024).
9 Biko, S. (1978). *I write what I like*. Bowerdean Press; Bradshaw, J. (2005). *Healing the shame that binds* (Revised ed.). Health Communications Inc.
10 Biko, S. (1978). *I write what I like*.
11 Thank you, Chantelle Wyley, for this conceptualization.
12 Attig, T. (1996). *How we grieve: Relearning the world*. Oxford University Press.
13 Attig. (1996). *How we grieve*.
14 Kübler-Ross, E., & Kessler, D. (2014). *On grief & grieving: finding the meaning of grief through the five stages of loss*. Scribner.
15 Dolny, H. (2018). *Before forever after: When conversations about living meet questions about dying*. Jacana Media, Johannesburg; Attig, T. (1996). *How we grieve: Relearning the world*. Oxford University Press.
16 Merleau-Ponty, M., & Landes, D. A. (1946). *Phenomenology of perception*. First paper. Routledge.

17 Thank you, Chantelle Wyley, for bringing in the notion of felt experiences from Gestalt coaching.
18 Lawler, J., & Ashman, I. (2012). Theorizing leadership authenticity: A Sartrean perspective. *Leadership*, *8*, 327–344.
19 https://dvdscoach.com/existential-coaching (Accessed: 15 June 2024).
20 van Deurzen, E. & Hanaway, M. (2012). *Existential perspectives on coaching* (p. 224). Palgrave Macmillan.
21 van Deurzen-Smith, S. (2020). *Existential coaching in a nutshell*. Available at: https://www.animascoaching.com/blog/existential-coaching-in-a-nutshell/ (Accessed: 10 October 2020).
22 van Deurzen, E. & Hanaway, M. (2012). *Existential perspectives on coaching*.
23 This terms comes from the title of this publication: Manganyi, N. C. (1973). *Being black in the world* (1st ed.). Ravan Press.
24 For example, Petriglieri, G. (2007). Stuck in a moment: A developmental perspective on impasses. *Transactional Analysis Journal*, *37*(3), 185–194.
25 Lewin, K. (1951). *Field theory in social science: Selected theoretical papers* (Edited by Dorwin Cartwright.). Harpers.
26 Argyris, C. (1990). *Overcoming organizational defenses. Facilitating organizational learning*. Allyn and Bacon.
27 Schön, D. A. (1983). *The reflective practitioner. How professionals think in action*. Temple Smith.
28 Kolb, D. A. (1984). *Experiential learning: Experience as the source of learning and development*. Prentice Hall.
29 Senge, P. (1990). *The fifth discipline. The art and practice of the learning organization*. Random House.
30 Reason, P., & Bradbury, H. (Eds.). (2008). *The SAGE handbook of action research*. SAGE Publications Ltd.
31 Freud, Sigmund. (2015). *Beyond the pleasure principle* (17th ed.). Dover Publications.
32 Winnicott, D. W. (1957). *The child and the outside world*. Tavistock/Basic Books.
33 Kiehl, E. (n.d.). *The transcendent function vehicle of psychic change*. Retrieved 19 July 2024, from https://iaap.org/wp-content/uploads/2021/09/The-Transcendent-Function-1.pdf.
34 Heil, D. (2011). *Ontological fundamentals for ethical management. Heidegger and the corporate world*. Issues in business ethics. Springer.

Bibliography

Argyris, C. (1990). *Overcoming organizational defenses. Facilitating organizational learning*. Allyn and Bacon.

Biko, S. (1978). *I write what I like*. Bowerdean Press.

Bradshaw, J. (2005). *Healing the shame that binds* (Revised ed.). Health Communications Inc.

Buber, M. (2010). *I and thou*. Martino Publishing.

Camus, A. (2012). *The myth of Sisyphus and other essays*. Knopf Doubleday

De Beauvoir, S. (2015). *The second sex*. Penguin Books.

Dolny, H. (2018). *Before forever after: When conversations about living meet questions about dying*, Jacana Media, Johannesburg.

Fogel, A. (2012). *Emotional and physical pain activate similar brain regions, psychology today*. Available at: https://www.psychologytoday.com/za/blog/body-sense/201204/emotional-and-physical-pain-activate-similar-brain-regions (Accessed: 21 January 2024).

Freud, S. (2015). *Beyond the pleasure principle* (17th ed.). Dover Publications.

Heidegger, M. (1927). *Being and time* (2018th ed.). Harper.

Heil, D. (2011). *Ontological fundamentals for ethical management. Heidegger and the corporate world.* Issues in business ethics. Springer.

Kiehl, E. (n.d.). *The transcendent function vehicle of psychic change.* Retrieved 19 July 2024, from https://iaap.org/wp-content/uploads/2021/09/The-Transcendent-Function-1.pdf.

Kolb, D. A. (1984). *Experiential learning: Experience as the source of learning and development.* Prentice Hall.

Kübler-Ross, E., & Kessler, D. (2014). *On grief & grieving: finding the meaning of grief through the five stages of loss.* Scribner.

Lawler, J., & Ashman, I. (2012). Theorizing leadership authenticity: A Sartrean perspective. *Leadership, 8,* 327–344.

Lewin, K. (1951). *Field theory in social science: selected theoretical papers* (Edited by Dorwin Cartwright). Harpers.

Manganyi, N.C. (1973). *Being black in the world* (1st ed.). Ravan Press.

Merleau-Ponty, M., & Landes, D. A. (1946). *Phenomenology of perception.* First paper. Abingdon: Routledge.

Petriglieri, G. (2007). Stuck in a moment: A developmental perspective on impasses. *Transactional Analysis Journal, 37*(3), 185–194.

Reason, P., & Bradbury, H. (Eds.). (2008). *The SAGE handbook of action research.* SAGE Publications Ltd.

Sartre, J.-P. (1943). *Being and Nothingness: An essay on phenomenological ontology* (2003rd ed.). Routledge.

Schön, D. A. (1983). *The reflective practitioner. How professionals think in action.* Temple Smith.

Senge, P. (1990). *The fifth discipline. The art and practice of the learning organization.* Random House.

Spinelli, E. (1989). *The interpreted world: An introduction to phenomenological psychology.* Sage Publications, Inc.

Tillich, P. (2000). *The courage to be* (2nd ed.). Yale University Press.

Van der Walt, E. 2012. Presentation to the South African OD Network on the neuroscience of creativity at work, 23 February. See http://www.neurozone.com/.

van Deurzen, E., & Hanaway, M. (2012). *Existential perspectives on coaching.* Palgrave Macmillan.

van Deurzen, E. et al. (2009). *Everyday mysteries: A handbook of existential psychotherapy* (2nd ed.). Routledge.

van Deurzen-Smith, S. (2020). *Existential coaching in a nutshell.* Available at: https://www.animascoaching.com/blog/existential-coaching-in-a-nutshell/ (Accessed: 10 October 2020).

Winnicott, D. W. (1957). *The child and the outside world.* Tavistock/Basic Books.

Yalom, I. D. (1980). Meaninglessness. In *Existential psychotherapy* (pp. 419–460). Basic Books.

Yalom, I. D. (2008). *Staring at the sun: Overcoming the terror of death.* Jossey-Bass.

Chapter 3

Understanding stuckness and fluidity from a context perspective

The previous chapter looked at stuckness from the human perspective; now it's time to look at the other partner in the stuckness dance, the context. The context is our dancing partner in life and in stuckness, and as such it is important to spend a little time exploring this before we get deeper into the Cycle of Stuckness.

What is a context?

A context can be the socio-political setting, an event, situation, or even the relationships surrounding a person. It is the container in which we grow and change and, more importantly, it plays a significant role in moulding who we are.

How do we determine our context?

A context can be an individual person and/or a collection of people, or physical, and/or intangible things. It can involve really anything that surrounds a person, including things that look close by (our bedroom, our partner), or far away (like human rights infringements in faraway places). The only criteria is that the context includes things that affect us in some way. The tricky thing is that on a systemic level, everything does interact with everything, and so we could argue that our context is actually everything in the world. But if we had to take everything in the world into account each time we acted, we would probably not get to acting. As a result, humans have conscious and unconscious mechanisms for deciding what is most important or figural,[1] a way of reducing our context to workable proportions so that we can actually act.

By way of example: my immediate context now is a dirty laptop screen (maybe I should be wearing my glasses), bed, you reading this, dog trying to get on bed, son upstairs doing something noisy on the floorboards, swimming pool looking at me through the window pleading to be relieved of leaves, garden shining contentedly because of the rain. Just a street away are people living in tents who have had a wet night, then beyond are shopping centres with

DOI: 10.4324/9781003536253-3

sausages waiting to be cooked, irritated residents without electricity, more poverty, an unequal society, racism, fraud, global inequality, Biden, Putin, Netanyahu, Sinwar, and Starmer, climate change, nuclear warfare, and the man on the moon. I am in a big place, and so are you. But how much of this do we see as our context?

The contexts we consider relevant differ from human to human, vary (often minute by minute), and happen both consciously and unconsciously. For example, I am not including Biden in my context now, much more present for me is the dog trying to get my toast leftovers off my side table.

The context thing is more complicated than one may think and I don't want to bog you down with this. I would, however, love you to understand that people's contexts can be very small (a kitchen) or very large (the world). They can focus on something like a war or a death or an overwhelming feeling, to like as in feeling like ennui. We can try to make them very small as a way to feel in control, important, and not at the mercy of a giant world. Alternatively, we can reach across the world to pull contexts in other worlds into our daily existence, a thrilling thought for some and terrifying for others.

Why is it important to understand context?

Humans adapt to contexts to survive and thrive. As a result, behaviours and attitudes that we see today are created by the context of yesterday, and hopefully also the contexts of today. This may seem like a bit of a no-brainer, but we often forget this, believing instead that behaviour is solely a function of personality or character. This is an attribution error, where we attribute the wrong causal factors to explain our own and other's behaviours.

This attribution error is most marked when we evaluate other people's behaviour. We often see our own behaviour as caused by a context or an intention, while we see other's behaviours as stemming from their (erring) personality. We can hear this in statements like, 'I was just trying to do my best', 'I got ahead through hard work only', 'He did it because he is mean' and 'He never got anywhere because he is lazy'.

To understand our *self* and *others*, we need to understand the contexts that created us/them. Without knowing this, we can easily respond with applause or judgement when neither is due. This attribution error distorts our experience, and this distortion is often in service of those who got the leg-ups, and judgemental of those who do not do as well in our world. When we understand how we or *others* may have been sculpted by a context, we can become more empathic to our *self/others*. We can view lives with more kindness and greater humility.

When we think about our *self* and *others* as a product of a context, we can view lives with less judgement. Judgement creates shame in our *self* and in *others* and, as we will find out, shame plays a significant role in causing stuckness. It is an enabler of stuckness, while empathy an enabler of fluidity. However, in order to do be more fluid, we need to learn how to read contexts more clearly, we need to become context savvy and not context ignorant.

How are contexts changing?

Globalisation and global media have brought more contexts to us and we have a sense of greater speed in our world. Technology, for example, seems to push us towards a faster and faster life. It impacts our lives hugely, telling us what to do, monitoring our behaviours, mimicking our thinking, and entrapping our sexuality. I am not a Luddite, I like a computer, and I think you get the picture of how the forces of technology impact our lives and the web.

The next point you after know as in know all about and that is the palpable increase in chaos and uncertainty in the world. We are at a stage of our civilisation where all sorts of things are now possible, including global wars, climate change disasters, global pandemics, massive displacements of people, global organised crime, political turmoil, AI, and more. There is much uncertainty.

The world is more complex, faster, bigger, and more uncertain. This means we have to work harder to make sense of our world and remain relevant. This does not mean we must panic and spin our heads, it means we have to notice what is going on and decide consciously how we are going to respond. Will we make our world smaller, will we avoid looking at other's suffering, will we cling on to the illusion that we can control our environment, or will we learn how to be more present and fluid to what is happening out there?

The five horsemen of the stuckness apocalypse

There are structural factors that increase our capacity for stuckness. The five that I think are most important include the neoliberal system, inequality, trauma, loss of humanity, and climate change. These five factors are all intertwined, amplifying each other's effects. They are presented below in no particular order because of their iterative and co-dependent relationship with each other.

Neoliberalism

Neoliberalism is a form of capitalism and the dominant global ideology for guiding the economies of organisations and governments, as well as international agencies. This approach recommends the reduction of state intervention in commercial and social activities and suggests that free competition reduces waste, increases efficiency, and ensures individual responsibility. In reality, this has meant more freedom for the rich and powerful and less protection for the poor and powerless. While some people would argue that this has led to economic flourishing, there is plenty of evidence that neoliberalism has created an increase in social inequalities in the countries where it has been applied.[2]

This system has had a huge effect on how we think about our *self*, where and how we take responsibility, and our capacity for being human.

The internal logic of neoliberalism is positivist and utilitarian, that is, based on science and numbers, and orientated around whether things and people have utility or not. Humans provide utility through the production and consumption of goods, and this utility is measured in numbers or put more bluntly, through currency.

Let's explore the idea of our *self* as objects of utility, that we exist to be used as tools or objects of commerce and our value is measured only by our economic contribution. When we generate a high economic impact we are more valued than when we generate limited or low economic impact; for example, CEOs earn more than school teachers, who earn more than beggars. When we don't add value to the system through economic output, we can be discounted, seen as disposable or even a drain on resources, for example, old poor people, or those with no education, or who have serious mental health problems.

We also provide economic contribution by consuming. The neoliberal context encourages us to consume because this is seen as the oil that keeps the wheels greased and the growth climbing. And we respond with enthusiasm, in fact, we go so far as to view our consumption as a measure of our lives, you with your Porsche are more important than me with my old Datsun.

Money moves away from the people who need it to those who already have it, and are considered economic contributors by producing and consuming. This system does not appreciate how we are all interconnected and that no money at the bottom of the pyramid creates problems for everyone, even the very wealthy.

This has several impacts on our psyche: firstly when we treat our *self* as an object of utility, we objectify our *self* and value our *self* according to our financial status. We organise our lives around enhancing this financial value and this limits our capacity to grow and be fully human. Objects can be enslaved, are disposable, and replaceable when they no longer render the desired value to the powers that be. When we are enslaved by a system in this way we become vulnerable to losing our *self* and our autonomy and, more critically, our capacity to grow becomes diminished. Neoliberalism has the ability to damage some of the fundamental aspects of our humanity.[3]

A further impact on our psyche relates to how we make sense of our own and other's success or lack thereof. When it comes to causality, the neoliberal way of thinking focusses on the individual and not the system. If you flourish in the system, it is because you are talented, but if you do not do well, it is because you did not take responsibility for your *self*, or were too lazy, stupid, or too rebellious to succeed. Critically, our impoverished situation is not the fault of the system and had nothing to do with you being born on the streets, excluded from education, forced into a life of crime to survive, or made ill from living in informal settlements.[4]

Neoliberalism individualises blame. So when it comes to fixing our unhappiness, or stuckness, or poverty, or mental health, then it is up to us because the system is not responsible. I don't want to totally remove personal responsibility as a factor here but we too often forget the systemic and structural causes of our problems. And yes, the *self*-help industry plays right into this, asserting that we and not the system are to blame for whatever is ailing us, and that it is our responsibility alone to remedy things. And yes again, this text has elements of a *self*-help book but hopefully one that also invites you to rail against the system and not just your-*self*.

Inequality

Related to, but not totally dependent on the neoliberal system is the issue of inequality. This can be understood on two levels: between a country and another country/ies, or within countries. The first type relates to the disparity between countries of economic wealth, control of the global narrative/s, bargaining power, land rights, migration movements, and more. I think you know how this works very well, especially if you come from a minority country.

The field of inequality within a country refers to how incomes and resources are spread across population groups within a country, notably how much they deviate up or down from the average levels of wealth and access to resources. This phenomenon is measured by the Gini coefficient with a score of zero meaning none or very little inequality. South Africa had the highest Gini coefficient in the world in 2024 with a score of 0.63.[5]

Countries with high levels of inequality tend to be more volatile internally with higher levels of social unrest, greater levels of health or social problems, and lower levels of economic growth. People living in unequal societies experience lower levels of satisfaction and happiness. Further psychological impacts of inequality include depression, anxiety, shame, anger, materialism, stigmatisation, trauma, loss of agency, and much more. These factors all contribute to creating an environment where people get become easily stuck in degenerative cycles.[6]

Loss of humanity

Many factors have led to a loss of humanity and community (colonisation, industrialisation, migration, globalisation, materialism, trauma, wars, poverty, technology, and inequality). The loss of humanity means the loss of respect for human life, and largely refers to using humans as objects for our service, pleasure, or wealth.

Individualism and individual achievement are built into and rewarded in our education system and economic activity. As a result, our community, family bonds, and other relationships have experienced significant stress; modern life can often be isolated and lonely. The collegial container that our worlds could offer has become weakened, and with this our capacity for remaining human and fluid.

Trauma

Trauma is a universally ubiquitous experience for humans. There are many factors that ensure trauma is never too far from our day-to-day lives (war; human rights violations; environmental disasters; accidents; poverty; slavery; being a refugee; crime; intergenerational trauma; domestic, social, and work-based violence; gender-based violence; bullying; adverse childhood conditions; racism; debt).

When we look at the histories of countries, a small number of which have not experienced the trauma of being colonised or being the coloniser,[7] we could come to believe that our entire civilisation is built on trauma. Trauma is possibly the bedrock of our civilisation and it is replicating itself over and over through the generations. When trauma plays out over generations and civilisations, it locks us into adversarial and stuck relationships between people, groups, countries, and the Earth. It is disheartening to think how many generations it will take to heal the current traumatising contexts and whether this is even possible.

Trauma limits people's lives, causes them to traumatise *others* and to damage the Earth in the same way that they have been damaged. It freezes our lives, objectifies us, disempowers us, addicts us, and destroys our relationships and our humanity.[8]

Now we know that there is such a thing as post-traumatic stress disorder and post-traumatic growth disorder, so the picture is not all bad. However, we cannot deny the role trauma has in shaping how we live, the relationships we have, and the futures we could inhabit.

Climate change

Climate change impacts on our capacity for stuckness in many ways. It causes contextual volatility, uncertainty, mass migration and refugees, wars for resources, mental health inequality, and a ripe context for the exploitation of minority populations.[9] These factors build a container ripe for stuckness because of their capacity to oppress, dehumanise, traumatise, isolate, and sideline people.

On an individual basis, climate change can cause anxiety, difficulties in envisioning and planning for a future, and depression. This has become more and more noticeable in millennials and Gen Zs who are also expressing anger towards previous generations for leaving them with a damaged and destabilised Earth.

Can contexts get stuck?

If we understand that stuckness is a relationship between parts of a system, be it human or environmental, then contexts can be stuck. In fact, if you look carefully, you will see couples, groups, organisations, and countries that are stuck in times different from today, in old repetitive warring relationships, or cycling outside mainstream economies into multiple generations of poverty. We live in a world where stuck systems are colliding with more fluid ones; no wonder we have such volatility in the world.

When societies are stuck, we spend all our energy on responding to the stuckness and have less time for our own growing and learning. It is very hard to be fluid in a context that is stuck. For example, it is very hard to grow and learn and emerge as a human when you are living in a war zone, or being trained to fulfil a societal role that is out of date. It is hard to be fluid while you are stuck in a downward poverty spiral, or age full of life in a care system where the focus is on geriatric compliance and control.

When organisations get stuck it can be because their purpose or way of working is no longer relevant. For example, an organisation that was set up to do x and has grown a culture appropriate for delivering x. This organisation would get stuck when the leaders failed to notice that x was no longer needed, and the culture had become stale and frustrated in its attempts to continue delivering x. Many organisations struggle with this problem, especially in the fast-changing environments such as we have now.

So, contexts can get stuck. This book is broadly about how individuals and pairs get stuck, although it can be applied to groups, organisations, and countries.

What contextual issues affect coaches?

When we coach, we are working with the context in which the behaviours were created as well as the current context in which they are being expressed. If we don't do this well, we can attribute behaviour to personality or maturity. Behaviour is not always just a function of intrapsychic processes but it is always a function of contexts. If we don't include contexts in our coaching, we are letting our clients down.

Watching the context is particularly important for executive coaching where we are paid by an organisation to work with their staff members. We do this work because we believe that it is useful to both the individual and the organisation. We know that both are our clients and that we have to serve both in our work. This is where it can as in get tricky, when we serve one at the expense of the other, and this has a significant impact on the way the coaching unfolds.

Coaching works best when it is voluntary and when client privacy is respected. It works best when the client sees it as an opportunity for growth and not remediation.

Coaching works badly when people are mandated to attend coaching for fixing, or as a last performative step before they are fired or moved, or supported to resign. These are potentially bad faith contexts where we are being paid to get the client 'fixed'. These contexts are not developmental unless we creatively find a way to make them so. Our job is to support people to grow, face the challenges in their environment, and make choices about how they want to respond. Our job is also to support organisations to be healthy and productive workplaces.

Sometimes, contexts come to coaching in the form of oppressive bosses/partners, unethical cultures, racism, and sexism. When this happens we need to think very carefully about how we support people to adapt, disappear, resist, or leave.

The psychiatrist and liberation theorist, Fanon, has some interesting suggestions about working with patients in oppressive systems. He was speaking to racial oppression in Algeria, under French occupation, and how this had caused mental illness. Fanon asks whether therapists should try to help clients to adjust and acclimatise to an oppressive situation, or whether they should be supporting people to decide how to choose their freedom within that context.[10] Perhaps there is a lesson in this for us? Wherever we stand on the role of corporates, the latter is always the best approach.

Questions to ask your *self*

- What was the context of your birth? What was happening in the world, what significant events happened in your ancestral line, how were your parents, and what life experience did they bring to your parenting? How would your early context have influenced the formation of your personality and orientation in the world?
- Has your orientation to the world changed as you have grown older? Has your approach to the world and coaching become more or less contextual?
- What contextual issue is currently top of mind for you?

Notes

1 Figural is a gestalt term from Clarkson, P. (2004). *Gestalt counselling in action* (3rd ed.). SAGE Publications Limited.
2 Wilson, J. (2018) *Neoliberalism*. Routledge.
3 Heil, D. (2011) *Ontological fundamentals for ethical management hedeiegger and the corporate world, issues in business ethics*. Springer; Mbembe, A., & Dubois, L. (2017). *Critique of black reason*. Duke University Press.
4 Wilson, J. (2018) *Neoliberalism*.
5 https://worldpopulationreview.com/country-rankings/gini-coefficient-by-country (Accessed: 28 June 2024).
6 Wilkinson, R. G., & Pickett, K. (2010). *The spirit level: Why greater equality makes societies stronger*. Bloomsbury Press.

7 Benjet, C., et al.. (2016). The epidemiology of traumatic event exposure worldwide: Results from the World Mental Health Survey Consortium. *Psychological Medicine*, *46*(2), 327–343.
8 Maté, G. (2018). *In the realm of hungry ghosts: Close encounters with addiction.* Vermilion; Hubl, T., & Jordan Avritt, J. (2020). *Healing collective trauma: A process for integrating our intergenerational and cultural wounds.* Sounds True.
9 Maté, G. (2018). *In the realm of hungry ghosts.*
10 Fanon, F. (1986) *Black skin, white masks.* Pluto Press.

Bibliography

Benjet, C., Bromet, E., Karam, E. G., Kessler, R. C., McLaughlin, K. A., Ruscio, A. M., Shahly, V., Stein, D. J., Petukhova, M., Hill, E., Alonso, J., Atwoli, L., Bunting, B., Bruffaerts, R., Caldas-de-Almeida, J. M., de Girolamo, G., Florescu, S., Gureje, O., Huang, Y., Lepine, J. P., Kawakami, N., & Kovess-Mas, K. K. T. (2016). The epidemiology of traumatic event exposure worldwide: Results from the World Mental Health Survey Consortium. *Psychological Medicine*, *46*(2), 327–343.

Clarkson, P. (2004). *Gestalt counselling in action* (3rd ed.). SAGE Publications Limited.

Fanon, F. (1986). *Black skin, white masks.* Pluto Press.

Heil, D. (2011). *Ontological fundamentals for ethical management.* Heidegger and the corporate world, issues in business ethics. Springer.

Hubl, T., & Jordan Avritt, J. (2020). *Healing collective trauma: A process for integrating our intergenerational and cultural wounds.* Sounds True. https://worldpopulationreview.com/country-rankings/gini-coefficient-by-country (Accessed: 28 June 2024).

Maté, G. (2018). *In the realm of hungry ghosts: Close encounters with addiction.* Vermilion.

Mbembe, A., & Dubois, L. (2017) *Critique of black reason.* Duke University Press. Available at: https://www.who.int/news-room/fact-sheets/detail/climate-change-and-health (Accessed: 21 November 2023).

Wilkinson, R. G., & Pickett, K. (2010). *The spirit level: Why greater equality makes societies stronger.* Bloomsbury Press.

Wilson, J. (2018). *Neoliberalism.* Routledge.

Chapter 4

An incomplete wound finds a salient context and hope blossoms

In this chapter I would like to deepen the idea of incomplete wounds that strive for completion. When this happens, we return to a previous state that results in the loss of *self*, *others*, and *meaning*. These losses are kept in place by a battery of stuck behaviours. Stuckness is a developmental impasse that ironically kick-starts a developmental surge.

What is an incomplete wound?

Incomplete wounds are wounds that need our attention; they want to heal and through this help us create a more satisfying life. Incomplete wounds are ambitious and want more than just healing, they want to be integrated into our lives and validated for the awareness and benefits they can bring. A wound wants healing, grieving, and also to be able to use the skills developed while being wounded to benefit the lives of our *self* and *others*. For intergenerational types of wounding, they also want to contribute to stop the cycle at our generation.

Our woundings create some of our 'flavour' and personality. They make us idiosyncratic and unique. They direct our lives in both positive and negative ways. We have to honour them and enable them to play their transformative role in our lives.

There are many kinds of wounding and just to give you an idea of this range, I have provided some examples below:

- Intergenerational trauma of all types.
- Trauma of all sorts, ranging from interpersonal (neglect, sexual abuse) to societal (race, gender, religious-based, national, ethnic) to environmental (climate-based) trauma.
- Wounding from growing up in poverty.
- Wounding from not being able to be our full *self* in early life.
- Wounding at experiencing oneself as not good enough.
- Wounding from not being adequately cared for as a child.
- Attachment styles that undermine our capacity to be with our *self* and *others*.

DOI: 10.4324/9781003536253-4

- Wounding from isolation and scapegoating.
- Unresolved grief.
- Too much or too little control, safety, love, attention, space, freedom, toughness, and conflict in our childhoods.
- Wounding from stuck patterns and being irrelevant.

Everyone has some wounding, but not all wounds are as severe as others. Just because our wounds may be less traumatic than others does not mean that they do not direct our life. We are always in some kind of wound completion process.

How do wounds complete their process?

Wounds have an inherent ambition to complete their process, that is, to heal and manifest their virtues, even if this has to be done over a couple of generations as in the case of intergenerational trauma. Completing wounds is not a one-off process but rather a repetitive cycle that occurs over time, again and again as we work with each layer.

The Cycle of Stuckness is one way that we intuitively work with our wounding. It provides us with the opportunity to digest our pasts and transform them into the seeds of our future *self*. Although the wound will lead us towards completion, it is better when we can support this process through other means. By doing so we can speed up the Cycle of Stuckness and make the digestion and incubation process easier for our *self* and *others*.

Why do wounds look for salient contexts?

Wounds often pop up for healing when we are relaxed and feeling more competent. They are also likely to become more conscious when our contexts are in some ways reminiscent of the original context or patterning of our original wounding. When wounds have a relationship to a context or a salience, we have a greater capacity to work with them.

My research suggests that there is a relationship between the wound needing healing and the contexts that manifest stuckness and ultimately prompt healing.[1] For example, if we are trained into being performative in our early lives, we may chose a vocational context that relies on this same behaviour. Through this matching we create a stuckness situation that ironically invites us to be more authentic.

For those that are Freudian in orientation, you could call this process 'repetition compulsion'.[2] For those more existential we call it a 'hermeneutic circle' in the Heideggerian sense. A hermeneutic circle is a learning cycle where we repeat old behaviours in order to learn new ways of being. The circle always starts in a known pattern of behaviour, but we don't notice it because it is so familiar.[3] This means we make choices based on what we know, and are familiar with, rather than on what may be immediately good for us. Luckily, this means we have a chance to work on our wounds.

Winnicott's work on rupture and repair is also relevant here. He speaks of ruptures as being breaks in relationships or wounding. Repairs are when we are able to repair this injury. We repair to a good enough state, not a state of perfection. As in the cycle, the rupture is less important than the repair process. Furthermore, like in the cycle, repairs are never totally complete but become good enough for us to move forward from or around them.[4]

Other ways of working with wounds

We can work with wounding in spiritual/mythological, somatic, psychological, and cognitive ways. Spiritual and mythological ways include ritual, religion, and spirituality. For some, it can include plant medicines and the use of hallucinogens. For *others*, it can be prayer, meditation, or sacred dance.

Psychological explanations relate to ways of understanding that are based on our emotions and thoughts. This includes most talking therapies, although many of these methodologies integrate somatic and mythological or spiritual work (like existential coaching can).

Somatic work refers to working with the sensations, discomfort, or disease that becomes embedded in our bodies as a result of the wounding and our attempts to live around this. We can discharge this through meditation, body interventions (massage, pressure point, body stress release, etc.), or physical experiences (exercise, yoga, TRE,[5] sex) or self-care (nutrition, sleep, hydration, minimising exposure to environmental toxins).

Cognitive approaches include explanations that provide scientific and rational explanations for feelings, senses, and insights. This could include biological explanations of disease, neuroscience, biofeedback, and more. Cognitive processes are conscious and involve the verbal articulation of what is going on inside us. As such they can be useful in making other non-verbal or 'rational' processes apparent to our conscious mind. There are, however, some things that cannot be explained in words.

When working with wounds, it is useful to use more than one of the process types mentioned above. We can use these approaches to understand the wounding as best we can, even if this means accepting the absurdity of life and our inability to understand it. We need a mourning phase through which we can discharge stuck energy created by the wounding or the unlived life resulting from the wound. We then must find a way to create an empowering narrative for our wounding and enable it to manifest its virtues into our lives. The empowering narrative is a way to 'file' the wound, log it into our *self*, or perhaps release it back into the wild. Shame prevents us from doing this well because it reattaches our *self* to the original form of the wounding. Thus, to complete an iteration of healing, we need to work with our shame as well.

I will mention these interventions all over this book, especially in the sections on growing *self*, *others*, and *meaning*. You will notice that when we work on the three areas (*self*, *others*, *meaning*) we are also working on our wounds.

So now that we know that our nascent wounds are out there for looking for salient contexts, it is time to see what happens when they connect, and through this enter a new iteration of the Cycle of Stuckness. We re-enter the cycle and hope springs anew.

Entering the cycle with hope

And so we arrive all fresh and new, with an ambitious wound looking for completion, and we enter this new relationship with hope. Hope that this time things will work out better than before.

Now we know humans repeat patterns in relationships, but this is not the point I am trying to make here. What I am trying to tell you is that no matter how badly the last 'thing' ended, humans tend to start the new one with the hope that it will work out better this time. This is a most beautiful quality of humans, that despite pain and suffering, off we go again, eager for another stint in the trenches. Obviously, not all people try again at everything, but I think that if you measured going again over a lifetime, you would see that most people do it. You see the quiet voice of hope never really dies while we are alive, and in some cases maybe even after we die. Perhaps it would be useful to explore this magnificent human quality before we enter the cycle more fully.

Hope

Hope is a combination of two things: a desire for something and an expectation, however small, that there is a chance this thing will happen. Both must exist for hope to be present.

The role of hope is to give us the courage and motivation to go for bigger goals, goals that make life satisfying. Desire gives motivation and expectation gives direction which we are then responsible for translating into action. Hope alone does not create change, we have to move into action. We must have desire, courage, motivation, and discipline for us to move through difficulties and achieve larger and more meaningful projects.

Desire and expectations can come from inside us and outside us – my sense is that the more powerful versions come from inside us. They are generated by a variety of thoughts, feelings, beliefs, assumptions, and can be very irrational, nonsensical, or downright idiotic. However, these factors don't stop us from having them. This is probably a good thing because it means we keep trying, and trying leads to growing, and growing leads to us being more fully human.

For desires to become activated, they need to be meaningful to us in some way. People have different ideas about what is meaningful to them, but there are general themes around what is meaningful for all humans. *Meaning* often relates to our own development (learning how to ride a bicycle, getting a degree), how we serve the world (helping needy people, getting a child through school), or grow something (making a beautiful garden or a business). These things have intrinsic *meaning* embedded in them, but there are other hopes that may be less meaningful. We can, for example, be easily confused by desires and expectations that come from outside our *self*, embed themselves inside us, and even speak with our own voice to us. We can also become easily distracted by things that are ostensibly meaningless, but that we have pushed meaning into, for example, a designer handbag, or a flat belly. We will get to this later.

Hope is unbelievably diligent and conscientious because it must be, it is a life-sustaining force. We really need it to survive, without it we have nothing but our *self* and our current situation, and that can make us feel homicidal and/or suicidal. We need the idea of something that transcends our here and now to keep us toiling on this mortal plane and continue engaging with death, isolation, meaninglessness, and freedom.

Incomplete wounds in coaches?

Coaches also have wounding and these can interfere in our coaching. They may even have brought us to become a coach in the first place. Our woundings may make us feel not good enough, or conversely a know-it-all, or even bully our clients. We can be triggered by client stories and we can project onto clients. Part of our duty as a coach is to review and clean out our wounding so that they don't interfere in our ability to be useful to clients. We need to learn to use our wounds to support our clients, not undermine them.

Questions to ask our *self*

- What did you think about the description of woundings and the critical role they play in initiating the Cycle of Stuckness? Does this make sense to you?
- Have you noticed any of your wounds popping up in sessions with your clients? What did you do about it, if anything?
- What do you think about hope? What do you do with hope when it pops up?

Notes

1 Kukard, J. (2021). *Bewitched, amputated or dead: An existential study of leadership stuckness*. DProf thesis Middlesex University/New School of Psychotherapy and Counselling (NSPC) Psychology.
2 Freud, S. (2015). *Beyond the pleasure principle* (17th ed.). Dover Publications.
3 Heil, D. (2011) *Ontological fundamentals for ethical management. Heidegger and the corporate world*. Dordrecht. Springer.
4 Winnicott, D. W. (1957). *The child and the outside world*. Tavistock/Basic Books.
5 TRE : Trauma Releasing Excercises.

Bibliography

Freud, S. (2015). *Beyond the pleasure principle* (17th ed.). Dover Publications.

Heil, D. (2011) *Ontological fundamentals for ethical management: Heidegger and the corporate world.* Issues in business ethics. Springer.

Kukard, J. (2021). *Bewitched, amputated or dead: An existential study of leadership stuckness.* DProf thesis Middlesex University/New School of Psychotherapy and Counselling (NSPC) Psychology.

Winnicott, D. W. (1957). *The child and the outside world.* Tavistock/Basic Books.

Chapter 5

Losing *self* and sedimentation

Physically, it's quite hard to lose parts of ourselves, however, psychologically and spiritually, we are fairly adept at this. This chapter explores what a *self* is, how we don't notice when we lose it, and how we lose it through becoming bewitched, amputated, or dead.

Self: the ground of our life

The most important relationship we will ever have is with our *self*. This is why this chapter is important, it is about our *self*; what it is, why we need it, how it grows, learns, and adapts, and how we can lose it and not notice.

Psychology, spirituality, and philosophy have many definitions of a *self*, there is even something called 'self psychology'.[1] When I use the term *self* I mean the sense of who we are that we get through our actions, impacts, thoughts, feelings, sensations, dreams, desires, relationships with *others*, and more. It includes our body (the source of our being in the world), as well as our spirituality (the source of our being transcendent in the world). Our *self* is our *meaning*-making machinery; how we make sense of life, as well as our own mini hall of mirrors; how we reflect on our *self*.

Some people believe that we are born with an essential *self*, some authentic core that is only us, is always the same, and that exists outside societal requirements and survivalist behaviour. This way of thinking can lead us to believe that the *self* must be uncovered and restored from the muck of ego, personality, and socialisation through a process of psychological excavation. The idea of an immutable central *self* gives us the idea that we are solid and stable and exist. This is comforting in our mad world where things are not always certain.

I like this idea, but I like two other existential ideas as well. The first is that the *self* is largely created in conversation with *others* and the world, and the second that authenticity is emergent. In this way of thinking we are formed by our interactions with the world. This means that most of our *self* does not exist before we interact with the world. Furthermore, that our authenticity is emergent and changing as we move through the world. Therefore, what is our

DOI: 10.4324/9781003536253-5

authentic *self* to us today may not be our authentic *self* tomorrow. In other words, we exist before we have an identity and that identity changes as we live our life.[2]

There is something else that may be useful here, and that is the field of epigenetics. Epigenetics is a scientific field that explores how context turns genes on and off. The initial research looked mainly at genes and disease, but more recently there have been applications to personality. The idea is that aspects of personality can be turned on and off in response to context, and that these same tunings can be passed on genetically across generations. As a result, we are not our own personality, we are in fact the personality genes that were turned on in our grandparents and transferred into us.[3] How curious and how interesting, and just another example of how mutable a *self* is and how difficult it can be to know who one's *self* is.

I am going to offer a pragmatic combination of the approaches: that there is some small central core that is our unchanging essential *self* and then a lot of other emergent parts that can be added and subtracted as the gene pool and context requires, and as we choose to be. The main point I am trying to make here is that we can and do change who we are and, in fact, should do. If we have not shifted our ideas about our *self* over the years, then we have not been learning and growing. So, don't go boasting as a 50-year-old that you are the same person you were at 20, its nothing to be proud of at all, it's a public declaration of stuckness.

A way to think about a *self* is that it is our central *meaning*-making machinery. It takes all kinds of data in from the world – our body, heart, and mind – integrates it and chooses how to respond to it. Some of the activities of our *self* may be less conscious, like instincts, and *others* more conscious, like thinking.

The *self* is the mechanism that holds us together in some sort of coherent whole; if we don't have a *self*, then we may be like a ship with no captain and a hundred passengers each having a turn at the wheel. We need a *self* to organise and integrate all the aspects of our *self*, including the nascent ones, and get us going on life in one direction.

When we have a robust *self*, we have the capacity to weather life's misfortunes and heal from life's blows. This is because a strong *self* gives us a sense of stability and direction and allows us to believe that we exist in some organised and solid way. It is this sense of *self* that also enables us to grow from adverse events, and not remain stuck or diminished by them.

Our *self* is formed over time and in conversation with our contexts. It contains current information generated through our experience now, but also a whole lot of historical data, some of which has been handed down to us from our parents and their parents. For many, if not most people, the *self* is dominated by historical data. We live in the present but our responses to the world are determined by the past. This is the aetiology of stuckness, when we use recipes from the past to deal with life in the present.

Having a broad and strong *self* where we have integrated many identities enables us to be more agile in our response to the world. When we have a narrow *self*, we tend to have a more limited repertoire of responses to the world. For example, if I think I am only a mother, then I will respond to the world only as a mother, and this may not be appropriate or useful in all contexts. When I have a *self* that has many aspects, including a mother, a leader, a spiritual person, a partner, etc. I have a broader range of behaviours from which to choose when I respond to the world. This makes me more agile and effective in the world and I can use this to move towards what I want from life more easily.

When I lose aspects of my *self*, for whatever reason, I diminish my range of responses and in some instances can become like a one-trick pony who has the same response to all situations. When this happens, I am unable to respond to changes in the context, and land up acting in historical ways that are less relevant and effective. I get stuck.

Maybe it's a good idea to just have a quick look at some theory on how people adapt or not; it's really a description of how the *self* sees and responds to information from the context.

How do we grow and learn and adapt?

Our *self* forms in response to the context, we are socialised into roles and personalities and behaviours. This happens through our interactions with *others* and the way we reflect on these interactions. *Self*-reflection is the critical function that lands the learning or not and, when agreed with, manifests it into thinking and behaviour patterns. This brings us to assimilation and accommodation, two ways of learning (or not).

Assimilation and accommodation[4] are Piagetian terms used to describe learning; that is how we take in new data and use it to adapt our *self* (or not). In both cases we notice information from inside our *self*, like feelings or senses, or from outside our *self*, like the world telling us to do something. What happens next is that we either use this information to adapt our *self* or we don't.

With assimilation, we process the data and make sense of it through our existing *self* or *meaning*-making machinery. The new data does not change this machinery and we get the same answers or questions that we normally do. Sometimes this is useful and energy efficient but sometimes this leads us to draw less accurate conclusions about our *self* and the world.

With the process of accommodation, we allow our *meaning*-making machinery to be changed by the new data. When we receive information that we don't like or that is confusing, or outside our version of the world and our *self*, we don't get rid of it by saying it's a personal attack from an idiot. We don't invalidate this information, we sit with it longer. We review whether the way we are making sense of something is useful, and where it is not, we then adapt our *meaning*-making machinery. This can require shuffling our assumptions around or minimising our generalisations, so that we start reading the information in a new way. In other words, we start to be able to see the world as it is, rather than how we are in it.

The world touches us in good, bad, and other ways. It can glance off us, lightly touch us, or enter our soul. The touch of the world can bore or entertain or depress us, or even motivate us to do things. It is largely up to us how deeply we internalise it. When we don't let the world enter us, it has no possibility to update our inner world, and stay relevant. Our inner programming remains stagnant, and we lose relevance and traction. This is the nature of stuckness.

How can we lose our *self* and not notice it?

The following sections of this chapter describe the processes of losing one's *self* through becoming bewitched, amputated, or dead. Losing some of one's *self* is often 'normal' and happens when we try to balance our own needs with those of another in a relationship. It is usually non-pathological but becomes a problem when we lose too much of our *self*, and through this our capacity to reflect and learn. This is when some other person or thing takes over the steering wheel of our lives and we are watching from the back seat but still think we are driving.

In early life, people generally hear their inner world and feelings fairly automatically, yes indeed, without therapy, coaching, or training. However, our childhood context and emergent sense-making may encourage us to stop doing this. Maybe our feelings are too scary, maybe the big people tell us that our feelings are not valid or appropriate, or maybe we see the bad stuff that happens when *others* have big feelings. And yes, sometimes it is useful for us to not feel our feelings, for example, when things are really bad and we need to focus on surviving rather than feeling. Not feeling in this case is adaptive, at least temporarily.

Socialisation and early life experience are important factors in how we connect to our *self*, in particular whether we are socialised to read and respond to our inner worlds, and whether we are rewarded or penalised for doing so. While we all need guidance from *others*, this needs to be balanced with our own inner direction, or we risk never finding our *self* fully.

A further influential aspect relates to our skills of *self*-reflection. We are often not good at this because it can be unpleasant or too pleasant, or because we are not sure how to think about our *self*. Sometimes we can use other's views as a way to *self*-reflect, for example, looking at my behaviour from the perspective of my mother or lover. In fact, and as this chapter demonstrates, reflecting on one's *self* through other people's eyes is a leading cause of loss of *self*.

It takes a solid sense of *self*, and a capacity to balance our 'bad' with our 'good', for us to face all our glory and imperfections and still have the courage to do life. This can be particularly hard for people who have experienced significant shaming in their lives, or for those who believe that they have found the recipe for life. It is often much easier for us to avoid *self*-reflection and externalise blame/praise, thereby avoiding facing our *self*.

Either way, most of us land up with a tenuous relationship with our feelings, sensations, and thoughts; not sure how to hear them, when to trust them, and what to do with them. Our feelings can then become inaudible or very distant and easy to ignore; like a baby ewe lost and bleating on one of the higher Alps while we are in the tavern in the valley below on our fifth beer and in the middle of an Arsenal game.

I don't want to omit a further aspect that enables our disconnection from our *self*, and that is a disconnection to our bodies. When we cannot connect to the information that our body provides, we are one step closer towards losing connection with our inner world.

Lastly, we can become entranced by the immediate outcomes of losing our *self*, for example, finding a new lover, so much so, that we don't notice the price we have paid. Ultimately, this means that we may not notice when we get stuck, at least in the early stages before it becomes painful. And so, as we will find out later, we need this pain to remind us to keep emerging and adapting and living life as it is and not as we are in it.

How do we know if changes to our *self* are adaptive or a loss?

So now that we know that our *self* can and should change, how do we know when this change is adaptive and grows one's *self*, or when it results in the loss of one's *self*. The answer is complex and simple; we need to get to know our *self*, even as it is emerging. This is, of course, a life's work because *selfs* are notoriously mischievous, oblique, and take a long time to get to know.

We may ask whether the changes we are making to how we think and be are expanding our *self* or making our *self* smaller. Additional questions could be: Am I learning new things? Do I have a greater behavioural repertoire, or am I making my life smaller in order to feel safe and certain? Lastly, we may ask, have I lost parts of me that gave me *meaning*, pleasure, joy, and belonging?

In the existential paradigm, much anxiety is the normal outcome of stretching one's *self* into life and embracing our freedom.[5] Healthy people are ambitious about learning and growing. They expose their *self* to the world and its influence, and this enables them to stay relevant. Change by definition induces anxiety in us humans, but it is how we respond to this anxiety that is important. Do we open our *self* up to life or do we foreclose on life as a way to reduce our inner anxiety. This is an important question that I will explore more deeply in the section on finding one's *self*.

What role does a *self* play in stuckness?

We need a *self* to direct our lives so that we can grow and learn and create value for the world based on our individual gifts. Our *self* is the source of our capacity to remain fluid in the world.

Without a *self* we cannot direct our lives towards meaningful purposes and relationships. If our *selfs* are too narrow, they lose their adaptive capacity, leaving us stuck in lives that are unsatisfying and irrelevant. We need many inner identities, a broad *self*, to be able to respond in an agile way to the world, so that we can manifest purposeful projects and satisfying relationships.

The next three sections provide more detailed descriptions of how we can lose our *self* through becoming bewitched, amputated, or dead.

Losing *self* by becoming bewitched

The first loss of *self* is through bewitchment, and before I go into the technical details I want to share with you the tale of Ashwin, the human spreadsheet.

Ashwin, the human spreadsheet

Ashwin was sent to me by his HR director. He was a full partner at an accounting firm in London after having grown his section of the business by 300% over the past two years. Mary the HR director explained that Ashwin had 'people problems' and that these had come to a head in the latest culture survey. His team had complained that he was transactional, competitive, pushed them too hard, and showed a lack of interest and respect for their lives. He was doing incredibly well on the numbers, but this was being undermined by his 'people problems' which looked like they may result in some of his team resigning, particularly the younger members. On top of this, Ashwin had thrown his hat into the leadership race and had been surprised when told that it was unlikely that he would get the CEO position because of his 'people problems'. Mary said Ashwin only focussed on the numbers and had very little idea of the relationship skills needed to lead people.

Ashwin arrived, dressed in a black suit as all committed accountants do, but with a more than average sprinkling of high-end brands decorating his person. We intended to explore the areas he wanted to work on in the first session, in particular, the results of his team's culture survey. This was challenging because Ashwin struggled to even see that there was a problem. He repeatedly noted that the numbers spoke for themselves and that this showed that he did not have a leadership or people problem. Despite this, I was however, able to get a picture of his life, finding that he was single, had a close relationship with his mother, but other than that, his work was his life and his identity.

Over the next few sessions, Ashwin told me about his life and how he had driven himself to become successful. He was the first in his family to go to university and the first to really make significant money. His parents had experienced poverty and powerlessness in the world, and the memory of this was still alive in Ashwin, internalised by the family stories and requirements his mother had of him and his life.

Ashwin's dad died young, leaving a small pension that would get him and his brothers through school, but money was still tight. His mom, Aisha, worked as an administrator for a bank where she learned the criteria for good investments, including how resources need firm and strategic management to come to fruition. Ashwin, the second born showed more than his fair share of discipline and intellectual prowess and, as a result, received more than his fair share of the familial investment. To Aisha, he was the golden child who would elevate the family name by being successful, and she made her dream for him very clear from an early age: no failure was to be tolerated.

This was a heavy burden for Ashwin, although there were moments of joy when he won competitions, or showed the more privileged boys at his school what hard work and brains could do. His excellent marks paved the way for scholarships for under- and post-graduate degrees, and finally a job offer from a consulting company.

Ashwin, who had been packaging himself for success since he turned nine, was once again able to chameleon himself into his consulting role. He learned how to dress, to talk and to present himself in a way that was reminiscent of an English country gentleman because it was this persona that seemed to get ahead at the European consulting company where he worked. He could live the elite company brand well, and if it were not for his skin colour, no one would have guessed his humble roots in India. He worked harder than his white counterparts because he knew that fighting the system would not get him the success he needed; better to join it and work it, no matter what cost to himself or his identity.

As his mother had predicted, Ashwin was the most successful child in the family. His other siblings seemed to flail about between jobs and in one case, brushes with the law. It was not clear whether this was a function of resource and attention allocation in the family during Ashwin's early years, or whether it was due to Ashwin's gifts and diligence, both were probably true. He was a clever and hard-working guy, but it looked like he had used up the entire family's quota for success all by himself.

Now at partner level, and 20 years into his career, Ashwin had a problem. The problem was that because he had only focussed on financial success, he had become like a spreadsheet. His numbers were doing well but the qualitative parts of his life, such as an intimate partnership, friendships, and a community, were underdeveloped. To be frank, he had the relational intelligence of a keyboard. He could rather woodenly strike the letters of a relationship but could not sustain a full sentence or narrative that a deeper relationship requires.

Over the years, Ashwin had had several encounters with relationships of all types but had only excelled at those with a transactional outcome; relationships where roles were clear and boundaried, and where the human element was less important. This had never bothered Ashwin, possibly because he had not noticed that it could be different. This was, of course, not entirely his fault coming from a conditional approach to love in his early life.

Ashwin had become bewitched by success, and yes his family's background and his mother, Aisha, had played a role; intergenerational forces are a critical aspect of many bewitchments. Ashwin developed the skills he deemed necessary for financial success, but not the skills of relationship, which in his mind were superfluous to his requirements for a life well lived. This had made him into a narrow person, one perfectly designed for achieving corporate financial targets in the short term and in a less senior role; a goal-orientated, unemotional worker bee. However, this skill set was less well suited to being a human, and nowadays being a human is a critical part of being a leader, especially at senior level (or so us leadership professionals like to think). You can understand how confusing this must have been for Ashwin.

We are going to leave Ashwin now for some theory, but don't worry, we will come back to him in the chapter on growing *self*.

Types of bewitchments

When one becomes bewitched, one becomes controlled by something outside of one's *self* and begins to act in the best interest of the external controller, and not our *self*. To become bewitched, one must disconnect from our inner world as a source of direction and follow the instruction of an externality. Being bewitched is often comorbid with amputation and death, but more on that later.

There are many forms of becoming bewitched; I am going to deal with only three. These include orientating around a magical external as with success in Ashwins case, becoming shame bound, and spiritual bypassing.

It is the nature of humans that we think something from outside our *self* can make us whole, feel permanently good, certain, and enable us to have meaningful lives. These outside things include the magical other: the magical wealth, the magical guru, the magical loss of weight, or the deeply transformative designer handbag. We continue to believe this despite all the religious, psychological, and philosophical literature which directs us to look inside for guidance, *meaning*, and joy.

Earlier, we explored the neoliberal system in which we live and how we provide utility to the system by producing and consuming. Within such a system we can easily become bewitched by material success and climbing various high status ladders. This can be particularly pronounced when we or our family have experienced poverty or been sidelined by history. In these cases, our decisions in life can become easily dominated by these versions of success as a way to keep surviving, rather than pursuing other things that may be more meaningful to us. (Another way to think about predisposition is that it is living the wound of our oppression so that we can complete it.)

Shame is a particularly insidious way of becoming bewitched. When we are shamed, we come to believe that we are in some way defective or abhorrent, and this then drives our thoughts and feelings and what we think we can do with our lives. We all have some level of shame but when it becomes the dominant thinking pattern in one's life, we can then become bewitched by it, believing that this badness is all of whom we are.

Sometimes humans orientate around a magical other such as spirituality; this is not intrinsically bad, it's all in how we do this. When we spiritual-bypass, we overidentify with what seems to be a spiritual version of our *self* denying our wounds, anger, greed, or lust; really anything about us that we consider unspiritual. In this state, we consider our *self* spiritual but have not done the emotional work that is required for this.

Bypassers can use potent technologies such as meditation, plant medicines, or somatic work to bliss out or avoid bad feelings and our embodied humanness. These technologies were designed to be used in the opposite way, as a way to connect with all of our inner world, including our pain, but this does not take place when we spiritual bypass.

We can also take on a language that presents us as spiritual but locks us into a narrow way of thinking where we can become impotent and narcotised, awaiting grounding and flowering by a magical outsider.

Spirituality always requires equal measures of downward and upward growth. Downwards into our humanness and shadows, and upwards into our capacity for transcending these. The big story of spiritual growth is expanding our range upwards and downwards, and not just consolidating our range at higher levels.

Losing *self* by becoming amputated

Amputation is often comorbid with bewitchment. When we become bewitched, we automatically lose or don't develop aspects of our *self*, much as Ashwin did with his relational skills. Like bewitchment, amputation can also be precipitated by external pressures as we shall see below with the tale of Celia, the coconut cheese girl.

Celia, the coconut cheese girl

Celia is a highly successful executive in her early 30s. She is a single Xhosa woman who grew up in the townships outside Cape Town, working her mother, sister, and herself out of poverty and finally positioning them in a firmly upper middle-class lifestyle. She came to me to talk about depression, love, and loneliness.

We met in my offices, her expensive perfume entering the room long before she did. I noted more than one brand adorning her body and she placed her LV handbag carefully on the table next to her. She was the carefully curated embodiment of corporate achievement.

In our early sessions, Celia took care to communicate her successes, and it became clear that she did not want to present herself as needy or wanting in any way. We finally got to her worries about feeling depressed and lost in life, and her struggles with finding a partner. She told me how she had dated quite a bit in her 20s and 30s – mainly black guys – but that there were always problems. Some seemed to be users who wanted her to support them, or they were not ambitious enough, or too sexist, or they were just too black. The few white guys she dated seemed to be touristic, curious but not actually that interested in her as a full-time partner. She did develop a friendship with a couple of white Afrikaans gay men who valued her over-the-top style and love of the finer things in life, but they were only available now and then. Celia was lonely and did not know where to look for a partner and proper companionship. She was not sure where she fitted in.

Celia's backstory was that she had grown up poor, her mother was a domestic worker in a white suburb, and she had very little contact with her father who lived back home in the Eastern Cape, South Africa. Despite the political change during her youth, the world still treated black people as inferior with black women receiving the brunt of this prejudice. For Celia, life looked and was still better for white people.

Celia's experience of the white lifestyle came initially through the hand-me-downs that she received from her mother's employer, Mrs Solomon. She would dress in scarves and dresses and pose with handbags imagining what it would be like to be in this upmarket restaurant or that corporate corner office. Her mother and aunties enjoyed these shows, encouraging them in the belief that they would inspire Celia to get ahead and out of the townships, that she could be more than her humble beginnings.

Mrs Solomon and Celia's mom conspired to send her to a school for white girls in the suburbs. There were not many black girls in the school, and it had not been easy for her to integrate. English was difficult for her because it was her second language and she struggled until her mother decided that no more isiXhosa would be spoken at home, and the TV could only be on English channels.

Over time and with hard work, Celia adapted well at the school and developed a persona that included likes and dislikes, dreams and nightmares that corresponded to the white culture of the other girls. This was a survive and thrive mechanism that worked, limited her outsider status, and got Celia good grades and bursaries. She could not invite her schoolmates home, however, and although this made her look a bit snooty, it was ok for Celia because it protected her schoolfriends from knowing just how black she really was. Named Hlonela at birth, meaning one who obeys and abides, she was abiding.

Celia did not have many friends back in the townships, other than the next-door neighbour Philli who loved to come over and dress up. And this ended all too soon after a dispute about a missing shirt; Celia said that she had stolen it because she was jealous and too lazy to earn her own things. To extract revenge, Philli spread rumours about Celia being a coconut and a cheese girl. For those of you who don't know what a coconut is, it is a black person who masquerades as a white person: white on the inside and brown on the outside. A cheese girl is a person who is considered to have money or be spoiled.

Celia did well in her first corporate job, she was used to white authority and showed no signs of inciting revolution or extracting revenge for Apartheid from her white managers. She was considered very professional which is another way to say she was very white. Once again, she did not socialise much outside work but was pleasant and hard-working enough to find herself in a managerial role within a few years, finally landing up as HR director for a large corporation in her 30s. By this time, she lived in the white suburbs, drove a BMW, shopped at the most expensive shops in town and had the best handbag in the building. She had arrived, and was no longer abiding, in fact, she was calling quite a few shots. It was through the shots, the address, the car, and the handbag that Celia engaged with herself; all these things told her that she was not abiding but had really made it in the world.

As I told you, she was struggling to find a partner, wanting to find someone as successful as herself, but not knowing where she fitted in the world, and where to look for such a person. She had built a persona based on white versions of success and had little connection to her black heritage. In this way she had amputated her blackness to survive and get ahead in life. However, this left her in 'no-man's land', not really fitting in anywhere and, as you can see, this limited her love life. Perhaps if she had met a similarly mixed black person or white person that grew up black, or even a liberal German, things would have been possible, but alas that was not to be.

Ashwin's story is similar to that of Celia's; a societal and socio-economic context that tells us where we fit in the world, gives us clues about where life is best and how to get there, and then a family context that amplifies this. And of course, finally, the personality of the individual which takes these external pressures, consolidates and integrates them, and lives them out.

I am not ging to finish Celia's story here, for that we will have to read on until the section on growing *self* by giving up curating our *self*.

Types of amputation

As we can see from Celia's story, amputation is a severe injury to the *self*. Once lost, it is very difficult to bring parts of our *self* back. I have provided two types of amputation below although there are many more ways in which we can remove aspects of our *self*.

For a more systemic understanding of amputation, we can look to the writing of Biko. He was, of course, speaking to South African black people during Apartheid, noting how this system and global racism had denigrated and defiled blackness. He comments that as a result of its denigration, some black people had discarded their blackness choosing to take on a whiter identity. This identity was treated with more respect by the world, and enabled black people to get ahead in an anti-black world. Biko notes that this strategy may have helped black people survive under violent and racist Apartheid. He does, however, warn us that this loss of *self* creates a loss of agency, and as a result black people could risk becoming sheep-like. Furthermore, that this sheep-like state, a form of inner oppression, was more enabling to Apartheid South Africa than any number of guns and jails.[6]

Celia was a victim of this type of amputation. Biko notes these as *self*-alienation, *self*-deception, *self*-evasion, a flight from freedom, impression management, losing one's place in the world, and the judgement of other black people.[7] These are severe injuries indeed, ones that take more than one generation to heal.

These same injuries are clear in Celia's case. The white identity she had initially created while at school was amplified later at work. She was not sure of who she was, and carefully managed how I would experience her. She had harsh things to say about black people who had not done well in life, calling them thieves, lazy, or stupid. She did not know how she fitted in, and as a result struggled to find someone to fit in with. We will come back to the story of Celia later on and see how she resolves her dilemma and finds love.

All families have a culture or way of doing things, and sometimes this culture means that members of the family need to lose or repress aspects of themselves to have parental and familial approval/disapproval. This could be anger or sexuality or even hobbies or, for the family scapegoat, being the good one. It can sometimes take a lifetime to reintegrate these lost aspects of our *self*.

School and peer pressure can also result in us losing aspects of our *self*. A common example is that of playfulness. Our education and our socialisation may teach us that playfulness is not useful for getting ahead, and so we consciously and unconsciously remove or reduce this aspect of our *self*. Over time we end up successful and conscientious but quite boring, lacklustre, and lacking in charisma (a bit like Ashwin). We also reduce our ability to learn because this is underpinned by the capacity to play.

The workplace is another context where we may lose aspects of us as we seek to portray our *self* in the way that will get us ahead. The requirement to 'be professional' can sometimes mean that we delete aspects of our *self*. These can include our feelings, our identity, our independence of thought, or our creativity. In Celia's case it was her blackness.

Aside from amputation through oppression, many of these factors are 'normal' ways in which we adapt to our lives, and maybe they are not all bad. The problem arises when we amputate so much of our *self* that we lose our capacity to *self*-reflect. We then forget who we are, make choices that don't meet our needs, and live a life we don't want.

Losing *self* by dying to our *self*

So far, we have explored processes that result in the loss of parts of our *self*, but what happens when we completely lose access to our *self*, when we are almost or totally dead inside? For this to happen we need to avoid developing a *self*, or experience trauma that decimates our inner worlds. Let's see what happened with Angelique, the 90-year-old coquette.

Meeting Angelique, the 90-year-old coquette

I met Angelique at an old age home after having been called in by the management staff because she was making inappropriate sexual invitations to the male staff and visitors. She had struggled to fit in, her children seldom visited her, and she had offered more than one male staff member a blowjob, even after receiving a firm warning to stop.

We met in one of the consultation rooms, where she waited for me in her wheelchair. She was fully made up, dressed in a velvet evening gown with matching gold shoes. Her hair was done, and her nails painted. She greeted me with, 'Hello darling, let me have a look at you, perhaps you could have done a better job with yourself this morning.' She asked, 'Surely you know that no man will pay you any attention in those lesbian shoes and jacket. Looks like I am not the one in need of help here'. I smiled, taking in the greeting that I knew would become our pre-session ritual.

During the first session, she regaled me with stories of her glamorous life starting with her being the fourth child in line, after three boys. She described them as large, uncouth, and feral during their earlier years, children one did not take to tea or dinner parties. She, on the other hand was just the type of child one did take to tea parties. 'You see I was a delight, with ringlets and a pretty smile, I could even be called upon to do fairy dances. My parents were so proud of me, they took me everywhere and later my mother helped me become a child model appearing in newspapers and even on billboards. I was famous overnight, people on the street recognised me, and asked for my autograph.' Later when I asked her about school, she said that she had a home tutor that taught her everything she needed to know, and no, education was not a priority for someone with her gifts.

Fast forward to her 20s and we find Angelique furthering her modelling career and dating older men, living in New York. Finally, she settled on an ambitious man by the name of Fred who looked like he would take the banking world by storm. This he did, building on his family's wealth and becoming extremely rich. During this time, Angelique was at her peak on Fred's arm, attending and hosting the most celebrated parties in town.

Of Fred, she said 'He always wanted me looking my best, there was no space for average in Fred's world, and of course, this meant for his wife too. He was happy to pay for gowns, treatments, and hairdos as long as I was able to put it all together into something outstanding. And I did, I was truly a beauty. I was quite a showstopper and with my charm it was impossible to keep the men away from me. Fred was quite good about that, he said, "flirt away, but you make it sure that they know you are mine", which of course I did.'

Angelique bore Fred four children, and in her words, 'returned to a flat stomach only two weeks after each birth'. As it was for many rich socialites, she was supported in her child rearing endeavours by maids, drivers, tutors, and governesses. All the children were reported as doing well in prominent places in society, except for the second; a girl who had 'made herself look so unfortunate that she had to join the feminist brigade and move to darkest Africa'. It became clear that Angelique had formal relationships with her children, and they all lived out of town, hence the few visits she received now.

According to Angelique, the main difficulties of her life were not her distant children, or the death of Fred, but what to do when you age and lose your power in society. Ageing was a constant threat to Angelique who bravely fought the passage of time with an unrelenting schedule of treatments and nips and tucks well into her 80s. She worried incessantly about disappearing altogether and this had been the source of constant and ongoing anxiety since her 60s.

Back then she had taken seat with an existential therapist who suggested that she had death anxiety and was struggling to come to terms with ageing. This did not come as a surprise to Angelique who knew all too well her fears of senescence. The therapist encouraged her to embrace her relationships with her children and grandchildren, but Angelique felt this was counterproductive. She did not want to be reminded that she was a grandmother. Her response then was to up the ante and become even more seductive in her interactions with men, and she continued now with this, even into her 90s. The strategy worked in some ways because she was seen and certainly not forgotten, but it was inappropriate, got the wrong kind of responses, and was upsetting to others.

And now we find her, after Fred's death, in her 90s in an upmarket retirement home. Make-up on by 8 am every morning, walks, massages, facials, and nail sessions still in place. And there she is, in her wheelchair feeling quite lost and looking for someone to flirt with. It's not a pleasant time for Angelique and she has not joined the gaggle of hilarious old gals who laugh at life, tell vulgar body jokes of decay and dementia, and bemoan the state of their offspring. Angelique does not laugh at life, instead she feels that life is laughing at her because after all these years of looking after herself, she has no one to validate her hard work.

Angelique lived a very narrow version of her *self*, she treated herself as an object to be validated and adored based on her beauty. Significant parts of herself had not been developed, like her education, friendships, her deeper dreams, and a sense of *self*. She had been prized as an object of beauty as a child and had not grown beyond this version of her *self* in later life. There was very little of her *self* available to enable her to adapt to her changing circumstance. She was stuck in the habits of a 30-year-old coquette.

I am going to finish this story here and not later in this book because with Angelique's age, time is short. Angelique began to really enjoy our sessions; she started to see me in my office because she was enjoying getting out more. Initially, she regaled me with stories of her glorious past but as months went by her stories started to champion her grandchildren more, and herself less. I tried to keep discussions to the present day and how she wanted to live before she died. As she moved towards accepting where and who she was in life, we explored how she wanted to be remembered by her grandchildren. As a result she made contact with them, sending cards and invitations to Zoom calls. Her care home began to enable regular calls which she looked forward to with great anticipation. At our last session she told me that she had started to distribute her jewellery amongst her children who had also become more regular in their visits and calls.

We ended because she felt happier and more content, there were no more complaints from the care home, and she was getting tired. I went to her funeral two years later and was glad to see it well attended not only by family but also friends and staff from the care home. She had clearly managed to find her place in her community and family and could finally rest in peace.

Types of dying to one's self

Dying to one's *self* sounds like a pretty serious condition; it is and we often don't notice it. It happens in various ways such as falling asleep to one's *self*, becoming an object, and experiencing trauma or toxic shame. There are more ways, but I think we should start with these.

Dying to one's *self* can be a kind of asleep state where one exists in a sort of daze following cues from outside one's *self* and never checking inside to see how one wants to respond. It's the zombie state where our inner director is in a deep slumber that very little seems to awaken. In this state we are easily bewitched or just follow the herd. It is possible that many of us are in this state most of the time, and that in some ways it is a normal state for humans.[8] A lot of us are often passengers of life; not knowing that we could be the driver, or even get off the bus altogether.

The idea of becoming an object is widely considered in psychology, politics, philosophy, and sociology.[9] Misogyny, oppression, colonialism, stereotyping, and religious hatred are all premised on making the 'other' less than fully human.

Objectification occurs when *others* treat us as objects, and when we treat our *self* as an object. This means we treat *others* or our *self* as having only one identity, such as slave or beauty queen, and not the full range of identities with which humans are blessed. We/they become one identity/thing only and as such are incapable of emerging and growing and becoming. They/we become an object in the sense of having a non-emergent identity like a stone.[10]

When we are treated as objects by *others*, we can internalise their gaze and through this build a very narrow concept of *self*, much like Angelique did. We see our *self* as only a trophy wife, or software developer, or refugee, or executive. When this happens, we lose access to the broadness of our inner world and through this our ability to emerge and change in response to the environment. We become stuck in one essentialised identity that determines all that we do. We become known to our *self* and *others* through only one aspect of our *self*.

We can die to our *self* through trauma and toxic shame. Trauma can be understood as a process of turning a person into an object.[11] It turns us into an object that is violated by another, or an experience. We become essentialised into the victim role which takes over our whole existence.

There are many ways in which trauma damages the *self*. We know the *self* is created through *self*-reflection and interactions with *others*. When we are traumatised, we have limited capacity to *self*-reflect, and also to have relationships.

Trauma tends to destroy our understanding of the world and with that, our understanding of our *self*. We may experience a disassociation from our *self* and life to cope with the pain of the trauma. When we try to come back and be present to our *self*, it can be so painful and overwhelming that it is easier to slip back into a more dead way of being. Processing trauma is processing pain, and if we are shattered by the trauma and have no resources for working through pain, it is very hard to come back to being present with our *self*.[12]

Trauma is a potent form of gaslighting as it separates us from our *self* and causes us to distrust our own experience of life. It weakens our sense of *self* and our capacity to strengthen and grow our *self*.

Lastly, we can also die to our *self* through shame. This is because having shame can cause us to disconnect from who we are, and create a cover story that papers over or amplifies the cracks in our *self*-esteem. We can then believe our cover story is all of who we are. When this happens, we will struggle to direct and organise our lives in a way that is satisfying to us.

Losing *self* and becoming sedimented

In this chapter, we have covered three broad processes that can leave us with a diminished or absent *self*: becoming bewitched, amputated, or dead. In many cases we do versions of this as an adaptive response to a situation; for example, fitting in with the corporate culture, or even getting married. When we do this, we tend to perform well in these roles/contexts because our identity is so well matched to them. When we lose our dear partner, a state of grief is appropriate; when we join a new company, dressing to fit in can help us get ahead; or even when we enter a new relationship, having no needs can help us seal the deal.

Typically, we don't recognise this change in identity as a loss because it does help us deal with the situation at hand. In some cases, we may even feel like we are blossoming, for example, when we get married or begin our MBA. The issue for me is not that we are getting ahead, getting ahead is great, the problem is the cost of getting ahead. If we get ahead by narrowing our identity, then it leaves us unable to adapt like the forementioned one-trick pony. If, instead of diminishing our *self*, we retain our usual broad range of identities and add in new elements, then we will have sufficient *self* to continue to adapt. This is a healthy way to adapt but we don't always do this. We throw our whole identity into the mix and reorganise our *self* around whatever has the most currency at the time.

Things tend to be working out during this stage in the process, and this provides a good enough reason for us to become even more devoted to our new ways of being. Old identities are forgotten and fall away, and our new *self*/ identity starts to consolidate, ultimately sedimenting into a concrete version of our *self*. We no longer see aspects of our *self* or the world that exists outside this sedimented version of our *self*.[13] We forget that we ever had other identities or ways of being. We come to believe that who we are in our bewitched, amputated, or dead state is who we have always been and always will be. This is not just *self*-deception; it really is who we know our *self* to be.

When we lose our *self*, we also lose *others* and *meaning*. This is because we are not there to connect with *others* or find our *meaning*. Our *self* needs to be fully present for us to be able to relate to the world and direct our lives.

At this stage, we are becoming more and more fixed in who we think we are and how we can be in the world. Our identity and our skills have narrowed down and we are starting to become one-trick ponies: good for one context only, like down a coal mine or in a circus ring, but never both.

What happens to coaching when coaches lose their *self*?

Our *self* is our most critical tool for coaching, we experience our clients and respond to them through our *self*. To use our self well in coaching sessions we have to know what our *self* is and what it is not. We need to be able to notice any other tricks that our *self* can get up to, like being a know-it-all when we sit on our coaching throne. We need to be able to use our *self* to mirror and affirm our clients' *self* and we need our *self* to validate our own and our client's humanity. It is for this reason that we spend so much of our training getting to know our *self*, why we must do our own work as a human, and have regular supervision as a coach.

When we start losing our *self*, and neglect to bring our human *self* to sessions, we lose a lot of the above capacity. As coaches, we must forget any ideas about being a blank slate; it's impossible and an existential approach to coaching demands it. We are not Freudian psychotherapists wearing our *tabular rasa* face and living a methodology based on this. We are existential coaches and our *self* and our humanity are our most effective tools. We must not sully this gift by offering an inauthentic, politically correct, airbrushed version of our *self* because if we do so, our clients may be seduced into doing the same.

Questions to ask your *self*

- What aspects of your *self* have you lost over the years, and when last did you add a new identity to your *self*?
- Do you relate to the idea of being bewitched, amputated, or dead? Where has this happened in your life?
- How much of your *self* do you bring to coaching? What parts of your *self* do you not bring in when you are coaching?

Notes

1 Kohut, H. (1971). *The analysis of the self*. International Universities Press.
2 Sartre, J-P. (1943). *Being and nothingness: An essay on phenomenological ontology* (2003 ed.). Routledge.

3 Wolynn, M. (2017). *It didn't start with you: How inherited family trauma shapes who we are and how to end the cycle*. Penguin Books.
4 Piaget, J. (1970). *Science of education and the psychology of the child*. Orion Press.
5 van Deurzen, E., et al. (2009). *Everyday mysteries: A handbook of existential psychotherapy* (2nd ed.). Routledge.
6 Biko, S. (1978). *I write what I like*. Bowerdean Press.
7 Biko, S. (1978) *I write what I like*.
8 Heidegger, M. (1927). *Being and time* (2018 ed.). Harper Collins.
9 Sartre, J-P. (1943). *Being and nothingness: An essay on phenomenological ontology* (2003 ed.). Routledge; De Beauvoir, S. (2015). *The second sex*. Penguin Books; Fanon, F. (1986). *Black skin, white masks*. Pluto Press; Biko, S. (1978). *I write what I like*. Bowerdean Press; Nussbaum, M. (1995). Objectification. *Philosophy and Public Affairs*, *24*(4), 249–291.
10 Sartre, J.-P. (1943) *Being and Nothingness*.
11 Spiegel, E. (2022). *Where is shame held in the body?* Attune Philadelphia Therapy Group. https://www.therapistsinphiladelphia.com/blog/where-is-shame-held-in-the-body/# (Accessed: 2 June 2024).
12 Hubl, T., & Jordan Avritt, J. (2020). *Healing collective trauma: A process for integrating our intergenerational and cultural wounds*. Sounds True.
13 Sartre, J.-P. (1943) *Being and nothingness*; Spinelli, E. (1989). *The interpreted world: An introduction to phenomenological psychology*. Sage Publications, Inc.

Bibliography

Biko, S. (1978). *I write what I like*. Bowerdean Press.
de Beauvoir, S. (2015). *The second sex*. Penguin Books.
Fanon, F. (1986). *Black skin, white masks*. Pluto Press.
Heidegger, M. (1927). *Being and time* (2018 ed.). Harper Collins.
Hubl, T., & Jordan Avritt, J. (2020). *Healing collective trauma: A process for integrating our intergenerational and cultural wounds*. Sounds True.
Kohut, H. (1971). *The analysis of the self*. International Universities Press.
Nussbaum, M. (1995). Objectification. *Philosophy and Public Affairs*, *24*(4), 249–291.
Piaget, J. (1970). *Science of education and the psychology of the child*. Orion Press.
Sartre, J-P. (1943). *Being and nothingness: An essay on phenomenological ontology* (2003 ed.). Routledge.
Spiegel, E. (2022). *Where is shame held in the body?* Attune Philadelphia Therapy Group. https://www.therapistsinphiladelphia.com/blog/where-is-shame-held-in-the-body/# (Accessed: 2 June 2024)
Spinelli, E. (1989). *The interpreted world: An introduction to phenomenological psychology*. Sage Publications, Inc.
van Deurzen, E., et al. (2009). *Everyday mysteries: A handbook of existential psychotherapy* (2nd ed.). Routledge.
Wolynn, M. (2017) *It didn't start with you: How inherited family trauma shapes who we are and how to end the cycle*. Penguin Books.

Chapter 6

Experiencing contextual shifts (or not)

This chapter takes us back to our dance partner in life, our context. We are always in a context; in our bodies and in a context. This partnership has such a great impact on how we experience life, and the sense we make of it.

Please know that this chapter could have gone anywhere in the losing or gaining sections because the context changes all the time. I decided to put it in here so we could hold the idea of continuous contextual change in the back of our head as we read through this book.

Context: Our dance partners for life

We are formed by our context and the *others* in it. They play a critical role in creating who we are now and who we will be in the future. This chapter explores what a context is, how it shapes us, and what happens when we are unable to dance with it.

At this stage in the cycle (after losing *self*), we are sedimented in our narrow sense of *self*, but doing relatively well at dealing with whatever our environment demands of us. Life would be fine if it was not in the nature of contexts to shift all the time. We know, however, that contexts do change, all the time, and without apparent rhyme or reason, and most often not to our tune. We have explored this extensively in the first section on some of the factors that create the all-encompassing volatility that we are experiencing in the world now.

Please refer to the diagram in Chapter 1 again, just so you can see where we are in the Cycle of Stuckness; we are in between losing *self* and losing *others*. We are at the point in which the context changes again. Once you have had a brief glance at the cycle, I want to introduce us to Avril and Arthur, owners of a small world.

Meeting Avril and Arthur, owners of a small world

Avril and Arthur found me in an old listing of coaches and therapists working near their home, as their main criteria for choosing a marriage counsellor was

DOI: 10.4324/9781003536253-6

that they needed to be close by. They came because for the first time in their married life, they were not getting on; bickering and fighting constantly and often about very small things. They both felt miserable, depressed, and anxious and, luckily, they had the energy and perhaps the will to do something about it.

It is common in couple therapy for the first session to be dominated by each party laying out the historical and current sins of the other person. Arthur and Avril were no different, but it took quite long to move beyond the sins of the other into learning about the relationship. They had been together for over 35 years and as a result there was a lot of history, some versions jointly shared, and others not.

The couple were in their late 60s, still too fit and young to commit to old age care, but not quite in the prime of their lives. They lived in a large house where they had raised their two boys, both of whom had left the country over two years prior in search of bigger lives. They had both been very involved parents, placing their children at the centre of their worlds. Although in some ways their children's departure had been expected and even desired, it was still a shock to be left alone in the big house with its emptied bedrooms and silence.

Arthur had always been a cautious man saving a good pension while he worked his way up in a local corporate. Avril had been a stay-at-home mom, contributing to the local community and even had a brief time (wo)manning the phone on the neighbourhood watch group. This experience had not left her feeling safer, but rather had reminded her that bad things happen in good neighbourhoods and that one needed to be careful, mainly with strangers but also with many of the so-called good neighbours who were in fact not so good.

On top of this all, the couple had come through the South African political transition in their late 50s. It was rather confusing to find oneself suddenly on the not-so-good side of history (they were white), but more worrying was the anxiety that the new black government would mess things up, especially for them – older white people who lived off private pensions. And then all the fraud cases started popping up and they were forced to face their worst fears; that their pensions would be depleted, that they would be attacked on the street, that their favourite mayonnaise would no longer be available, and that medical care would become third world.

Arthur and Avril's health started deteriorating and the money and medical aid worry became more pronounced. Physically, they felt less able to cope with daily life and they became troubled that their frailty would make them an easy target for criminals. The world also seemed to be changing in ways that they could not understand or learn; for example, banking and even communicating with their children now required significant IT literacy. It was all very confusing and frightening.

So, what did they do to feel safe? Well, Arthur and Avril started restricting the size of the world in which they lived. First, they stopped listening to the news, then they stopped long car trips, then driving at night, then they stopped all trips over 20 minutes (unless driven by friends), and this in turn resulted in fewer visits to friends, only trips to the closest mall and no expansive trips to nature.

Their world got distinctly smaller, and they were less anxious if a little bored with each other. But over time, the boredom and worry turned into a perpetual stream of grumbling and anxiety that boiled between the two of them. Their small world was keeping them safe, but it was also killing them from the inside.

For Arthur and Avril, much had changed in a short amount of time. They began feeling old physically and this was something they had to get used to. Growing old is really not for sissies, but (sadly?) many of us must do it. Then there was the empty nest bit that they had gotten used to, but it still meant no strong person to call during the night in an emergency. And then there was the whole political change and the fear of the new regime and crime. A lot had changed, in fact there was a lot of new uncertainty pushed in where it really was not wanted. And how it manifested was in the amplified sense of a lack of safety and fear for their physical and financial wellbeing.

These are understandable and big worries for older people and worries that are not restricted to older white people in South Africa. The tricky bit for Arthur and Avril, was that they experienced vulnerability inside themselves, and this amplified their sense of vulnerability outside themselves, and they became focussed on where things were dangerous or where they might be harmed.

The strategy they then adopted was to stay in worlds that they could control even if this meant that their worlds were very small and that they got bored and irritated with each other. You can see how very logical this was, and that this may be an entirely appropriate approach to life in the late 60s. My sense is yes, AND life could have been so much more exciting for them; they could have travelled to see their kids, walked in nature, helped people in need, learned new skills, and had a few parties. They could even have gone to tantric sex workshops and taken mushrooms. Nearly turning 70 is not necessarily a moment for foreclosing on life.

Losing one's place in the world can be disorientating and confusing. To remain in life fully, one must have the wherewithal and desire to change. When change is not desirable, it is even harder to accept and adapt to it. This kind of adaptation means letting go of past ways of being, and moving towards a new way of being, even if one does not know how to do this. This can feel like letting go of one lifeline without knowing where the next one is, it's terrifying.

This was Avril and Arthur's problem, they lost their life as it was and were not sure how to make a new one. This created anxiety for the couple, who responded by making their world smaller rather than engaging with the newness of their lives. It was too hard for them to change and adapt into life, so they adapted away from it.

We can adapt away from life when our role in the world suddenly changes, for the worse or for the better. This can include changes that we expected, such as having a baby, moving countries, and/or unexpected changes, such as losing a limb, a house, or a spouse. It is when we notice that our identity has changed, we are no longer who we were, and we have not yet stepped into a new identity.

Just so you know, I did not see Avril and Arthur beyond a couple of sessions. They turned down my suggestion of being more in the world. They saw their issue as an interpersonal one, they just did not get on anymore. This may have been true to some extent, but who knows. I suspect they are still out there arguing about where objects need to be stored, and waiting for a call from their children.

Not noticing or responding to context changes

I think we all understand the idea behind the boiling frog metaphor; that is, that the frog does not notice the water heating up around him until it is boiling and it's too late to save itself from death by scalding. This is true for humans as well.

We don't recognise changes in the context for many reasons. A first reason is that neurologically and psychologically, we don't like change and experience it as energy sapping and confusing, even when it may be positive in the long run. An excellent defence against having to expend the energy required for change is to deny or minimise, or avoid a contextual shift.

A second reason for not noticing changes is that at this stage in the cycle, we seem to be doing ok by staying the same. We know how it is for humans; 'don't fix it if it ain't broke'. Don't change for change's sake. Our way of being and our behaviours still have some relevancy and traction in the world, so we just carry on as usual.

We have several additional defences against noticing context changes, including 'shoulding' (it should not be happening) or 'coulding' (it could not happen to me) the change. These defences can be useful in the short term because they can allow us to step back from our panic and review our lives. But they are never useful in the longer journey of our lives where we need to accept changes so that we can adapt to them.

If we don't notice context changes, we cannot adapt our way of being. Furthermore, even when we do notice context shifts, we may be unable to adapt. This is because we have sedimented our way of being into something narrow, permanent, and non-emergent.

Being contextual in coaching

When it comes to working with our own context for coaching, we must start with our relevance as coaches. What training have we received, and what supervision do we get? Where and how do we engage with clients, and what metaphors and resources do we use? We need to consider all these factors.

When it comes to working with our clients' contexts, the more mature we are as a coach, the more contextual our coaching will become. When we are contextual in coaching, we see the impact of past and current contexts in the behaviour and lived experience of the client. We do not see the client's behaviour as an acontextual function of their inner world alone.

When we are contextual, we are less likely to locate blame in the client and can support the client to do the same. This approach is useful because it minimises *self*-criticism and shame, two factors that create and sustain stuckness. Shame holds us in stuckness and so any strategy that can limit this experience is hugely useful. Clients do need to take responsibility for their lives, but this does not need to happen in a way that creates further stuckness.

Contexts can be useful in many ways. We know that they can create behaviour and even make us look at things differently. This means that we can also use contexts in our coaching, that is, we could invite the client to step into new contexts and let these influence the way they make sense of the world. I will develop this idea further in this book but I just wanted to plant a small seed in your head on the way.

Clients as salient contexts for our healing

I suspect, coach, that you knew this would come up; yes our clients can be the very contexts that enable our own healing. Lucky us, we are paid to grow (that is, if our inner wounded healers allow us to charge for our services).

Our clients can present a familiar and emotionally engaging 'movie' that we can watch, feel, and sometimes even star in. This offers us vicarious ways of healing our *self*. This is, however, something to be careful of because we can project our *self* onto our clients lives. We can become confused about what is theirs and what is ours. We can see our client's lives as we are in our own, and not as they are in theirs. And, as we know, this does not make for good coaching.

Starting to get stuck

When we don't notice and don't adapt to the external context, we become stuck in a way of being that is not relevant now. We are like the one-trick ponies who are only good in a coalmine but must turn down a party invitation because we don't know how to be at a party. We are starting to disconnect from our context, even as it changes, and with this disconnection, we start to lose relevancy and traction in the world. We may notice this but probably not because, after all, noticing may require us to change, and we try to avoid that at all costs.

Questions to ask your *self*

- Have you ever had the experience of the world changing around you so much that you are not sure if you still are connected to it?
- How easy is it to move with your context and how has this changed over the course of your life? What are the factors that make you more or less contextual?
- Which of your clients offers or has offered a healing context for you, and why?

Chapter 7

Losing *others* and isolation

Perhaps it's just me, but sometimes it seems like the coaching world overvalues individuality, individual growth, and undervalues community. This of course means that we can understand coaching problems as intrapsychic or monadic and fail to recognise the influence of others and context. Let us be rebels, let's devalue individualism (just briefly), and embrace our communities. Let us understand that coaching problems always involve *others*. This is the chapter that will help us do that.

We are now on the right side of the stuckness cycle, where we grow our relationships with *others*.

Others: The with whom of life

The Cycle of Stuckness shows us how losing *others* is the next stage of the process. By now we have a diminished sense of *self* and have started to disconnect from the context because our capacity for adaptation is diminished. We still have some connection to others, and this gives us some sense of place and validity. This, however, is about to change. Before we explore this change, it would be useful to understand why others are important, what kind of relationships are useful to us, and some of the structural issues around contemporary relationships.

Why are *others* important?

Loneliness is a very clear and painful symptom; it tells us we need companionship. It is a survival mechanism that reminds us that we need *others* to survive. I guess we have all had lonely times in our lives and therefore know intuitively why *others* are important to us. However, it may be useful to provide a fuller picture of why other people are important, especially with all this *self*-love and *self*-help going around, we may become bewitched into believing that we don't need *others*.

A good place to start is with the Ubuntu idea that *others* enable us to be human; we cannot be human on our own. We need *others* to 'make' us human,

DOI: 10.4324/9781003536253-7

and *others* need us to 'make' them human.[1] We cannot become human alone.[2] This humanising process happens through how we treat each other; critically that we treat *others* with respect, validation, and a recognition that they have an inner world of feelings and thoughts.

When we don't treat *others* in this way, we dehumanise them. They become objects to us, and their dehumanisation in turn dehumanises us. It is a vicious circle, with the chains of dehumanisation held at both sides. When one side loses their humanity, so does the other.

Consciously and unconsciously, interacting with *others* also creates who we are. We come to know our *self* through our impact on *others*. The traits we attribute to our *self* come from the knowledge we gain when comparing our *self* with *others*.[3] They witness us and help us consolidate and integrate our *selfs*. In this way we are not singular or *self*-generated but rather created through our interactions with *others*. Even if we are rebelling against *others*, it is still the *others* that are telling us what not to be.

An important outcome of this interaction is our growth; we need others to grow. We need *others* to enrich and validate our own inner world and encourage us to leave the safety of our own *self* to explore that of *others* and the world around us. This growth is easier when the relationship is supportive and caring because we are less defensive and more motivated towards adaptation.

This leads us back to exploring the kinds of relationship that we need to be human, to define our *self* positively, and to grow. The kinds of relationships that will enable us to weather stuckness more easily.

What kind of relationships with *others* do we need?

As humans we need different kinds of relationships; familial, lovers, partners, friends, acquaintances, technology-based friends, and more. In the world of stuckness it is less about the varieties of relationships we have, and more about their quality.

We know from earlier on in this book that when relationships are characterised by respect, validation, and the recognition of inner worlds, they can humanise us, support us to grow, and get stuck less often. These are what one could call engaged relationships.

How can we lose *others* and not notice?

We can lose *others* and not notice it because it can become the norm in our community. In a world that values getting ahead, autonomy, *self*-love, and *self*-help, we can forget the importance of *others*. The loss of *others* can happen slowly, like the boiling frog story, and one day we wake up and realise that we are not surrounded by friends and a community.

In rarer situations we can also lose others and not notice because we did not ever have *others* in the first place. This can happen as a result of traumatic early events or even in competitive cultures at work.

Structural factors play a critical role in how we lose *others* and not notice it.

The structural factors of contemporary relationships

Structural factors create the container in which relationships take place. They refer to the way in which our environment and culture shape our relationships. This includes broader factors such as our bigger context (did we grow up during wartime, social unrest, during a dictatorship or in peace), and the political and ideological context (conservative or liberal approach to relationships). Our family, education, religion and work culture also play a role here (open and engaged relationships or hostile and competitive).

There are many factors that we could look at here to get some insight into how our relationships are influenced, I would like to explore three; structural isolation, neoliberalism and technology/social media.

In 2023, the US Surgeon General Murthy warned of a growing epidemic of loneliness and social isolation in the USA. He continued that this posed a serious risk to health, including an increased risk of premature death (26%). His most famous quote was that lacking social connection can endanger our life more than smoking 15 cigarettes a day.[4] Perhaps this growing isolation is not true for the whole world, but there is much research suggesting this is the case with Western nations. This trend is driven by globalisation, individualism, urbanisation, low birth rates, and increased longevity. People are more isolated than before, and it is starting to affect our health. Isolation is a modern-day epidemic.

Earlier on, we explored neoliberalism and its tendency to use humans as objects of utility. We can see this in some organisations, where people are treated as numbers and not whole humans. We can also see this in other relationships such as with trophy wives (Angelique) or the use of our children to enhance our social status, or even how we relate to our celebrities. When we exist in these environments, we can be treated as objects and we can be tempted to treat *others* in a similar way. This then undermines our capacity to have engaged relationships.

One of the biggest contemporary influences on the nature of relationships is technology and social media. These are ostensibly neutral, but have indeed spawned an avalanche of superficial relationships online, and are starting to influence the structure of offline relationships. Social media enables the objectification of *others* and our *self*, for example, selfies are curated versions of our *self* that we present to the world. With selfies we tend to amplify the aspect of our *self* that we want people to see; our wealth or our wide friend set or the expensive or spiritual experiences we have had. We can even present a completely false version of our *self* online that we may then attempt to live out in our real lives. This can cause a lot of identity confusion as well as a narrowing of our version of our *self* as we are tempted to only see and grow aspects of our *self* that are beneficial to our online identity.

A further issue with social media is that of our relationship to *others*. Friends and followers can become objects; a measure of our status, entities that can be cancelled, ghosted, or whose image can be exploited as we wish.

I am not being a Luddite here; I do know that technology has also opened and deepened some relationships. However, many technology-based relationships are not engaged relationships. They are too speedy, efficient, and brief to do so. Engaged relationships need patience, understanding, and commitment. They also require authenticity and imperfection to be integrated within the relationship. This is not always likely or possible online.

Relationships with *others* play a critical role in humanising and defining our *self*. They enable our learning and growing. For relationships to play this role, we need at least a few to be engaged ones. Structural factors such as those mentioned do not always create an appropriate container, and in fact they may limit how much *others* can touch us. The next sections of this chapter will describe how we can easily lose *others* through our attachment styles, through living in a castle, through trauma, and by treating *others* as objects or tools.

Losing *others* through our attachment styles

Attachment styles are the inner, often hidden guidelines that we use for identifying, understanding, and managing our relationships, particularly our intimate ones. They tell us what to want, what to expect, how we should behave, and what perfection looks like. Before we go into the details of this, let's explore the tale of 'Horace the horrible' and see if you can figure out his recipe for intimate relationships.

Horace, the horrible

Horace was a huge man: big chest and a limping leg, in fact, his whole body looked sore when he came in. After he lowered himself into the chair, he said, 'I am here because my girlfriend says that I am a horrible man and I need therapy to become nicer.' He went on to describe in angry tones how the world and his girlfriend had bullied him, how people had taken advantage of him, how he was always blamed and a victim, all the while looking like he had significant talent in the perpetrator department.

To be honest, I found him quite scary, foul of tongue, sexist, racist, and physically in your face. It took me a while to steady my inner world and calm my judgement so that I could look hard enough to see the frightened vulnerable person he was. And he was feeling vulnerable, perhaps even for the first time in his life. He really did love his girlfriend and did not want to lose her; also he had been experiencing terrifying panic attacks that left him paralysed and unable to leave his house.

Horace told me about his painful childhood with a physically and emotionally abusive father and an emotionally unavailable mother. They had sent him to a posh boarding school away from his home in London, and there he learned that the ones that love you the most will abandon you, send you away to a place where only the fittest survive, all the time while saying how privileged you were to be sent away to such a great school.

Initially at boarding school, Horace suffered at the hands and mouths of bullies, until he learned how to bully back. He discovered that he had a natural aptitude for bullying and making money (even at school), and that these skills generally got him what he wanted, including friends, food, marks, girls, and even weekends away.

As a young working man, it was easy for him to forget his difficult early years; he was making lots of money and could afford all kinds of narcotisation including human, liquid, pill, and powder forms. He was very entrepreneurial, excellent at seeing angles for personal benefit, and never had to worry about taking advantage of others because he felt so very victimised by the world, no one had it worse than him.

Despite all his wealth, Horace was hypervigilant about staff stealing sugar or business partners taking more than a penny more than what he thought they deserved. He even felt that nature was an intrusive thief, trying to steal his money by requiring expensive waste processes at his factories. Climate change remedies, whatever they were, were just another blood sucker on his life.

You could be tempted into believing that during this time Horace was unable to attract a partner because he was so horrid, but there were many candidates interested in sharing his life and wealth. Gorgeous women were lining up to partner him, and he took more than a few of them up on their availability. He would control them through strategic giving but over time they always got beyond themselves and slapped his plastic card about a bit too much. He secretly gave them each a financial limit and once this had been reached, they were dismissed. You see, he felt that you can only let ourself get used so far and then you had to put a stop to it.

It was only much later, in his 40s, that he started to experience the idea that maybe things were not so good, that he did in fact have pain, soft spots, and 'weaknesses'. It was then that he started to experience the panic attacks. Horace had met his current girlfriend during one of these panic attacks, which had occurred on an airplane. She happened to be sitting next to him during a very turbulent flight and landed up holding him as they touched down. Horace had never been held that way before and it was so good that he pursued her. She was reluctant because she knew that Horace was possessed by demons from his past but could see enough good in him, if only he would go to therapy and work through some of his pain. She wanted to have a real relationship, not one where she was expected to obey.

I am not going to finish the story of Horace here, we will have to wait for the section on growing *others*, but don't worry things do work out for Horace.

Attachment patterns

We have tacit and often unconscious attachment styles for everything: animals, objects, work, and especially our significant *others*. Research in the 60s suggested that these recipes form in early childhood based on the child's experience of the parental figures, largely the mother.[5] Subsequent research has shown that attachment styles don't just come from the influence of parenting but from multiple other environmental and relational factors.[6] Over the years, four attachment styles have been identified: secure, anxious-ambivalent, anxious-avoidant, and anxious-disorganised.[7]

If the parental figure is available, supportive when needed, but does not overwhelm the child, then the pattern created is considered secure. When the secure base is missing, the child will form an anxious attachment recipe, also known as a conditional attachment pattern.

There are three kinds of these, formed through different parental experiences. When parents are inconsistent in their attention, the child may develop an anxious-ambivalent attachment recipe where they can over-serve the caregiver in order to preserve the relationship. An anxious-avoidant attachment style stems from a parenting style that prematurely encourages the child to be independent. The child then learns how to look after themselves as much as possible, including soothing themselves, and creating strong boundaries against the impact and needs of the parent. With the anxious-disorganised or disorganised attachment style, the environment would have been a source of both love and fear, possibly scary or dangerous. The child learns to do both the behaviours, alternating between over-serving the parental figures and seeking autonomy. They may learn to expect abandonment and experience emotional extremes.[8]

If we have a secure attachment pattern, we are more likely to be able to trust other people, be independent and receive support, hold boundaries, and ask for what we want. People with an anxious-ambivalent attachment pattern tend to get caught up worrying about relationships ending and focus on performing services to keep them. People with anxious-avoidant patterns worry more about the possibility of being hurt in relationship and tend to prefer autonomy rather than merging with another. They are less likely to ask for support, and more able to hold boundaries. When we have an ambivalent attachment pattern, we exhibit both anxious-avoidant and anxious-ambivalent behaviours, and this can result in chaotic relationships, where we are in and out.[9]

Horace had an anxious-avoidant attachment pattern; he was avoiding real attachment to stay safe from pain. This was because his early experiences of relationships were characterised by pain and abandonment, and he was trying to avoid a repeat of this at all costs. However, as you can tell, the pain of having no real connection was beginning to outweigh the safety of isolation.

These attachment patterns are recipes that we use to formulate and structure a relationship, including the kind of people we are attracted to, the role we play in relationships, and even their value to us. They form in early childhood experiences, but we use them again and again in various forms over the course of our lives. This is because we as humans tend to seek what we know and are comfortable with. We can change our attachment recipes; this is, however, quite difficult and usually needs to involve a professional.

I know that by now you may be scanning your childhood for signals of what your attachment style may be, and yes there are great sources on the web for helping you do this. Please go ahead but know that attachment patterns are more complicated in reality than what I present here. These are centres of gravity more than absolutes, but useful as a way to start thinking about your own relationship patterns. Just as a warning before you point your finger at your parents; know that they are generally human and fallible, cope with extraordinary life events while raising you and, with a very small exception, have done their best. And, if you think your parents are perfect, please don't hesitate to get professional advice.

If we understand our attachment style and how it prevents us from having engaged relationships, we can change them. We can become less fearful, more consistent, and more equitable in our relationships with *others*.

Losing *others* by living in a castle

We can disconnect from *others* in many ways, including by avoiding them completely. As I shared earlier, many of us live out of community and isolated, it's a part of contemporary life. This is the story of Alice who was a natural introvert, but further isolated by COVID, and living in a new place. Have a look and see what happened to Alice, who was caught by an algorithm.

Alice who was caught by an algorithm

I saw Alice online for coaching, she was a remote working manager in an IT company in the US. This was during COVID when everyone was working from home. The company wanted to implement an Agile[10] approach to work and had introduced a team and individual coaching process to enable this methodology. As you know, the Agile approach demands strong team relationships and skills to be successful. The team had remote workers from around the world; different nationalities, races and languages, although everyone could speak English. A further objective for this programme was to enable greater inclusivity and appreciation of difference within the team because this would deliver richer and better work with a global outlook.

Alice's isolation became clear in the first few sessions, not only as the leader of the team, but also because she was isolated in her apartment with her cats. She was new to the town she lived in and working across timelines and into the night meant that she did not have much time to build a social network. She did not go so far as to say she was lonely, just that it might have been nice for her to have someone to do things with.

We began to discuss ways in which she could find others, but she was not entirely convinced that having a social life would be useful to her. We started to build a business case for engaging with others, but she did not find it compelling, and I became curious about her historical experience with other people.

After we had built up some trust, she started wondering aloud about who she would meet in the world and making comments that could be interpreted as racist, revealing very right-wing beliefs about problems caused by certain people or by liberal politicians. I wondered where these attitudes had come from, they appeared very different from what I would expect, given what I knew about her upbringing, youth, work, and intelligence.

Then she started sharing video clips, at first quite cautiously, as if wanting to see my reaction before she sent me the next one. I asked her where she got them from, and she told me how YouTube had started suggesting videos to her and that she had watched them, and then more videos came, and she watched those too. At first, she found them a bit farfetched, but over time they became more and more compelling. Stories that initially seemed conspiratorial now seemed to be realistic and she started to change some of her more liberal views judging these as idealistic, unrealistic, and immature. She decided that she had been a victim of left-wing lies and vowed to never fall prey to liberal media again. Alice had been caught by a fascist algorithm.

She had shared her interest in right-wing ideas with some of her old friends from school who had reacted very badly. Their geographic separation from Alice became further amplified by an ideological gulf. Even her best friend Geordie had drifted away, leaving Alice and the cats on their own.

This is a sad tale, especially for liberals like me. I think you understand how the absence of others created a vacuum that the YouTube algorithm filled with fascist ideas and videos. Alice had no one to distract or warn her about the algorithm that was sending her videos, or to provide her with a more realistic idea of what happens in the world, including the value of diversity and equality for all humans. She was clever, so it wasn't a brain problem here. I would venture that it was the pain of isolation, and her difficulty in understanding what caused this, that drove her to seek solutions and relief in blaming and stereotyping.

Poor Alice, it would be nice to think that once she re-entered the world after COVID, she would open to a broader way of being and that she did not remain an introverted fascist. I had a couple of sessions with her after COVID and she was considering the idea of going face to face with other humans and building a social life. She had attended a company face-to-face meeting that went off well and built her confidence for being present with others. I am not sure what happened to her political beliefs, but I hoped she could open herself to more of others and the world.

Alice lived in a castle, with too little of *others*. Like Alice, we need *others* to humanise our *self* and to help us stay responsive to the world. When we don't have this, we can stop growing and learning and even become susceptible to predatory ideas – like that fascist algorithm.

Losing *others* through trauma, death, and addiction

I spoke earlier about us living in a time of trauma, and how much it informs our way of being in the world. Solomon's story below illustrates this.

Solomon, the sad

I met Solomon for four sessions after he was released from jail in Cape Town. On the phone he mentioned that he was seeking career advice because he was not sure what to do with his life. I explained that I was not a career coach, and he said yes, he knew, but had heard good things about me from someone else and wanted to see me. He was a pro bono client from a referral NGO with whom I worked.

When I answered the door for the first session, I was struck by his slightly sheepish look, head hung low between his shoulders. He moved quietly and sat upright in the chair and started telling his story in a surprisingly neutral way. He said his recent stint in jail was not too bad, he had learned from the army how to survive in a macho culture. He was used to routines, structure, hierarchies, and violence. It was a world he understood, and he had the skills and physical strength to get what he wanted or at least protect himself. Over the two years he had spent in jail he found kindred spirits and a community of allies, and together they had built a life in jail. In other words, Solomon had joined a gang, he had moved almost seamlessly from an army life into gang life.

His dilemma was what to do with his life now that he was out of jail; the gang was calling him to new roles, but he wanted to try to live a normal life, meet someone, maybe even have children. The world outside jail and gangs was, however, not offering him any opportunities, and he was sitting at home with his mother, trying to avoid gang emissaries and becoming depressed. He had no friends and his mother was wanting to move to her sisters in another town, so he would soon have no place to stay.

Over the next four sessions Solomon told me that he went to war at 18. He was conscripted, received some basic training, and then sent to the battlefield. His father felt that being a soldier would help him toughen up and stay off the streets. His mother felt it was too soon for her baby to be exposed to combat but by law, she had to give him up to the state. They had been ok parents to Solomon in general, a little too heavy-handed on the corporal punishment and drinking, but typical of the community that he had come from. They had reared him in challenging times, when the streets were owned by gangs and police, and they had managed to get him through school with limited mishaps.

Solomon came to understand the difficulty of life deeply. While in the army he was sent into horrendous circumstances; saw friends die, saw enemies killed, and refugees impoverished, displaced, and desperate. He only encountered one of the people he killed, the rest were slain at a distance. But this one person that Solomon shot and killed, died right in front of him, the same person who minutes before had tried to kill him. She was of a similar age to Solomon, and left her face etched on Solomon's brain and in his dreams.

When he came back from war, going home to his mom, he intended to find a job and get on with life. He was different; definitely older, angry, and lost. He was happy to see his family but reluctant to tell of what had happened on the battle-field. These things were best kept away from those who loved him in case they found out who he really was, and the family had their own problems anyway.

During this time, sleep evaded Solomon, and when it came, as it could when assisted by alcohol and weed, it was broken by nightmares and cracking head-aches. This, along with mood swings, did not put him in the best shape for job interviews or even getting along with others. Solomon got into fights with family members and strangers and was finally jailed for beating up a fellow drinker who had insulted him. The judge found him to have used excessive force, force that resulted in the fellow drinker having brain damage and Solomon was given a jail sentence.

I know by now you have been watching how much trauma Solomon suffered in his life, maybe even starting in childhood. You can also see from the symptoms he expressed that he was suffering from PTSD, and it is likely that this played a significant role in the bar fight. My sense was that he not only had PTSD but also additional negative combat-based beliefs and behaviours that were locked in dur-ing his formative time in the army. Together these made him awkward, difficult, and sometimes aggressive socially, undermining his ability to make friends out-side gang life. And, as we know PTSD can severely damage relationships with others, limiting empathy, connection, and creating isolation.

At the fourth session, Solomon said that his mother had left town and he was sleeping at one of the gang's houses. They had needed some muscle for a job and he had provided it. He looked like someone who had given up resisting the mag-netic pull of life's underbelly and was stepping into a slipstream. A year later, I read of his death in a shoot-out with the police.

I think Solomon's story says a lot about how trauma can shatter life and relationships. He was living in a repetitive nightmare that undermined his abil-ity to have the engaged relationships that may have allowed him to process his past and incubate a new Solomon. Solomon became stuck in a way of being that ultimately resulted in his death.

Solomon's story is very sad, a life destroyed by trauma. Experiences of death, grief, and addiction can do the same.

When someone close to us dies, we lose them. However, the impact of this death may cause us to lose further people as we grieve. We can feel the need for isolation and can be misunderstood in our grief by those around us. Our grief can make us aggressive or behave in ways that further isolates us. We can also focus on our dead companion instead of the living as we come to terms with their death. These are normal processes of grieving; however, if we stay iso-lated and are unable to rebuild our lives without our beloved, then we become stuck in a cycle of grief that turns us away from life. (Just FYI the chapter on losing *meaning* contains the case study of Gertie who could not stop grieving, which illustrates this well.)

I have no doubt that you understand how addiction can interfere in relationships; addicts prioritise their addiction over people and then they leave. This limits the people addicts can call on to help them move out of stuckness and addiction, and underscores the importance of post active addiction communities where we can find support, help, and community.

Losing *others* by using them as objects or tools

The earlier section on neoliberalism and those on objectification speak to the dehumanisation of *others*.[11] Sadly, there are many short-term benefits to dehumanising *others*. We can use this to justify taking a larger slice of the pie (migrants don't warrant getting paid fairly; retrenching in the lower ranks but raising pay in higher ones), to justify acts of violence and land theft (they were just cockroaches; their religious practices were inhumane; they were living like savages), show us up in a good light (I always help the poor and needy; I always have a young attractive man on my arm) and much more. Dehumanisation is also, as we know, the precursor to colonialism and genocide.

A common way to dehumanise *others* is through words: 'words create worlds'.[12] For example, in Rwanda, Radio Télévision Libre des Mille Collines[13] calling Tutsis cockroaches in order to enable genocide.[14] We can use the term 'fatalities' when speaking of deaths at work, tell addicts to get 'clean' as if they are dirty, call professional women 'dollies', slut-shame on social media, and describe opposing football club supporters as 'scum'. We are very quick to objectify and dehumanise through words.

Dehumanised relationships do not offer us an easy opportunity to become more human and emergent. They are more likely to offer further dehumanisation, unless we are very careful to find ways to rehumanise *others* and our *self* within the relationship. This is why it is so hard to reunite perpetrator and oppressor, coloniser and colonised, white and black/brown people. These patterns of relationship are often just cycles of dehumanisation.

We have spoken at length about the objectification of humans, and I provided an example of someone who had been objectified and in turn, objectified herself, Angelique. This time we will look from the other side of the objectification continuum to understand the objectifier, who is in this case a coach.

Hatchet Harriet

Harriet became a coach after a stellar career in HR. She had held positions in two large organisations as HR director, both in the UK. In both organisations she was known for her toughness, especially when it came to retrenchments. By her late 50s she decided she wanted to be a coach. She wanted a job that was easier, less exhausting, and more flexible. Five years on, all trained up and with all her credentials in place, she became a victim of her own success, and her work became more exhausting and less flexible.

The back story is that Harriet's leaving corporate had happened at the same time as her husband left her. Their relationship had always been rather neutral but this had taken a turn for the worse as it became clear to her husband that she was married to work and not him. She had been the sole earner in the family, and the courts ruled that a 50/50 split was fair. In Harriets mind, her assets were halved, including her pension and she became anxious about money and her ability to live the luxurious retirement of her dreams. Harriet believed that she needed to earn more money.

Harriet's reputation for toughness meant that she was referred more and more remedial clients. Senior leaders in organisations for whom she had worked had seen her in action and they needed more of that on their shift. She was seen as the fixer of bad attitudes and behaviours, the panacea for wayward difficult execs. They would be sent for ten sessions to be slapped around and remodelled into the right shape for the job.

Harriet believed she knew how to identify types, how to leverage their ambitions, and re-shape them to the epitome of a successful corporate executive. She ignored clients' existential dilemmas about life and finding meaning, saying that they needed to be practical. Harriet helped them to think strategically, competitively, and politically, build their stakeholder networks, and promote their brand. None of these are bad things in themselves, but when overused, can promote inauthenticity, unbridled ambition, and the loss of self. In fact, Harriet was a bit of a sausage machine creating bland, inauthentic corporate machines. She was an expert at this.

She was seeing too many clients and following the organisation's lead more than the client. Her approach did not value the individual but sought to create homogenous executives. She did not seek to build her client's agency or find freedom in the context, but rather create compliance to a corporate identity.

Harriet had names for her clients, which she used behind their backs when speaking to her executive secretary Maria. She called them names like 'flabby Bob', 'sulky Sheila', 'last-chance Lila', or 'defiant Dan'. She called them the names of their 'development area'.

Over time, Harriet became more tired, more cynical, and more robotic. Her work became less meaningful, and she became more fixated on seeing as many people as possible because she felt her time as a coach could be coming to an end and she still needed more retirement money.

Harriet came to me for supervision, only because a client put this in as a requirement for a new contract. The client had heard that best practice coaching required supervised coaches.

At first Harriet was quite performative in coaching, giving me the pat lines of a 'good' coach. During these sessions it became clear that she was dehumanising her clients, essentialising them into their 'problem' area and pressuring them into a mould. I suspected she was doing the same to herself as well.

We can see all the signs of Harriet treating her clients as objects here. An overworked coach with empathy fatigue, referring to people as 'problems', not treating them as full humans. Furthermore, she used the same process for all clients and this undermined client individuality and agency. Lastly, her relationship accountability was always tipped towards the organisation, and away from the client.

My suspicion about her treating her *self* in the same way was based on the following factors. She worked her *self* excessively hard, her financial success had superseded client success, and she was performative and stereotyped in her behaviour. In fact I felt quite nauseated and irritated by her constant use of coachisms like 'reaching out', 'managing our emotions', '*self*-regulation for performance', and much more.

We catch up with Harriet later in the section on growing *others* and see how she became more her *self* and how this allowed her clients to be more their *self*.

Losing *others* and becoming isolated

When we lose *others*, we lose their capacity to humanise us as well as the opportunity to grow. When we are isolated, we are disconnected from other humans, we cannot draw on *others* to pull us away from our own stuckness and towards our humanity in life. Isolation is a deeply painful state for most people.

When we are isolated, we become vulnerable to being scapegoated and objectified. This is because people tend to scapegoat those who do not have social or other forms of explicit power. As a scapegoat, we can be shamed and made responsible for ills we have nothing to do with. Shame itself has many poor outcomes for stuckness, including that we will be less likely to seek the help of *others*. We will also be less likely to act on changing our situation because we may believe that we deserve our isolation and rejection. We may also become objectified in our scapegoated identity.

When we lose *others*, this depletes our sense of *self* and *meaning* as well.

At this stage of the Cycle of Stuckness we get more stuck, we have not only lost our *self* but also *others* and we are increasingly unable to change our situation. All we can do now is keep moving with the momentum of the cycle into losing *meaning*.

What kind of relationships do we need in coaching?

Coaches of all kinds value the coaching relationship above all else. This is because it is the relationship that brings the transformation. Engaged connections between coach and clients are bridges that birth insight, accountability, energy, courage, and much more. Here are some the things that the coaching relationship can do:

- Build trust that supports an honest relationship.
- Enable the client to improve their relationship with themselves.
- Provide a safe space in which clients can express themselves.

- Support clients to choose enabling narratives for their dilemmas.
- Enable better thinking.
- Witness and validate the client's inner world.
- Empower the client to muster and align themselves to overcome obstacles and achieve goals.
- Provide a bridge over which to transfer information and feedback.
- Act as a proxy for relationships outside coaching; a way to understand how clients enter and remain in relationships.
- Provide a low-risk development opportunity for the client to learn how to express needs and solve problems in relationships.
- Enrich the coach's work and impact.

It is clear from this long list above that the coaching relationship has magical properties indeed. We know that humans grow and humanise in engaged relationships, but how does this look in its professional form, what makes a good coaching relationship?

As we know, this is a very well-worn question and there have been many answers. Some of the qualities that have been used to describe an engaged coaching relationship include trustworthiness, integrity, openness, presence, authenticity, equality, and more, and there are many good books that demonstrate how to do this. I would like to talk to two aspects of this relationship: the quality of the coach's humanity and the coaching frame.

A critical part of coach training includes working on our *self*, building *self-*awareness, unlocking mind traps[15] and, most importantly, the loosening of behavioural fixations and attachment patterns. This is working on our humanity and when we do this, we learn humility, an essential skill for coaching. Our work as coaches is to engage and build our full humanity and not seek to erase it.

Some of the things we need to know about our humanity could be how needy we are in relationships (including the coaching relationship), how much affirmation we desire, how desperate we are to be of service, and how we think about emotional depth. When we know about these things, we have the choice to bracket them[16] out or use them constructively in the coaching relationship. For example, if I know how my desire to be of service can sometimes overshadow clients' goals, then I have the opportunity to work more consciously with these impulses. This is the way we learn to see the client as they are and not as we are.

An area that I enjoy thinking about and working with is the coaching frame. This includes the opening of the relationship, the parameters, and responsibilities of the relationship, what happens when the frame changes or needs to change, and the closing of the relationship. These are the guardrails that focus and intensify the connection so that it can manifest its potential. Without these, the relationship will be too diffuse and undirected to be able to stimulate and support change. We are not in the business of providing friendship, although that may happen, we are in the business of co-creating energy and direction for change.

Our attachment patterns (see below for more detail of these) play a huge role in influencing how we are able to implement the coaching frame. Someone like me with poor boundaries and a desire to be liked may find it harder to do than a coach who has stronger boundaries and is more goal orientated. Either way, we all have to develop disciplines around the frame.

I like using the frame to understand how clients do relationships, work in partnership, or commit to their own development. Some clients need tighter frames than others, others push back at frames to retain autonomy or stay in control. Some clients want to endlessly shift meeting timings, others argue for special conditions and fee reductions, some are often late, some submit pre reading, and so on, and so on. All of these behaviours relate to the coaching frame and provide hugely valuable information about the client.

What happens to coaching when coaches lose their clients?

A critical skill for coaches is that of being able to have and sustain a productive relationship, even in extreme situations where the client seems intent on undermining this. There are many ways in which we can lose clients, including by being irrelevant, not listening well enough, and pushing them into acting in ways that suit us. We can also lose clients by treating them as objects, by not holding them firmly enough, by being vague, by not stepping into the relationship, and more. Our primary focus needs to be on holding the relationship with the client because without this, we have limited capacity to support their transformation.

We want to close client relationships in a structured and orderly way, with no unfinished business. We want our clients to leave us feeling confident that they can continue on their own, we don't want them forever hankering after our influence in their lives. Exiting well is critical for this.

Our own approach to endings, and yes death too, influences how we close client relationships. We may be uncomfortable with endings and make the last session short and sweet, with a sigh of relief. We may linger longer and invite clients to contact us whenever they have the slightest whim. For some of us, closing well means to stay in the 'pain' of this ending, and be present to the client. For others, we need to be more transactional and create a sharper exit. My best coaching endings have been when my coach honoured my growth, noticed how well I was prepared for the future, and wished me well. It was best when my coach was able to create a clean break with no stickiness created by their needs.

Questions to ask your *self*

- What attachment patters do you have (secure, anxious-ambivalent, anxious-avoidant, or anxious-ambivalent)? How do you think your attachment style plays out in coaching?

- What is it like to be a client of yours?
- How good are you at closing coaching engagements?

Notes

1 Louw, D. J., & Fourie, D. P. (2011). Towards a definition of philosophical counselling in South Africa. *South African Journal of Psychology*, *41*(1), 101–112.

2 van Deurzen, E., & Iacovou, S. (2013). *Existential perspectives on relationship therapy*; van Deurzen, E., Craig, E., Laengle, K., Schneider, K., Tantam, D., & du Plock, S. (2019). *The Wiley world handbook of existential therapy* (1st ed.). Eds. E. Craig et al. Wiley Blackwell.
van Deurzen, E. et al. (2009) *Everyday mysteries: A handbook of existential psychotherapy*. Second, *Everyday Mysteries: A Handbook of Existential Psychotherapy*. Second. London: Routledge.
van Deurzen, E. (2012) *Reasons for living: Existential therapy and spirituality*. Available at: https://www.researchgate.net/publication/307967655_Reasons_to_Live.

3 Spinelli, E. (1989). *The interpreted world: An introduction to phenomenological psychology*. Sage Publications, Inc.

4 Murty, V. H. (2023). *Our epidemic of loneliness and isolation* (pp. 1–82).

5 Ainsworth, M. D. S. (1969). Object relations, dependency, and attachment: A theoretical review of the infant-mother relationship. *Child Development*, *40*, 969–1025; Bowlby, J. (1969) *Attachment and loss: Volume 1. Attachment*. Basic Books; Bowlby, J. (1973). *Attachment and loss: Volume 2. Separation: Anxiety and anger*. Basic Books.

6 Levi Levine, A. (2011). *Attached: The new science of adult attachment and how it can help you find--and keep--love*. Jeremy P. Tarcher, Penguin.

7 Vansloten, J.A., & Henderson, M. (1997). *Attachment orientation and leadership style: The effect of avoidant attachment priming on relational leadership* (pp. 60–64). Available at: https://cpb-us-w2.wpmucdn.com/campuspress.yale.edu/dist/a/1215/files/2015/11/2011_VanSloten-Henderson-2011-19gnxp9.pdf (Accessed: 2 June, 2019); The Attachment Project (2024) https://www.attachmentproject.com (Accessed: 5 March 2024).

8 The Attachment Project. (2024). https://www.attachmentproject.com (Accessed: 5 March 2024).

9 Levine, P. (1997). *Waking the tiger: Healing trauma: The innate capacity to transform overwhelming experiences*. North Atlantic Books.
The Attachment Project. (2024). https://www.attachmentproject.com (Accessed: 5 March 2024).

10 Agile is a methodology for managing IT processes and software development. It contains all sorts of processes that help things flow, but these processes need to be backed by good relationships for the system to work well.

11 Heil, D. (2011). *Ontological fundamentals for ethical management hedeiegger and the corporate world, issues in business ethics*. Springer.

12 Heschel, A. (2020). *Words create worlds*. Available at: https://beingfullyhuman.com/2020/10/16/words-create-worlds-6-doctors-against-fascism/#_ftn1 (Accessed: 12 January 2024).

13 Ndahiro, K, (no date) "In Rwanda, We Know All About Dehumanizing Language" https://www.theatlantic.com/ideas/archive/2019/04/rwanda-shows-how-hateful-speech-leads-violence/587041/, accessed 02/09/2024.

14 Ndahiro, K, (no date) "In Rwanda, We Know All About Dehumanizing Language" https://www.theatlantic.com/ideas/archive/2019/04/rwanda-shows-how-hateful-speech-leads-violence/587041/, accessed 02/09/2024.

15 Garvey Berger, J. (2019). *Unlocking leadership mindtraps: How to thrive in complexity* (1st ed.). Stanford University Press.
16 Van Deurzen, E., Craig, E., Laengle, K., Schneider, K., Tantam, D., & Du Plock, S. (2019). *The Wiley world handbook of existential therapy*. Hoboken and Chichester.

Bibliography

Ainsworth, M. D. S. (1969a). Object relations, dependency, and attachment: A theoretical review of the infant-mother relationship. *Child Development, 40*, 969–1025.

Bowlby, J. (1969). *Attachment and loss: Volume 1. Attachment*. Basic Books.

Bowlby, J. (1973). *Attachment and loss: Volume 2. Separation: Anxiety and anger*. Basic Books.

Garvey Berger, J. (2019). *Unlocking leadership mindtraps: How to thrive in complexity* (1st ed.). Stanford University Press.

Heil, D. (2011). *Ontological fundamentals for ethical management Heidegger and the corporate world, issues in business ethics*. Springer.

Heschel, A. (2020). *Words create worlds*. Available at: https://beingfullyhuman.com/2020/10/16/words-create-worlds-6-doctors-against-fascism/#_ftn1 (Accessed: 12 January 2024).

Levi Levine, A. (2011) *Attached: The new science of adult attachment and how it can help you find--and keep--love*. Jeremy P. Tarcher, Penguin.

Louw, D. J., & Fourie, D. P. (2011). Towards a definition of philosophical counselling in South Africa. *South African Journal of Psychology, 41*(1), 101–112.

Murty, V. H. (2023). *Our epidemic of loneliness and isolation* (pp. 1–82). US Public Health Services.

Ainsworth, M. D. S. (1969b). Object relations, dependency, and attachment: A theoretical review of the infant-mother relationship. *Child Development, 40*, 969–1025.

The Attachment Project. (2024). https://www.attachmentproject.com (Accessed: 5 March 2024).

Spinelli, E. (1989). *The interpreted world: An introduction to phenomenological psychology*. Sage Publications, Inc.

van Deurzen, E., & Iacovou, S. (2013). *Existential perspectives on relationship therapy*. Palgrave MacMillan.

van Deurzen, E., Craig, E., Laengle, K., Schneider, K., Tantam, D., & du Plock, S. (2019). *The Wiley world handbook of existential therapy* (1st ed.). Eds. E. Craig et al. Wiley Blackwell.

van Deurzen, E., et al. (2009). *Everyday mysteries: A handbook of existential psychotherapy* (2nd ed.). Routledge.

van Deurzen, E. (2012) *Reasons for living: Existential therapy and spirituality*. Available at: https://www.researchgate.net/publication/307967655_Reasons_to_Live.

Vansloten, J.A., & Henderson, M. (1997). *Attachment orientation and leadership style: The effect of avoidant attachment priming on relational leadership* (pp. 60–64). Available at: https://cpb-us-w2.wpmucdn.com/campuspress.yale.edu/dist/a/1215/files/2015/11/2011_VanSloten-Henderson-2011-19gnxp9.pdf (Accessed: 2 June 2019).

Chapter 8

Losing *meaning* and falling into the void

Humans are *meaning*-making machines, this is what we do. Despite this inclination we can become confused about what *meaning* is, and how to create it in our lives. Let's see how.

Meaning: the why of life

Meaning is the source of why and how we continue to live, given our toil on this mortal coil. It is the forever horizon that keeps us moving in a direction. This chapter looks at how *meaning* is critical to living a fluid life and how we might lose it.

By this stage in the cycle, we have lost our *selves* and lost *others*, but we still have some form of *meaning* that can sustain us in a limited way. However, if we keep flowing with the momentum of the cycle, we shall lose this too. Before we go there, it would be useful to understand what *meaning* is for humans and why it is important for humans.

Why is *meaning* important?

Meaning is important, without it we are likely to do very little with our lives. It gives us energy, purpose, and direction. *Meaning* gets us going towards bigger goals, and encourages connection and service. It helps us get over daily struggles so that we can leave a positive mark on this Earth. The last point is important; *meaning* has a transcendent quality, it enables us to transcend the difficulties of daily life by giving us the courage to face our struggles and move beyond them. It can even help us to transcend death, with our good deeds and memories of our loving and life, keeping us alive beyond our bodies. These are the two most important functions of *meaning*; it enables us to transcend our life and our death. This helps us to feel that we exist, and our lives are valuable.

Meaning creates a values structure for our lives that builds an inner coherence, and directs us to act in ways we desire. It keeps us on track for the moment of our death when we must account to our *self* and others (for example, God),

DOI: 10.4324/9781003536253-8

for what we have done with our moments on Earth. *Meaning* creates structure and values, and this allows us to feel a sense of control over life. And lastly, together *meaning*, values, and structure, how we have sculpted our lives in alignment with this, gives us a sense of *self*-esteem. This allow us to feel that we exist and our lives are worth something. So, all in all, *meaning* is vital for our survival as humans.

Meaning also allows us to transcend ourself and our lives; for many people it is deeply intertwined with spirituality. Like religion/spirituality it sits outside our *self* and between people holding us together like a spiritual glue of collective cohesion. It can have a life of its own winding around us and *others* and directing us towards connection and healing.

Meaning is a central interest in the world of existential philosophy, and there are two schools of thought. Firstly, there is the Camus orientation which argues that there is no meaning in life at all because life is essentially absurd and meaningless. For these thinkers, nothing is connected, no dots join to lead towards a higher goal, and there is no real purpose for doing anything. Camus himself, went so far as to argue that the most important question philosophy could answer was why live at all when life is meaningless.[1]

On the other side of the continuum and across the existential wasteland, is Frankl. He suggests that *meaning* can be experienced in many things, especially those that involve and benefit *others*. He claims that we can make *meaning* by doing something useful, experiencing *others* deeply, or by the attitude we take to inescapable suffering in our lives. For Frankl, *meaning* is what enables us to live, even in inhumane conditions.[2]

Meaning gives us coherence, direction, and purpose as well as courage to keep living when our mortal coil is unliveable.

How can we lose *meaning* and not notice?

We can lose *meaning* without noticing when we are not tuned into the importance of *meaning* and therefore do not seek to cultivate it all over our lives. We lose *meaning* when we attach to the wrong types of *meaning*. We don't notice this when we are working so hard in other ways that we never get to reflect on our lives. We also lose *meaning* when we have trauma and are so entrapped by pain that we do not see how this loss has also damaged our *meaning* of life.

Remarkably, there are many ways to lose *meaning*; these are described in the next section but first let us look at the structural factors impacting how we make *meaning*.

Structural factors affecting *meaning*

A contemporary existential philosopher Joel Vos,[3] suggests that specific economic systems promote different types of *meaning*. He talks about Capitalist

Life Syndrome where *meaning* is primarily materialistic, hedonistic, and *self*-orientated. Materialist *meaning*-making leads us to value material possessions, status, education, and professional success. Hedonistic *meaning* invites us to build *meaning* around experiences with our *self*: food, drink, sex, pain avoidance, animals, and nature. Lastly, *self*-orientated *meaning* leads us to personal development, resilience, *self*-efficacy, being in control, and achieving goals as a way to live a meaningful life.

Vos says that people living within a capitalist system are less likely to chase *meaning* through social types of *meaning*, including being connected to *others*. We may also not engage with conformist, altruistic, and community forms of *meaning*, favouring individual success and autonomy. He continues that people within this system are also less likely to look for higher purpose types of *meaning* related to *self*-transcendence, authenticity, wisdom, justice, ethics, spirituality, and religion. And lastly, we are less likely to use existential and philosophical sources of *meaning* that include the *meaning* inherent in being alive and moving towards death, uniqueness, connectedness, freedom, and taking responsibility for our lives.[4]

According to Vos, a significant part of the Capitalist Life Syndrome is that the offer of freedom is an illusion. We are told that we can choose our life and the material, hedonistic, and *self*-fulfilling forms of *meaning* we want. However, the gravitational pull of the system does not allow for this. Socialisation, education, advertising, and professional mores corral us into certain choices. Only the very rich and powerful can choose to operate out of this gravitational pull. For most of us, we don't notice that we think we are free but are not.[5] For most of us, we think we can choose our own *meaning*, but we may not be able to.

The impact of the Capitalist Life Syndrome is that we focus on the more superficial forms of *meaning* to guide our lives and less on finding *meaning* through being authentic, individual, purposive, and connected. According to Vos, this has an impact on our mental health: we experience existential crises, internalise blame for external events, experience a sense of helplessness and fatalism, and can become depressed and anxious.[6]

Losing *meaning* by not knowing how to create *meaning*

Many of us believe that *meaning* is automatically bestowed upon us, along with life. This is not entirely true; we often have to make it.[7] For example, it is relatively easy to find *meaning* in rearing children; you look after them and they grow, and it all feels generally meaningful. In this case *meaning* is intrinsic and easily accessible. It is far less easy to find *meaning* in life situations that have no intrinsic *meaning*, a lot of pain, unrelenting boredom, or even perhaps when it would be a relief for us to die. Below is the story of Mohammed who had lived a life full of *meaning* but was not sure how he would find it in his retirement.

Mohammed making meaning

Mohammed was a charming man who came to see me during his first year of retirement. His wife Amani had sent him because she thought he was depressed and was getting irritated with him hanging about the house. He was not so sure about being depressed, he said all the newly retired people he knew went through a phase, and this was his. He was happy to have someone to chat too as he had found coaching beneficial before during his corporate career, and hoped to get some clarity on what was ailing him now.

Mohammed had had an illustrious career, circulating in the C suite for his last ten years of work. He had worked in and run the EMEA (Europe, Middle East, and Africa) division, which meant he was always off to places there. In all his years, the work had never stopped flowing over into his personal life, taking away time from his wife and children.

He felt that his kids were amply compensated for his absence because his work had given them access to the finer things in life: good schools and an influential network to kickstart their careers. They had lived all over the world as he moved jobs from London to Jeddah, Dubai, Moscow, and back to London. They had had global exposure, and this had paid off in terms of their confidence and ability to interact with anyone. They had launched Aisha and Tariq in London and Nasir in Dubai. Soon they would bring partners home and hopefully children too.

When they moved back to London his wife Amani had re-found her old friends and was fast becoming enmeshed in a close-knit community. She was popular and fun to be with, found beautiful words to say to everyone, and was the centre of any community advisory group. Her life was busy and meaningful.

The problem was not Amani, she was fine, it was Mohammed who was starting to feel a little lost in his retirement. For starters, he was not sure what to do with his day. He had become more involved with managing the house and cooking meals, but Amina found him irritating and in the way, it was after all her turf, and she wanted things done the way she had always done things. His friend Adam had advised him to take up hobbies and go see the world, but he had no interests outside work, and he had seen as much of the world as he wanted to. There were obviously things he could do like manage his money, mow his lawn, learn how to cook, or spend more time with God, but it just did not feel enough. He did not feel useful or productive enough and he wondered what he would do with all the years between now and his final resting place.

Not only was Mohammed looking forward, but he was looking back as well. How had he got so old so quickly, how had he stayed with the same company for so long, why had he not spent more time with Amani and the kids, and why had he always been an accountant? He had had other dreams from time to time, but none were followed, he had spent his life counting units and grouping numbers in pre-ordained ways. Was this enough to constitute a useful life?

During our discussion he described how the early years of his career were meaningful, he had focussed on getting ahead and providing for the family. He remembered the moves, the new jobs, finding schools, and acclimatising Amani

and the children to new places and lifestyles. This had been exciting and challeng-
ing and meaningful, and fast. In the later years of his career, things were not as
exciting, it seemed like a lot of repetition, sitting around, and listening to people
who didn't know what they were doing, or who were playing games. What was the
meaning of all the rushing about, all the panic, late nights, anxiety, cynicism, and
exhaustion? Was his work meaningful, had he contributed to the world in some
way, would he even be remembered?

We unpacked his question, exploring when his work felt meaningful and where
there were years of vague blur created by blind busyness or boredom. He said that
he liked creating stories with numbers, helping businesses to see what was really
happening so that they could be better managed. And then finally he shared what
was said at his farewell speech, when many of his colleagues told stories of how
he had impacted on them, as a person. Quite a few mentioned that he had listened
to them or believed in them or helped them solve problems, one mentioned that he
had spearheaded the inclusion programme for the company bringing in people and
voices from different races and religions. As a minority staff member himself,
Mohammed was not sure if that had really worked, but he liked the idea that he
had been helpful to others. In fact, he liked this more than the fact that he had
played a pivotal role in building new markets and achieving stretch targets.

We had finally gotten to an understanding of what was meaningful to
Mohammed, and it was helping *others*. The problem was he did not have *others*
to help now; his children were gone, Amani did not want help, and he was not
sure how or where he could be helpful to *others*. We catch up with Mohammed
in the section on growing *meaning* so hang on for the resolution of his dilemma.

Losing *meaning* by choosing the wrong kind of *meaning*

Some *meanings* are more meaningful to us, for example, *meaning* that enables
our growth and for us to transcend our lives. However, as we will see below, it's
easy to get distracted by materialist and other shiny, ersatz *meanings*. Let's take
a look at Cas, the curator, and get to a deeper understanding of what this is
about.

Cas, the curator

Having a coach can be a status symbol for some people, at minimum it shows you
can afford one, either by paying for it yourself, or by being valuable enough to
have someone else pay. I suspected that this may the case with Cas, the curator,
especially after I found that she had been posting pictures of herself at my gate
titled 'what a day, can't wait for my sesh with my coach'.

Cas was self-employed and ran her own business writing copy for social media. She
was 29 years old and single. Cas was a looker and a dresser, always ready for a selfie
or group shot. She was also very obsessed with presenting a self that was special and
different so that she could stand out from the flotsam and jetsam of social media.

Cas said she was pleased with how her life had developed, she had done better than her school friends and was doing well in her business thanks to her strong social media presence. In fact, we spent a lot of time looking at pictures of her in various places, unpacking what the pictures said about her and who she was, and whether she stood out.

Initially, I asked questions aimed at getting her to explore deeper issues like her childhood, her life, relationships, and where she was going. I was probably a bit old-fashioned and judgemental about what appeared to me as the superficiality and performance of her life, and I wanted her to have more depth and authenticity in line with my existential ideas about what makes a life worth living. But she was not interested in pursuing any of these topics, and so I finally started flowing with her more fully through the collections of her posing here or there.

I started really engaging with the pictures, noticing clothes, props, contexts, and even make-up. These were very varied and when grouped together, it was hard to find connections between the pictures. She was definitely showing me something, but I was not sure what it was, and then it finally hit me, slow learner that I am. She was showing me her various special and curated selves and maybe she was not sure where she was in all of this. Perhaps she was playing with possible identities and maybe she was asking me to help her identify where she actually was in all these various disguises. Perhaps too, all these multiple identities had flowered so individually because she had limited coherent underlying and integrated meaning in her life. Maybe she was also not sure about who she was.

I went in with the meaning hypothesis and asked her what meaning these pictures were in her life. She looked up at me and said, 'Its where I am now, it documents where I am now.' I went in through this tiny gap that had opened and asked, 'Where are you in all these pictures, where is Cas'? She scrolled through the pictures and said, 'Here, here, and here,' and then she kind of crumbled inwards and said, 'I don't know where I am. I am not sure who these people are and what they are doing in my life.'

I am sure that you can by now see that this is a case of losing one's *self* and also a case where Cas was struggling to find her place in life. Meaning gives us coherence, purpose, and direction in life, and if we don't have this central compass in place, we risk fragmenting into multiple world-inspired ways of being, just as Cas had done.

I suspect that Cas was suffering from Capitalist Life Syndrome to some extent. She had built her identities around those most valued by capitalism and social media. We will catch up on Cas in the section on growing *meaning* and you will get to see the astounding things this woman achieves.

Losing *meaning* by not having *meaning* in all the right places

Even though we know how to create *meaning* that is meaningful, we may still have a *meaning* problem. This is because having *meaning* in one place in one's life may not be enough, we might need *meaning* in more than one place. Let's see how this plays out for Jane, the justice fighter.

Jane, the justice fighter

The morning before I met Jane, I saw her in an online newspaper being interviewed about her latest bust (not her breasts, nor a sculptured head – a crime bust). I checked her name with the name in my calendar, it was the same. The morning was spent in anticipation of her arrival, wondering if she was coming with PTSD or something related to her work. I was right, it was something related to her work but not PTSD.

Jane was an intelligent and thoughtful client who wanted someone to talk to about her life. She had been experiencing a sense of heaviness and depression in her life. She was also fairly burnt out, having invested 30 years of excessively hard work in crime fighting.

She was a justice fighter, not your average cop but a super crime fighter heading up the Organised Crime unit for the state and sending countless criminals, dealers, and money launderers to jail. This was very meaningful work and people were grateful for how she contributed to society. It was, however, all consuming and over the years, her friendship group had reduced to those with whom she worked, and she had not had a partner for many years. You see, work crept into every empty space in her life, and it only stopped creeping in when she was dead tired and flopped, fully clothed on her bed asleep.

Jane did feel that she missed having a private life; something pleasant and meaningful to do on the weekends other than sleep and watch Netflix in bed with a few glasses of wine. But she was often too tired for being with others, they could be quite draining and, in her words, 'full of shit'. Due to her high profile, people knew about her work and when she went out, they always wanted to get an inside view on the current trial in the press or offer her some advice on how to proceed. Jane found this very annoying, especially the advice from back seat crime fighters.

Instead of seeing people, she tried to fill her companionship gap with animals and plants but landed up giving them away, or in the case of plants killing them. After a day at work, she had little capacity left to curate a home or nurture other living beings. And so she spent much of her down time getting back-ache from watching movies in bed. Her private life continued to wait, inactivated, in service of a demanding and meaningful work life. She had what one might call a doughnut life, with everything happening on the outside and a big hole in the middle.

As Jane aged and started thinking about retirement, in particular what to do with all that time on her hands, she became more and more anxious about the lack of meaning and companionship in her private life. It became a heavy weight on her shoulders that ironically made her fill her weekends with more work.

We know that isolation is a killer, but Jane was not totally isolated, she had work, work companions, and more work. We know that a lack of meaning is also a killer, but Jane found much meaning in her work. The problem here was the distribution of meaning and companionship. There was just not enough of it to go around to her weekends and her retirement loomed like the sword of Damocles waiting to drop a void on her head. Ironically, her solution to this anxiety was more work and more solitary red wine and Netflix. This as you know is not an easy source of meaning and companionship, but rather some ersatz stand-in for a private life that is going to cause more pain in the long run. Jane needed to fire the faux actor, and invite her own self back in to her private life; she needed to claim the doughnut hole as her very own terrain.

We catch up to Jane, the justice fighter in the section on growing *meaning*. However, maybe you can hold this story in the back of your mind now, so you have some ideas to offer later when we come to solving her predicament.

Some of us have very meaningful jobs, we are changing the world and helping people, but when we go home, it is to an empty home. Some of us have very meaningful home lives but work is meaningless. Only you can tell how much *meaning* is sufficient for you and how you need it spread across your life. There is no one easy answer to this, we need to discover it on our own.

Losing *meaning* through death, trauma, and addiction

I have put death, trauma, and addiction together in this section because they are often linked. The deaths of *others*, whether they be friend, foe, or nameless can leave us traumatised and wondering about the *meaning* of life. As with trauma, there are many kinds of addiction, some more noticeable than others. One form of addiction that is not easily seen in our neoliberal environment is shopping addiction. Maybe we can look at the story of Li and see how this works.

Li, the shopper

I was working with Li's uncle in his business in the USA, running a leadership development programme with his executive team. During one of our meetings, he mentioned that he was worried about his niece, Li, and would I mind having a chat to see what was happening and how she was. He was particularly worried about her spending as he was on the paying end of her credit card. The uncle was not a direct coaching client of mine, so I felt ok about agreeing to go ahead with this.

Li and I met online, at first for one exploratory session which was then extended to 12 sessions over the period of six months. She said that she had been diagnosed with anxiety and depression and was receiving medication for both. During her time at university, Li had consulted with a therapist and a psychiatrist, both of whom put her symptoms down to being away from home or long-term impacts of her mother's death. She had curtailed her interactions with these professionals because she felt awkward in the sessions and could see no reason to keep engaging after she had her diagnosis and a prescription.

I have paraphrased Li's story below describing the parts that relate to her being a shopping addict because this is a story about shopping addiction. Li was not fully aware of her shopping addiction, only that she did a lot of shopping, and this had become a problem for her uncle who was threatening to cut her off. She thought that her problems related to her depression and that her shopping was not in question. From what she could see, her level of shopping was normal for an affluent college student so not worth mentioning at all. Initially, all I knew was that her uncle thought she was a big spender but that this could be because he was tight, out of date with student needs, or because she actually was a big spender.

We spoke at length about her depression, her feelings of isolation, and her lack of interest in her studies. I thought we could start with some practical steps like clearing and structuring her residence room so she could socialise and work in there more comfortably. It was then that I became aware that her room was overflowing with objects. She said she was messy and turned her zoom camera to her room to show me. It really was stuffed to the gills with clothing and toys and other objects, all lumped together in piles, some still in their store bags.

Li's backstory was that she lost her parents when she was very young and was brought up by the servants of her wealthy uncle. She spent her childhood moving around cities in the USA as her uncle opened businesses and grew wealthier. Servants came and went, and she did not stay in one place long enough to settle into long-term relationships with her peers. There were, however, things in her life that she did have long-term relationships with, and that was objects.

Her interest in objects was sparked off by the luxurious gifts given to her by her uncle, especially when he was not around for her birthdays. He meant these as a symbol of his love for her because he did love her, he just had no time for her. Each time the arrival of the object would excite her, and she would play with it incessantly, but this wore off quite quickly.

Fast forward to now when she was at university trying to make friends and integrate in a residence with other girls. Not only were there racial complexities, but Li had few social skills with which to engage her peers because she had always been alone. She did, however, have access to desirable objects which she could use to trade for social experiences.

This of course meant that Li had to shop a lot, which she did, online and in person. She preferred in person because when the shop assistants saw her coming, they heaped her with praise, chatted to her, and seemed to offer some kind of relationship. Li also experienced pleasure in making the payment, a sort of dopamine hit, I guess.

The purchased objects were sources of joy for her when she got them home, she could admire them and herself sometimes in or with them, and she could also trade them for invites and temporary connections with other girls. But ultimately the joy was short-lived, and she would have to start the cycle all over again which was to feel depressed and isolated, to shop and share and feel joy and then to be depressed and isolated again.

I think that you can see this is a story of isolation as well as addiction and perhaps you can also trace her behaviour back to the loss of her parents and her subsequent isolated years with her uncle. In fact, Li's story has aspects of trauma, addiction, loss of self, loss of others, and loss of meaning. It is a story where the medication for the trauma and isolation (objects and shopping) had become the disease (shopping addiction). It is also a story of how an addiction can distract us from creating real meaning in our lives.

Shopping addiction is a much under-diagnosed condition. People don't tend to go to coaching because they are addicted to shopping, and furthermore, shopping is encouraged in our capitalist system. With shopping, it is difficult to know the line between buying what we think we need and becoming addicted to this pursuit, especially when budget is no object.

I referred Li to an expert on this problem, someone who could provide the specialist addiction treatment that she needed. Li was a bit reluctant to go and I suspected that she thought I had abandoned her like her parents had. We kept in touch for a while through phone calls and then she disappeared.[8]

With addiction, the meaningful object is the object of addiction. This of course can be heroin, sex, shopping, or really anything that we can use to transform our inner state to something more desirable. In this case, the *meaning* of the addiction subverts and dominates all other sources of *meaning*. It locks us into a repetitive cycle of partially satisfying our needs that keeps us stuck and out of life.[9]

Earlier we saw the damage that trauma can inflict in the story of Solomon, the sad. Trauma also has a huge impact on our capacity to have *meaning*. Trauma can take us to the end of our ability to make sense of the world. It can shatter our understanding of the world, leaving us devoid of *meaning*. We don't know how to create *meaning* because all our assumptions about the stability or generosity of the world become lost to us. Not only that, but trauma reduces our cognitive flexibility[10] and we can fall back into old rote ways of being (stuckness) because they offer some stability in a world without reason. We lose relational capacity[11] and so lack the influence of *others* to pull us back into life and *meaning*.

When we experience death, especially of our loved ones, our sense of *meaning* can be shattered and we can remain stuck in a vacuum, unable to get a foothold back into life. Let's see what happened to Gertie, who could not stop grieving.

Gertie, who could not stop grieving

Gertie came to see me in Cape Town three years after the death of her dearly beloved partner Siya. She had had three years of watery misery and insomnia, was desiccated, and desperate. She described that when she was not crying, she had a running nose and when she did not have a running nose, she was crying. Water poured out of Gertie constantly, so much so that she considered upping her water intake to accommodate these excessive outflows.

Gertie was a scientist and the scientific paradigm of rationality and linear causation had colonised her inner world. She did not know what to do with her irrational and overwhelming feelings of grief and felt that her response was inappropriate, irrational, and out of character. Her only defence was to put in longer hours at the lab and avoid home as much as possible.

The backstory to Gertie and Siya's union was that this unusual cross-cultural marriage between two introverts had taken many years to come to fruition. They had fallen in love, found each other emotionally but found it hard to integrate their two worlds. Siya was a geologist with a spiritual bent who liked working unsociable hours and was happiest alone with his thoughts, meditating, or walking in nature. He had seen how complicated relationships could be from his parents, with their shouting and screaming and abuse, and it was hard for him to imagine that a relationship could offer a person anything other than pain.

Gertie is a microbiologist interested in life on a microscopic level. Her work is often solitary, and she liked it that way because she could control the environment when it was just her and her lab equipment. She had discovered earlier in life that the more people there are, the more problems there are, and had actively sought to reduce this type of chaos in her life. Irrational pursuits like spirituality and relationships were less interesting to Gertie, certainly in her earlier years.

You could imagine how slowly the relationship would have taken to form and how much compromise would have been necessary for those two to give up alone time and invest in another human, but they did. Slowly their worlds opened up to let each other in. This happened slowly as I said, because both were passive-aggressive and conflict-avoidant so setting boundaries and asking for their own needs was a complex process with much second guessing and many starts and stops.

After about ten years of dating, they moved in together, ensuring that each had their own private caves as well as some communal areas. They found that merging was less overwhelming when combined with science, especially biology, and spent many delightful hours creating their own indigenous garden. They were in fact very happy, and the world seemed to have worked out for them. This was of course until Siya's untimely demise in a car crash.

We catch up with Gertie in the section on growing *others* because *others* can also be a source of *meaning*, as you well know.

Losing *meaning* and falling into the void

Meaning and purpose give direction to one's life. They also provide a measurement for how well we are doing at living. When we don't have *meaning* we can flip flop around directionless and expend our last drops of energy on activities that may not matter. Being lost is exhausting and frustrating and depressing and lowers our self-esteem.

When we have no *meaning*, it is hard to have direction and have the courage to face everyday pains and boredoms. It is even harder to change because there is no reason and no direction for the change. Every event becomes amplified and isolated because there is no grander scheme of things to put events in their place. As a result, we can become anxious and confused and lost. Being lost in life can feel like falling into an existential void where we circle and circle and nothing that matters happens. We are alone in an unfamiliar world, not knowing who we are, or where we are. All of this leads to an inability or lack of courage to adapt to the world, and so we get stuck.

There are many understandings of the void, including a version in *Minecraft*. Generally, the void refers to a place of darkness and nothingness where one has no sense of oneself or the world. Inside the void we have a sense of emptiness both inside and out, and this of course terrifies us because it makes us question whether we even exist. When we have a sense that things are meaningless, it can feel hopeless, and even terminal. There are no signposts or dropdown menus offering us a way out.

I like to think of the void as an experience of deep stuckness where we and the world grind to a halt and disappear. It is the final reminder that we cannot continue to exist in the way we have been doing. It is the final slap on the wrist to remind us to forge a new path. Voids, however, can be endings as well as beginnings. That is if we can just get out of the dark and undifferentiated zone of nothingness. But more on this in the next few chapters.

When we lose *meaning*, this depletes our sense of *self*, and our relationships with *others* as well.

By this stage we are very stuck. We have lost our *self, others*, and *meaning*. We are still doing our old dance routines, but they are not rendering any useful outcomes. We don't know where to turn or what to do, we are stuck wading in the treacle of nothingness.

What is the *meaning* of our job coach?

Why do coaches become coaches and why is coaching meaningful to us? The answer probably starts with our desire to be helpful to *others* and share our learning. Then there are other layers of *meaning*, including the flexible nature and structure of the work, how it can enable lifelong learning, and that we can do it in our old age. We may also gain *meaning* from being able to influence people who are influencing the world.

We can also have less productive versions of *meaning* in our work as a coach. We may gain *meaning* from having the status of a coach, and being a know-it-all on human beings at work and in life. We may also rather like influencing and fiddling in places that we would not usually get access to, and with little accountability. This can be related to our own unlived lives, for example, the senior management role that we never got, or maybe even to get back at the bullies who took us out at school.

We must understand the light and the darkness of our motivation to coach, and how we create meaningful work from this. We have a duty to create *meaning* in our work that is useful to our clients. Without this, we may inadvertently cause damage.

What happens to our coaching when we lose *meaning* in our work?

There are times in our coaching life when our job becomes less meaningful. Here are some examples that I have seen and experienced:

- When we feel we are not making an impact.
- When we struggle to demonstrate our value in a system that demands this to be done in a very specific and quantitative way.
- When we have agreed to unrealistic outcomes and know we are going to fail.
- When the client is too busy for coaching sessions or when they fail to take responsibility.
- When we feel cynical or demoralised about the system in which the client is working.
- When we know the coaching contract is part of a broader game that will not benefit the client.
- When we are scared of our client.
- When we are burnt out.

Meaning keeps us in the work. When our work is not meaningful, we struggle to commit to the client and this undermines our impact. As a coach, we have a responsibility to make our work meaningful. We have to engage with our cynicism and decide on a positive role for ourselves in difficult systems, even ones we despise. We have to face up to what we despise and respect it because it is our client's world. We also have to be brave and vulnerable and talk about our own and our client's perception of our value, instead of just playing the game until the contract is over.

It is hard to have a meaningful relationship with a client when we are scared of them. Over the years, I have been cautious of a few clients, largely because they have been highly reactive when I have challenged their world view, even softly and empathically. Clients with bullying habits can be frightening.

My only advice in these instances is to decide what you need to do given your responsibilities as a coach, your ethics, and your capacity to be of value in that system. If you decide to go ahead and take the plunge, then empathically describe your experience of being with the client, and gently explore the possibility that *others* may also have this experience. This can be very helpful to the client and the relationship. Or it can go very wrong if you do this badly or perhaps when the client has narcissistic or sociopathic tendencies.

I guess it would be good to end this section with something on burnout and how bad we coaches can be at *self*-care. Burnout comes from working too hard in a context where *meaning* becomes eroded. We sell *self*-care and *meaning* to *others* but we don't always do it for our *self*. Enough said.

Questions to ask your *self*

- What is meaningful about coaching for you? How does this *meaning* connect to your wounding?
- How do you feel about your clients' contexts?
- Have you ever been afraid of a client and if so why?

Notes

1 Blomme, R. (2014). The absurd organization: The insights of Albert Camus translated into management practices. In Blomme, van Hoof, B. (Ed.), *Another state of mind: Perspectives from wisdom traditions on management and business* (pp. 161–174). Palgrave Macmillan; Camus, A. (2018). *The myth of sisyphus* (2nd Intern). Vintage Books.
2 Frankl, V. E. (1946). *Man's search for meaning* (1st ed.). Language (1st ed.). Random House.
3 Vos, J. (2020). *The economics of meaning in life: From capitalist life syndrome to meaning-oriented economy*. University Professors Press.
4 Vos, J. (2020). *The economics of meaning in life*.
5 Vos, J. (2020). *The economics of meaning in life*.
6 Vos, J. (2020). *The economics of meaning in life*.
7 Sartre, J. P. (1943). *Being and nothingness: An essay on phenomenological ontology* (2003rd edn.). Routledge.
8 Thank you Dr Simon Kettleborough for sharing the learnings from your doctoral research on shopping addiction. I have used these to build this case study.
9 Kemp, R. (2018) *Transcending addiction: An existential pathway to recovery*. Routledge.
10 Thompson, N., & Walsh, M. (2010). The existential basis of trauma. *Journal of Social Work Practice*, 24(4), 377–389.
11 Hubl, T., & Jordan Avritt, J. (2020). *Healing collective trauma: A process for integrating our intergenerational and cultural wounds*. Sounds True.

Bibliography

Blomme, R. (2014). The absurd organization: The insights of albert Camus translated into management practices. In Blomme, R. & van Hoof, B. (Ed.). *Another state of mind: Perspectives from wisdom traditions on management and business* (pp. 161–174). Palgrave Macmillan.

Camus, A. (2000). *The myth of Sisyphus*. (J. O'Brien, Trans.). Penguin Classics.

Frankl, V. E. (1946). *Man's search for meaning* (1st ed.). Language. Random House.

Hubl, T., & Jordan Avritt, J. (2020). *Healing collective trauma: A process for integrating our intergenerational and cultural wounds*. Sounds True.

Kemp, R. (2018). *Transcending addiction: An existential pathway to recovery*. Routledge.

Sartre, J. P. (1943). *Being and nothingness: An essay on phenomenological ontology* (2003 ed.). Routledge.

Thompson, N., & Walsh, M. (2010). The existential basis of trauma. *Journal of Social Work Practice*, 24(4), 377–389.

Vos, J. (2020) *The economics of meaning in life: From capitalist life syndrome to meaning-oriented economy*. University Professors Press.

Chapter 9

Experiencing stuckness

By this stage, our wounding has found a salient context in which to be healed. We are re-living the wounding. The situation creates the loss of our broader *self*, *others*, and *meaning* as we cling to an older *self*, and the milieu of the wound. When we lose aspects of our *self*, *others*, and *meaning*, we lose our adaptive capacity and direction. This is because our *self* and our actions relate to the context of the wound and not the current situation. To continue this way of being, we develop defensive behaviours that take us nowhere. We are stuck.

Stuckness is loss and grief

As mentioned earlier, stuckness is about loss and the grieving of that loss. Grieving provides a release that in turn softens us and readies us to engage with the world. The process of grieving allows us to start relearning our *self*, *others*, and our life.[1] It initiates the rebuilding of *self*, relationships with *others*, and *meaning*. When we can't grieve our losses, we remain fixed, separate from *others*, and feeling lost.

People generally only start feeling stuck as soon as they start feeling the pain of the losses. However, by this time, our losses have already happened. So when the pain and grief of stuckness comes, know we have been on this journey for some time already. Furthermore, that we still have a way to go. Settle in, this is where it gets interesting.

Let's have a deeper look at the experience of stuckness.

The experience of stuckness

There are common feelings that we all may experience when stuck. Some of the these include feeling numb, frustrated, lonely, *self*-critical, disconnected, disorientated, unfocussed, useless, helpless, angry, fearful, spinning out of control, or fragmenting.[2] It can also make us feel split in half, with one half of us taking a position against the other, much like soccer fans shouting and throwing bottles at their opposition supporters in a pub. In polite conversation, this

DOI: 10.4324/9781003536253-9

could be called being stuck in a dilemma.[3] We can also experience existential anxiety or guilt at not living our life fully enough.

There are some specific experiences of stuckness that deserve more focus in this chapter, these include the experience of oscillating inner worlds, *self*-criticism, and shame. We can become isolated and scapegoated, or experience the void and lose one's soul. This can make us respond by running and trying harder. Lastly, stuckness impacts on our bodies.

When we are stuck, we can go from feeling numb to feeling angry to feeling sad to feeling numb, all in one split second. We can flip between blaming *others* and blaming our *self* for the situation. We can experience contradictory emotions all at the same time.

I suspect that the biological intention behind this oscillation is to 'let off steam' without being engulfed by the pain of stuckness. It allows us go in and out so we can process our experience, view it from multiple perspectives, test out theories, and experiment with how we want to proceed.[4] We need time to allow these inner narratives to boil and then finally settle, however, this process can be exceptionally disorientating, especially if we are used to an affirming, certain, and placid inner world.

Self-criticism and shame are an integral part of the experience of stuckness.[5] They play a significant role in ensuring we stay stuck. *Self*-criticism can lead to guilt or shame in the context of stuckness. Guilt is a better option than shame because it refers to something that we have done, and not ourselves as a whole. And that's the problem with shame: it denigrates our whole *self* and can thus be deathly in experience. We can lose our *self* in shame, just as we can lose our *self* in death.

Shame is so intense a feeling that it manifests physically in our posture, for example, we might slump or try to make our bodies smaller as if we wanted to disappear. It also startles our limbic system, the emotional centre of our brain, we feel frozen, and our hearing sounds like we are under water.[6]

Shame is a terrible feeling, one that we all seek to avoid. Some of the strategies we might use to avoid shame are to attack *others*, attack our *self*, withdraw from *others*, or deny that there is a problem.[7] These are all defences against feeling the pain of shame, but they often make life worse, or at least lengthen the experience of shame. This is how shame keeps stuckness in place.

When we feel ashamed of our *self* we may isolate, and this further entrenches our stuck position. Isolation and loneliness reinforce the idea that we are defective, unworthy, and unlovable. In this state we are more likely to receive the projections of *others'* fears and unwanted *self*. This means that we can become a likely target for scapegoating and gossip. We, the stuck person can feel this, even when said behind our backs. We begin to wonder if the scapegoaters and gossips speak the truth after all, that we are in fact defective, unworthy, and unlovable.

As a stuck person, we can feel like we have lost our soul and are falling into the void. This experience, together with that of shame, can give us a zombie-like experience and appearance, because we are living life outside of our *self*. Our soul and *self* is somewhere else and we know it, but we don't know how to get them back inside our *self*. We are living in an existential void.

For many people, running faster and harder seems to be the automatic response to stuckness. Sadly, this is likely to be more of the same, but done faster. This strategy is also more exhausting than walking or lying down. It is not the antidote to meaninglessness nor a solution for finding *self* or *others*. However, it is the false 'solution' many of us go for because it makes us feel that we are in fact doing something. The real 'solution' is to stop running and trying so hard. It is to lie down and rest so that we can gather our energy for getting out of stuckness.

Stuckness is a physical experience, we can feel it in our body. Sometimes we get fatter or thinner from stuckness, our sleep gets messed up, and it can even affect our toilet habits. When we get stuck we can easily disconnect from our body so that we miss its information and needs.

Stuck people tend to be tired or over wired. We are tired because we are in a state of grief, and we may even be experiencing insomnia. We can also be over wired; wired up by stimulants, anger, unmitigated drive, or misplaced euphoria to keep going. When we are tired or over wired, our head can get locked into downward spiralling narratives. As Nietzsche said, when we are tired, we are attacked by ideas we conquered long ago.[8]

What does a stuck person look like?

When we or *others* are stuck, we can look isolated, angry, flat, opinionated, critical, argumentative, grumpy, tired, and irritable, all at once. It is confusing, and there are other signs that we can look for.

I love looking for linguistic clues. The linguistic translation of stuckness is the term *yes but*. Listen for this both in words and concepts. Some stuck people use a lot of platitudes and can divide people and situations into only good or only bad. Listen also for metanarratives that circle unresolved.

We can also see stuckness in environments, clothing, and even food. Stuck people can wear clothes that speak to an earlier time (not in a trendy way). Their homes can be filled with objects and pictures that celebrate the past but speak nothing to the as in present and future. Sometimes, food preferences can become limited and repetitive. None of these signals on their own are indicative of stuckness, but a nest of these clues is probably pointing towards something.

Right at the beginning of this book, I spoke about stuckness being a black hole, sucking in everything around it. By this I mean the stuck person or couple might invite us in to their world in some way, maybe to reinforce their views. They may blame us, get us to validate how victimised they are, or use us as witnesses or alliances in relational machinations.

As coaches, we can have an uneasy feeling about stuck people, knowing intuitively how we may become used in their troubled inner worlds. When we feel this, we need to step out of the gravitational pull of their stuckness black hole. We as coaches and even as friends cannot help stuck *others* if we slip down this slippery slope. Someone needs to stay on the bank and think clearly.[9] I show how this can be done in the case study on successful Shane and suitcase Sarah.

Successful Shane and suitcase Sara

Sarah and Shane had been together since their 20s, and were now in their early 30s. They had moved in together fairly early in their relationship intending to get married and have a family, but when there was time for and interest in marriage, there was no money, and when there was money, there was no time or interest.

Shane had a very busy career in an asset management company; he was on the partner track, and was putting in the steps up the ladder. He was proud of his daily step count, mentally noting how each step was one in the right direction, and that he would soon be encased in the celestial light that hovered over partner's heads.

Sara was unemployed and looking for a job; she had moved to Johannesburg with Shane but had found it difficult to find her feet.

Sara was a suitcase that Shane carried around, not one from a James Bond movie that could be used to shield oneself during a gun battle, but an old-fashioned, brown one with straps that buckle up at the top. Generally, the buckles were done up, but sometimes they flapped open threatening to release the suitcase's contents. When this happened, Shane would leave Sara the suitcase at home: it was not becoming when the dirty linen spilled out in public, not something with which Shane wanted to be associated. And yet, just like your own old brown suitcase in the attic, Shane could not throw her away because she held all his memories and secrets.

Now I know you are thinking how cruel I am calling Sara a suitcase. I know, it's a horrible metaphor but it's very useful here because it gives a sense of how Shane thought about her, and how Sara thought about herself.

Although they came to see me together, they came for different reasons: Shane because he wanted Sara to clean up her act and do something with her life, and Sara because she wanted Shane to stop being so mean to her. Shane needed a wife that he could take to work events, and Sara wanted a partner who could share her feelings, believe in her, and help her take steps into her life. I am not going to bother you with their backstory, or what secrets they shared. Instead I want to talk about how stuck couples can create a black hole that, if you are not careful, will suck you in. When coaches are in the black hole with the clients, they cannot help them.

In sessions, both Shane and Sara were lining up narratives and causation lines that supported their experience of victimhood in the relationship. One way my job could have gone was to try to integrate these narratives into some sort of shared history and experience, with which they could work. However, neither wanted to create a shared narrative, nor find an easier way to live with their differences, nor even break up. Conversations were downward cycles cementing pain and victimhood.

I alternated between investigating dynamics and details and standing on the bank noticing the process. Each time I extended a hand to lift one of the couple on to the bank, they would try to pull me in. They did this through comments such as, 'You see I am right', 'She agrees with me', 'It's your fault'. When I didn't get into the hole, they would sometimes rather unexpectedly band together and turn against me; complaining about my skills or presence, or even the care of my plants. My sense was that they were not looking for a solution, but rather a witness or an extra to appear in their drama. Or maybe I just did not have the skills necessary for this complex situation.

After three sessions, I realised that I was in fact getting stuck in their drama, even as I tried not to be. With this in mind, I went to see my wonderful supervisor. He validated my desire to stay on the bank, and wondered why it was so hard for me to stay there. Of course, it's always tricky when you are in between two people, but this situation felt more activating to me than the average 'in-between-two-people' scenario. My supervisor helped me think and feel through previous experiences of being in between two people, particularly in my family of origin. I recalled experiences where I had been hurt by being in between two feuding people, and the fear I still had in these situations.

Bracketing my own response out of the situation helped me decide that the next move for this couple was for them to explore themselves and what they wanted individually. I suggested separate therapy for both, so that they could find themselves more fully before they started finding their relationship. It felt like the drama of their relationship had taken up so much space in their lives that they had not developed themselves in other areas like friendships, hobbies, and other interests. We set a date to reconnect in six months' time.

Six months later they returned. Only Sara had completed the full six months in therapy although Shane had been to a few sessions which he considered sufficient for exploring his contribution to the situation. They had, however, created a lot of space for pursuing their own interests and friendships and this was working well for them. Sara had found a job in an advertising agency, made some new friends, and things were generally looking up for her. Shane had had a lot of time out with his friends, and was getter bored with their lack of ambition. He wanted to settle into a quieter life with Sara. Greater separateness had worked for them and now they were ready to think about their relationship.

The burdens and benefits of stuckness

Stuckness is exquisitely designed to be a temporary experience of pain whilst we change gear and bring in a new version of our *self*. It does, however, become a problem when we don't know how to get out of our stuckness, and what should be a temporary experience becomes a lifelong identity. This is probably the biggest danger of stuckness, and one that I am hoping to help people avoid through this book.

When we stay stuck for long periods of time, our *self*-esteem can take a knock, and it can take a while to rebuild this, especially if we are not intentional about doing so. We can also experience existential guilt, anxiety, and depression.

When we get stuck, we have an opportunity to complete incomplete wounds. We can do this through repetitive behaviours, possibly repeating traumas, or behaving as if we are living in the time of the wounding. We do this until we are ready and able to engage in the present as it is now.

Stuckness is a time when our inner and outer worlds cohabit at odds with each other. This is until our nascent inner world becomes strong enough to start interacting more fully with the outer world. When this shift occurs, it is a reboot that can allow us to update our relationship with the world, to change unproductive habits, or to enter new relationships. Most people live in this state of ambivalence in the short term, while a few get stuck here, permanently between worlds.

Stuckness can be a survival mechanism, a way to survive an untenable and inescapable situation. Sometimes people resort to living in a stuck, zombie-like state to survive a world that is unpleasant or destroying them. This could even be as simple and innocent as commuters shutting down into a rote pattern of sleep, commute, work, commute, TV, and drink, sleep (repeat). We can sometimes see this in commuters in big cities, soldiers at war, and people working in jobs they hate. Stuckness is the coping mechanism for keeping going when we must.

There is significant research showing that a substantial majority of addicts come from a background of trauma.[10] In these cases, the addiction can initially offer symptomatic release, a distraction from pain. However, sooner or later, the addiction starts to dominate our whole system, and stuckness takes over.

One of the more beautiful impacts of stuckness is that it can allow us to build empathy for *others* and loosen our hard-heartedness. This service is crucial to our future as humans sharing a planet.

There are many very good reasons to get stuck: survival, adaptation, facing up to past trauma, building empathy, and learning how to live better. One of the biggest benefits stuckness grants us is the ability to adapt and grow beyond our own painful life experiences.

The turnaround is announced by grief

One can see grief as marking the end of the old or the beginning of the new. In the case of stuckness, it is the clarion call of change, announcing the emergence of a new state of fluidity. The experience of stuckness is either one of emptiness or rigidity, or both. Grief is a melting of that emptiness and rigidity. As such, grief is not an experience of stuckness but rather the early warning of fluidity creeping in.

I have included comments on grief in the chapters on gaining *self, others,* and *meaning.* We need to grieve each of these losses fully in order to leave the past behind, and start a new way of being.

How does it feel to get stuck as a coach?

All coaches get stuck from time to time, and so a stuck coach looks like us. We may not notice that we are stuck, and keep on going. We may notice that sessions are not as satisfying as before, or that we have lost confidence in our coaching skills. We may also fantasise about other professions, ones where we actually make something.

One of the ways in which coaches can get stuck is to cling too tightly to a methodology, instead of flowing with the client. When this happens we can find our *self* defending our methodology against the client. While this may be temporarily amusing/horrifying to us, it is not helpful to the client.

It is important for us to not panic when we get stuck as coaches. We need to remember that stuckness is a normal part of our growth as coaches.

Questions to ask your *self*

- When have you got stuck in coaching, how did it feel, and what did it look like? How did you get going again, and what was the value you got from being stuck?
- Are you going to supervision for our coaching, if not, why not?
- How good are you at grieving, do you grieve too little or too much? What does your grief look like?

Notes

1 Attig, T. (1996). *How we grieve: Relearning the world.* Oxford University Press.
2 Petriglieri, G. (2007). Stuck in a moment: A developmental perspective on impasses. *Transactional Analysis Journal, 37*(3), 185–194.
   Bella, K. (2011). *The tao of stuckness–A heuristic art base.* Institute of Integral Studies.
   Kukard, J. (2021). *Bewitched, amputated or dead: An existential study of leadership stuckness.* DProf thesis Middlesex University/New School of Psychotherapy and Counselling (NSPC) Psychology.
3 Van Deurzen, E., Craig, E., Laengle, K., Schneider, K., Tantam, D., & Du Plock, S. (2019). *The Wiley world handbook of existential therapy.* Hoboken and Chichester; Kukard, J. (2021). *Bewitched, amputated or dead.*
4 Van Deurzen, E., Craig, E., Laengle, K., Schneider, K., Tantam, D., & Du Plock, S. (2019). *The Wiley world handbook of existential therapy.* Hoboken and Chichester; Kukard, J. (2021). *Bewitched, amputated or dead.*
5 Bella, K. (2011). *The tao of stuckness–A heuristic art base.* Institute of Integral Studies; Kukard, J. (2021). *Bewitched, amputated or dead.*

6 Spiegel, E. (2022). *Where is shame held in the body?* Attune Philadelphia Therapy Group. https://www.therapistsinphiladelphia.com/blog/where-is-shame-held-in-the-body/# (Accessed: 2 June 2024).
7 Poulson, C. (1999). *Shame. The master emotion?* 61(December).
8 Kaufman, W. (1974). *Nietzsche: Philosopher, psychologist, antichrist* (REV-Revised). Princeton University Press.
9 Thank you, Simon Cassar, for this excellent piece of wisdom given during a supervision session.
10 Mate, D. G. (2018). *In the realm of hungry ghosts*. Vermilion.

Bibliography

Attig, T. (1996). *How we grieve: Relearning the world*. Oxford University Press.

Bella, K. (2011). *The tao of stuckness—A heuristic art base*. Institute of Integral Studies.

Kaufman, W. (1974). *Nietzsche: Philosopher, psychologist, antichrist* (Revised ed). Princeton University Press.

Kukard, J. (2021). *Bewitched, amputated or dead: An existential study of leadership stuckness*. DProf thesis Middlesex University/New School of Psychotherapy and Counselling (NSPC) Psychology.

Mate, D. G. (2018). *In the realm of hungry ghosts*. Vermilion.

Petriglieri, G. (2007). Stuck in a moment: A developmental perspective on impasses. *Transactional Analysis Journal, 37*(3), 185–194.

Poulson, C. (1999). Shame. The master emotion? 61(December).

Spiegel, E. (2022). *Where is shame held in the body?* Attune Philadelphia Therapy Group. https://www.therapistsinphiladelphia.com/blog/where-is-shame-held-in-the-body/# (Accessed: 2 June 2024)

Van Deurzen, E., Craig, E., Laengle, K., Schneider, K., Tantam, D., & Du Plock, S. (2019). *The Wiley world handbook of existential therapy*. Hoboken and Chichester.

Chapter 10

Growing *self*

This is the first chapter which describes activities on the left side of the cycle. Growing *self*, *others*, and *meaning* are all interrelated activities, and growing one will result in the enlargement of the other two. This process is iterative and complex. It's important to remember that the cycle exists as a map or prompt for our development, it is not the territory.

In the past, I thought that one had to first find *one's self* fully, and then find *others*. I was wrong, we find our *self* as we find *others*, we get to know our *self* as we get to know *others*, and we build our *self* as we build our relationship with *others*.[1] It's ok for gurus to sit on the mountain alone searching for themself but for the majority of us, we need *others* to enable our journey.

However, to get going with *others* we must have something to get going with and so, the first step is identifying, consolidating, and amplifying what we know already about our *self*. Before we look at how we can do this, it would be useful to understand the importance of knowing our *self* including how we can know this.

Self: the ground of our life

To live life and to live it well, we need to have a good sense of our *self*, as well as a good enough relationship with our *self*.

Our *self* integrates our inner world into a coherent person, and gives us a stronger sense of certainty and knowing from which to launch our lives. Furthermore, when we are directed by our *self* and not externalities, we have a greater opportunity to manifest our unique value to the world. If we don't have access to our *self*, then we lose this critical north star, and become subject to the vagaries of the world. As a result, we land up in places where we don't add value, may even be destructive to *others*, or that make us unhappy.

We need a *self* to grow, heal, learn, and adapt. If we don't have a *self*, we have little to draw on to heal from the pains of life, or find direction when we are lost. Our *self* is the rootstock of our life, rebirthing us over and over again.

DOI: 10.4324/9781003536253-10

Lastly, our *self* is also the source of our humanity, reminding us of our frailty, our strength, and our need for connection and *meaning*. If we don't have our *self*, we don't have our connection to humanity.

Our best hope with regards to living life well is to understand our *self* as best we can, even in our paradoxes and contradictions. This is not easy to do as *selfs* are notoriously mischievous, oblique, and take a long time to get to know. Understanding our *self*, however, is not enough, we need to have a positive and enabling relationship to our *self* as well.

By an enabling relationship to one's *self*, I mean a relationship that is encouraging, safe, and grows our *self*, you know, like a good companion would. This is not a relationship where we punish or shame our *self*.

Shame is a theme that comes up again and again all over this book. It creates long-term stuckness and depletes our courage for life. Shaming our *self* is not helpful to the world or to our *self*. It shrinks us, and our contribution to the world. No *self* is worthy of being discarded and abandoned, but we all do it from time to time.

In the earlier chapter on *self*, I described how we can lose our *self* through the processes of becoming bewitched, amputated, or dead. Do you remember the examples of Ashwin, the human spreadsheet, Celia, the coconut cheese girl, and Angelique, the 90-year-old coquette? We don't know we are losing our *self* because our *self*, and therefore our capacity to *self*-reflect, is not present or weak.

How does one know one's *self*?

The odd thing about learning about one's *self* is that the thing we are studying, is also the thing doing the studying. If we are not aware of how and what we are looking at when we look at our *self*, we might miss crucial pieces of data. This could result in situations where the blind is leading the blind. This is how we create stories about our *self* that may not be true.

So, figuring out how we can know ourself is a thorny question, and with all thorny questions it is useful to ask it in many ways. So here we are; how do I know what I know about myself? What data do I use or ignore or distort when constructing my version of myself? What happens when my inner data collector collects data that reinforces my worldview? Academics might call this understanding an epistemology of one's *self*.

So, the data part is relatively simple; we use thoughts, feelings, insights, bodily sensations, and experiences with the world, as well as other people's feedback. However, not all this data gets through into our version of our *self*, some is blocked by defences or other ideas about who we are (accommodation and assimilation). For example, if I believe I am a nice person, I might forget the time that I was mean to someone and continue to believe I am only good. In this way we defend our versions of our *self* even when it does not serve us, and sometimes even to the death.

We defend our versions of our *self* for various reasons, ranging from attempting to be good enough, bad enough, successful enough, etc. These injunctions or needs to be good, bad, or whatever, often come from our child-hoods and messages from the big people. We can change these later in life, with some introspection and healing, perhaps even by using this stuckness methodology.

A further reason why we defend our versions of our *self* is that of certainty. Humans like to have certainty about who they are and can struggle with having a mixed *self* that is both good and bad. At later levels of maturity, people can start to accept that they are both good and bad, successful and unsuccessful, and don't have to resolve or defend against these so-called contradictions.

We manage to do this when our *self* has become large enough to accommodate all aspects of us. We do this when we get used to the idea that we are emergent in identity and our inner worlds do change. We can do this because we are not trapped forever in an identity created by some past behaviour or feeling that we experienced. Indeed, we can and should be more than our past and current *self*.

Generally speaking, our capacity to receive and use data is fairly limited, especially at earlier levels of maturity, when we have a more fixated version of our *self* or our recipe for life. This is why we must be extra vigilant when using feedback from our *self* and *others*, and make sure we pay attention to discon-firming data. When we do this, we have the chance to build a more realistic idea of who we are, and how we are experienced. This understanding enhances our ability to learn and grow and adapt. This is useful to bear in mind as we explore ways in which we can find our *self*.

Lastly, it is useful to notice that sometimes it is adaptive to defend our *self*, and stick with what we know of our *self*. Perhaps this is because we are living in a crisis and we need to prioritise where our energy goes. Ultimately, we all have to face our *self*, either here or in the afterlife.

The journey of growing more of our *self*

The rest of this chapter is about how we find more of our *self* and these ways are many and varied. Take what you have use for and leave the rest. But notice what you decide is relevant to you and feel into why this may be so. Even our choices of remedies are projections and reflections of who we think we are.

With each of these chapters on growing more *self, others,* and *meaning* I will always start with two sections, one on grieving and then one on completing the process of the wound. Each loss needs both processes.

How to grieve the loss of one's *self*?

We need to grieve properly; appreciating the goods and the bads of our previ-ous *self*, laugh at our frailty and humanity, and prepare for change. If we don't grieve well enough for our lost *self*, we may long for them and be tempted into bringing them back and going backwards up the stuckness cycle. If we grieve our past *self* too much, we risk re-entering them.

Our grief must unravel the 'what ifs', the 'if onlys', the 'whys and the wherefores', as best we can. We can throw shame and *self*-blame into our pot of grief, but this only serves to complicate the grieving process even more. This is because shame binds us to our previous *self* instead of allowing us to separate out from it and emerge as something new.

We need grief to help us soften and relearn our *self* and the world, melt the rigidity of our previous existence, and allow something new to emerge.

Completing wounds related to *self*

Stuckness is precipitated when a wounding pops up for completion. The three losses occur because we stay in the wounding and not in life, and our stuck behaviours are organised around this. As we grow our *self, others,* and *meaning*, we will automatically work with our wounding as well.

It would, however, be useful to work directly with the wounding itself. This includes identifying it, tracking its influence in our lives, grieving its impact, and limiting the shame related to it. Finally, we must create an enabling narrative that allows us to log it in our being. When we do this, it's as if we have closed a file on something, at least temporarily. In the language of Winnicott, we have created a good enough repair to a previous rupture.[2]

We can do this through talking therapies, somatic work, cognitive work, and spiritual work; the best approach integrates all four. Therapy, coaching, trauma-informed talking therapies, mindfulness, artistic expression, prayer, ritual, and body work are also very useful here.

Building a container for our *self*

When we are seeking to regain our *self* more fully, the most productive way to do this is to focus on creating a context for connecting and staying in touch with our *self*. This is a much more sustainable way of being with our *self* than selecting specific targets such as *self*-knowledge and *self*-love.

The rest of this chapter describes how to do this through the following tips:

- Maintaining a stable inner world that is also emergent.
- Being a good companion to our *self*.
- Taking responsibility for our *self*.
- Live with and through shame.
- Igniting our life force.
- Building our capacity for discomfort and pain.
- Laugh and play.

I know this is starting to read like a shopping list but never fear, it is impossible to do it all well. My suggestion would be to choose one or two of these areas of growth, read up on those, and experiment with the ideas therein. If it does not work for you, or it works very well, then move on to the next one or two. Take it easy, you have a whole lifetime to do this work.

Maintaining a stable inner world that is also emergent

We have spent a lot of time in this book on the importance of knowing our *self*, and remaining emergent. This is an important paradox to manage rather than resolve into one polarity, we need both. Most of this book covers the process of staying emergent, so I am going to cover the other half of this polarity more deeply here, maintaining a stable inner world.

The world is pretty chaotic at the moment and we can't control it, so our best response to this is building our inner stability. This is not an arbitrary best response, it's our only choice. This way we can interact with the storm thought-fully and carefully.

When we have stable inner world, we are less volatile, less reactive, more thoughtful, kinder, and, quite frankly, less exhausted. It is exhausting to always be emotionally volatile, reactive, and hypervigilant. A stable inner world enables growth because we are not just knee-jerking in response to the world and we can make better choices.

There are many things we can do to build our inner stability. We can build our awareness of our inner world and work through triggers more fully so they are not so triggering. We can build our capacity for holding pain and not acting on it by *self*-regulating and *self*-soothing. We can also structure our environment to lower our stress. Critically, we can create safe inner worlds that enable rather than disable us (see below). Working with these factors can help us to build a stable container for our *self*, one that enables our fluidity.

Being a good companion to our self

The objective of being a good companion to our *self* is to keep our *self* feeling relatively positive, able, and confident in the world. When we are in these states we learn and grow better and are less likely to get stuck for long periods of time. We are also more *self*-reflective, and this results in greater learning. If we do not accompany our *self* like this, we run the risk of creating unstable, critical, negative inner worlds that diminish our capacity to grow and learn.

I can just hear you saying, 'what happens when it is authentic for me to be in this state because I am an idiot and my life is shit'. What happens then? Well, the answer is the same and amplified. We have a responsibility to get our *self* into a state that is enabling, especially when we are feeling disabled. While we may have some aspects of our lives where we do not feel good enough, it is unlikely that this experience will stretch across our whole life. We are always doing well at something, even if it is just the washing up. This is not denying our failures or inadequacies, it's about balancing our view of our *self* and taking responsibility for getting our *self* into a state where we can engage with life.

Good companions notice the good in the people they are accompanying. They also notice where things are not so good, but the emphasis here is on noticing where we are good. If we want to discourage and disable our *self*, then we should only notice the bad. If this reminds you of you, then be sure to pay attention when you read the section on *self*-criticism and shame. And remember that if we don't talk to our *self* nicely, *others* might not either because our relationship with our *self* is mirrored in our relationships with *others*.

Being a good companion is also about understanding and seeing the context in which we grew up and now operate. Sometimes we forget that the context has a major impact on where we find our *self* now. So, instead of blaming our *self* for our apparent lack of achievements or dysfunctions, be kind. Create explanations that encourage rather than discourage our *self*. And then paradoxically, as we will find in the next chapter, we should not take our *self* too seriously. I know this is a tricky balance to create but that's life.

Below is the story of Ashwin who learned how to become a good companion to himself.

Ashwin becomes a good companion to himself

I think you may remember Ashwin in London who was bewitched by success. He was a good companion to success but not to himself. He had lived out his mother's dreams but not his own. This section describes just some of the ways in which Ashwin created a supportive container for his self by learning how to be a good companion to his self. Ashwin did much more than just these processes, but you will have to look at the other chapters on finding others and meaning to understand what this involves.

The first thing Ashwin did was seek help, or rather he followed the advice of the HR director who sent him to me. It may have been his ambitions around the CEO position that drove him to my door, but either way he came. And then he kept coming every two weeks for over a year. We covered many topics but Ashwin's relationship to his self was the core theme; how he might get to know, support, and grow his self.

It took Ashwin a while to get to know who he was, collect his history of his life (until now he had relied on his mother's version) and decide how he wanted to go forward on his own journey. He struggled to find his feelings in the beginning and had to dig quite deep to locate and actually feel them. To demonstrate the value of feelings to his work (his primary area of interest initially), we created the Ashwin's Business Case for Deliberately Engaging with feelings (ABCDEF).[3] Once he understood how feelings could help him at work, he felt more justified in his pursuit of them.

As Ashwin started to feel more of his feelings, more of his older and unfelt feelings started to pop up. We were able to venture into other more sensitive feelings like his relationship with his mother and how she had shamed him as a young child when he had failed or not achieved enough success. This work was exhausting for Ashwin who had low levels of stamina for feeling feelings. Furthermore, many of the feelings were negative and it became disheartening for Ashwin.

We needed to find ways in which he could have pleasure and fun in the world as this would give him courage and motivation to keep going. He said that he liked cooking and drinking, but aside from that he had no hobbies. So, he enrolled on a social cooking course for singles which seemed like fun, but perhaps the real clincher was that he met Sully who really made him laugh. They got on like a house on fire and when the course ended, the cooking continued at Sully's. This was fun for Ashwin who later went on to meet Sully's friends and have more fun.

Being a good companion for one's self also involves looking after your body, clothes, and environment. Our initial discussions were just about sleeping patterns and then a brief check on drinking habits. He was not up for changing these, so we left drinking where it was, at least initially. Ashwin agreed to start walking along the river in the evenings with the long-term view of one day jogging there.

I asked if Ashwin ever invited Sully around to his apartment and Ashwin said no, his apartment was not so cool, having been designed by his mother. We explored how he could make his environment more fun, cooler, and show more of his emerging personality, and so he ordered some pictures and some cushions for his lounge. Bravely, Ashwin threw away his plastic TV table, the ageing coffee table books, and the second-hand cushions from his mother. He also started thinking about expanding the kitchen so it could accommodate two cooks at once.

The change in his home environment had a surprising impact on Ashwin's wardrobe; the lounge had become cosy, and his wardrobe of suits and 1980s tracksuit pants felt inappropriate. He went online and bought himself some trendy lounging pants, and then a purple shirt, just for the days when he felt more exuberant and needed something other than his daily diet of white branded shirts.

Exploring his history, feeling his feelings more, having fun with Sully, moving his body more, exploring new identities through his clothes and redecorated apartment, all added up to making Ashwin more excited about life. These moves were initially difficult for Ashwin but over time became self-reinforcing and amplified, preparing him for even greater changes in his life. Although these changes were remarkable, they were not full changes out of stuckness, however, they are useful here to demonstrate how being a good companion to one's self can get one going with a new relationship to self, a new identity, and a new life.

And, as Ashwin's relationship with his self changed, so did his relationships with others, as did his leadership style. His leadership scores in the next culture survey went up, and the last I heard he was back in the race for CEO, this time with 'people skills'.

Taking responsibility for our self

Taking responsibility for our lives is critical for supporting our fluidity. While this can be an unpleasant and difficult course, when we don't take responsibility, we will be forced to wait until the world decides to 'save' us. It will be the world that decides our fate whether we like it or not. We can cite oppression and abuse as much as we like, but until we do something about it for our *self*, we are just enabling the oppressive relationship while moaning from the sidelines. I know this is a hard pill to swallow and quite simplistic for some contexts, but chains are always held at both sides, and perhaps it is time we dropped our side.

Taking responsibility for our lives can take a lifetime. We often do it in small steps moving from initially blaming *others* to seeing and finally changing our role in situations and relationships. It is often easier to blame *others* and victimise our *self*, because it can be painful to see our own culpability.

We need a strong *self* to witness our imperfections up front and be compassionate with them, especially when we have shame and anxiety about being lovable or good enough. We need to find a way to work with our negative past behaviour that is not shaming but rather compassionate and understanding. When we can't do this for our *self*, it makes it even harder to take responsibility for who we are and our life. This is a moment of radical responsibility when we take our *self* compassionately by the hand and choose the attitude we have towards our lives.

This brings us to a further idea and that is taking responsibility for how we make sense of the world. This is an important skill because how we read the world impacts on how we read our *self* and our life. Let me explain: Our inner world and how we make sense of things is determined by who we are and have been (our personality, demographics, experience, place in the world, etc.). Our reflective and *meaning*-making machinery is not a neutral and objective computer but rather is constructed from a whole lot of qualitative and idiosyncratic data and programming (personality, demographics, etc.) As such, it has quirks of interpretation that sometimes have more to do with our inner worlds than our outer worlds. We tend to see the world as we are in it, not as it is.

When we know our habits of making *meaning*, we can interrupt them and seek a deeper and possibly more productive understanding of the world. We can try to know the world as it is rather than as we are in it. For example, if we see our *self* as being constantly victimised by the world, we could become suspicious that this may be a habit of *meaning* making. We could then look for disconfirming data and see where that takes us. Transformation always begins with a transformation of how we see the world and the *meaning* we make of it. When we see the world differently, we behave differently and the world responds in a new way. And there we go; fluidity starts to seep in and our life changes.

When we realise that our inner narratives are just stories weaving points of fact and fiction together in a particular way, we begin to have options. If we are making it up anyway, then why don't we make up an empowering rather than a disabling story.

Live with and through shame

We can experience toxic shame when we have been abused, violated, or in some way made to feel less than. It can, like normal shame, encourage us to be better, but it often comes with negative side effects. These include being defensive, angry, shaming *others*, criminal activity, suicidal thoughts and actions, *self*-harm, addictions, and much more.

In the case of toxic shame, we are often not to blame, even though we may spend our lives feeling in some way deficient, broken, or unlovable as a result. In a World of Shoulds, we should not have to be responsible for fixing our shame. However, we don't live in a World of Shoulds and so it is our responsibility to do so. It is our responsibility to find out where our sense of shame comes from, and work to heal and live with it more amicably. It is not our responsibility to internalise it and live it out.

In my 20 plus years of coaching, I have still to meet a person who does not have some level of shame and *self*-criticism. Perhaps it was an intergenerational or parental gift, the mark of belonging to a minority group, an experience from school or maybe from later. We all use the voice of *self*-criticism as a defence against us doing something bad in the world. We *self*-criticise to stay safe against our *self*, and perhaps the more we fear our *self* and our possible badness or brokenness, the more we *self*-criticise. This is not all bad, because it can help us to avoid doing bad things. But when *self*-criticism comes to dominate one's inner world, it can make living horrendous and exhausting. In these cases we need to work with our shame so that we can create an inner world that is safe enough for us to live and grow in.

We have spoken at length about working with shame in this document. I also provided the idea that we can externalise it to our earlier contexts, thereby reducing *self*-blame.

Igniting our life force

Inside us is a life force that drives and directs our life. Stuck people have limited access to this drive because they are tired, dazed, or feel hopeless. They generally also have less access to their *self* as we have discovered in earlier chapters.

There are many ways to activate our life force, including activities that are pleasurable and intrinsically rewarding. By intrinsically rewarding, I mean that we get rewards while we are doing it, it's not just outcome orientated. This includes things like creative projects, good conversations, walking in nature, playing silly games with children, gardening, and good sex. The idea is to fill our *self* up a bit with pleasure so that we are reminded of how good it can be to live. Another idea would be to have a few skulls hanging around like the Stoic philosophers do, they remind us to live now because death lurks around the corner.

Part of reviving our sense of life is to experiment with new things, people, and situations. New roles, contexts, and people can create openings into the parts of our *self* that are dormant. They remind us that our *self* is not fixed but loves to grow and learn and adapt. Variety is indeed the spice of life.

Lastly, an easy and quick way to begin reviving our sense of life is to clear out or move things around in our context. See what happens when you move the furniture in your bedroom around, do you feel different now that you wake up facing the door versus the cupboard? Even the shifting of a chair can create a sense of newness or disorientation that can help build momentum for change.

Before we go on, I want to share the story of Paula and the sexy panties. It's a quick vignette based on one of my client's experiences with lingerie. It illustrates the point that sometimes an object can be a call to action by reminding us of a previously enjoyable, but currently amputated, way of being. You may think it a superficial story, one that is lacking in rich philosophy and not orientated to greater good, but believe you me, the sexy panties has power when used in the right way.

Paula and the sexy panties

The backstory is that Paula had birthed, weaned, and almost completed the schooling of three children. She had done this with George, who had been helpful most of the time. They had worked like a trojan couple on those children, the house, and on George, and his job. Money had flowed out to the house and the children, and they had tightened their belt on their own personal luxuries. In fact, they very rarely spent anything on themselves at all.

At the time I met her, Paula was in a peri-menopausal patch of getting fat, having heavy painful periods, sprouting hairs, and clouded by bad moods. She felt like a tired workhorse; disinterested in herself, George, sex, and even the children. She described her body as something extra and heavy to carry around. It was undisciplined; slinking over to the fridge, lurching off to chairs, slumping at tables and waiting for when it could slip into bed with Disney+ with a gin (Disney+ and gin were, to all intents and purposes, her primary loves at this stage in her life).

Over the years, Paula's underwear had moved from girlish panties to feeding bras to supermarket panties to corrective and restraining shape wear, to period panties, and then to shapeless granny bloomers whose bottoms bunched up under jeans like a nappy. Her undergarments never once veered into the realm of the sexy panties, and the string was never welcomed into the grey drawer holding her smalls which were in fact quite large. Furthermore, these grey misshapen things were not replaced regularly enough, because they were not shown to the outer world, or so Paula thought. In her mind, bush coverage was a practical affair aimed at keeping clothes fresh and gussets unsullied.

So, at the ripe age of 46, Paula ordered a pair of sexy panties by mistake online. She was multitasking at the time, clicked and bought the wrong pair. And then it was too late, the universe had intervened, and her life would be changed forever.

She was alone when they arrived, and still not dressed, having spent the morning cleaning the fridge and kitchen floor. After a shower and a brief look in the drawer of smalls (larges) she realised she was fresh out of undergarments and in a desperate attempt to make the lift club, she slipped the mistaken order on. They went on all satiny and smooth, gliding over her body like it was 18, and finally falling into place as if they had been made for her. It was quite surprising how she felt in them and so she walked over to the mirror to see what had happened to her bottom half. There before her was a sexy woman, the panties revealed the good bits and hid the parts she felt less attracted to. Oh, my word she was a goddess after all.

For the rest of the day, Paula slithered about in her sexy panties; they did not stick to her jeans, push her belly up into a muffin or waterfall into the ravine of her butt. She felt sexy and sassy, and it reminded her of a previous life when this feeling had been more regular. This same sensation led her to activities of a nocturnal nature, and then on to a shopping trip for more pantie products. You see, the sexy panties had woken up a part of Paula that had been asleep but once woken and acted upon, was intrinsically rewarding, and built up a momentum of its own that moved beyond the bedroom and into her life.

So, not all panties are born equal and not everyone's life force is so ready to burst into flames. But in this case, the panties were truly gorgeous and sexy, and reminded Paula of a previous way of being. The sexy panties had in some mysterious way added just enough excitement and life force to get the ball rolling towards a more fluid and enjoyable life. The powerful panties were the catalyst for change.

This is not a treatment I would prescribe to all, especially those of us who have shopping or sex wear addictions. But I am sure that you get the idea of how an object can remind us of parts of our *self* that we thought we had lost and through this remembering invite these discarded parts back. It is also a story of how so-called mistakes are often the openings for change, and that Freudian slips are often the best way to crack open the door into a new life.

Growing our self by building our capacity for discomfort and pain

Have you noticed that happiness is the new status symbol and human right? We live in a world where we see discomfort and pain as things that we should not have to endure, an indication of failure, abnormality, or being unfairly treated. It can be these things too, but the idea that we can get through life without having pain is sheer madness.

The Stoic philosopher, Marcus Aurelius, asks whether we have been made to lie under blankets and keep warm.[4] By this he means is it our due to always be comfortable and pain free in our lives, is this what life is really about? Should we not be pushing our *self*, stretching our *self* in some way to become more than who we are now. Maybe if we are not feeling some sort of discomfort, pain, or anxiety, then we are not stretching our *self* fully into life.

If we believe that a life well lived has no pain, and seek this out in our own life, we may become hypervigilant to every twinge of pain. Each twinge becomes a reminder that we have failed to achieve our goal of happiness and ease.[5] When we do this, we have organised our lives around pain avoidance rather than at grasping life itself.

There are many sources of pain and I have commented on this in the first chapter. I also mentioned that physical and emotional pain are the same neurologically.

A difficult source of pain for most people is uncertainty. We like to plan, know how things will roll, and many of us believe that we can create some measure of control over the world outside ourselves. The idea of control is enormously seductive, it offers us safety and security, and a future when everything is certain. But it is capricious, a malevolent Lorelei, and will dash us on the rocks if we become too dependent on it for direction.

The promise of certainty is malevolent because we cannot control other people, we cannot control nature, and we cannot control the world. There are some solutions, including focussing only on what we can control and this means our *self*. However, I know from personal experience that this is not always possible. A better option would be to try to create a safe inner world, one where we can hide and wait for things to clear.

Pain can be very useful to us, it brings information that we need to change. When we narcotise or dull pain at the slightest twinge, or toe over our comfort zone perimeter, we lose this vital source of motivation and direction. When we narcotise or hand on pain or even when we amplify it beyond its natural proportions, we lose the message embedded in the pain. What we need to do is learn how to read our pain, know its source and size, and it is only then, when we have this information, that we should start to soothe, dull, narcotise, or distract our *self*. This can be hard for us to do because who really likes to be uncomfortable or sit in pain, even for a short time.

We learn the skills of pain management in our childhoods or not, based on what the big people tell us. They tell us this implicitly and explicitly through what they say and do. The messages can include directives like suppress our pain, or externalise our pain on to someone else, or 'you have no capacity to handle pain', or even, 'you are a pain'. We build our capacity to hold our own pain around these directives.

We manage psychological pain by using defences; these help us tolerate the ebb and flow of our inner worlds. Defences are intended to reduce the level of pain so that we can function and/or step back to review the situation and process what is going on. This is useful because sometimes we cannot think or even act when we are in pain.

When we can't handle our own pain, we often hand it on. This is normal for kids and for adults too from time to time. Pain can be handed on in a useful or non-useful way. An example of a useful way is when we talk our pain through with our best friend and they are not injured by it, even though they may be a little tired or bored by our loquaciousness.

A less useful way of handing on pain is to hand on the wounding; for example, when we feel pain, we go out to a bar and beat up *others*. We can hurt *others* through physical means, through projections and stereotypes of people, through political systems, and through limiting access to resources. We can also do this through damaging nature and through entitlement.

There are many ways in which we can grow our capacity to notice and hold our own pain. The first step is accepting that you have pain and that you are going to try to feel it, at least a little. This does not mean that we must freeze in fear, we can and are already managing our pain, even if unconsciously. We can employ this skill when things start to get overwhelming; there are always distractions, narcotics, and other people around that we can use to distract our *self* from pain. Ultimately, we as humans must learn how to tolerate our own painful inner worlds without having to express them negatively in the world.

Humans are accretive, this means we learn best in small increments. Large increments of pain can be overwhelming and cause our pain tolerance to diminish, as well as our courage for experimentation. So, we need to expand our comfort zone for discomfort and pain slowly.[6]

Two ways to reduce our pain are *self*-soothing and working on our triggers. *Self*-soothing techniques can be very helpful in allowing us to hold our pain. We can do this through breathing techniques, movement, and body techniques, sweet talking one's *self*, doing one job slowly, remembering pleasant and calming things or getting into nature.

We can also work on our triggers using them as pointers to aspects of us that need healing and growth.[7] When we start to see what triggers us and can unpack and understand how certain things activate us, then we can start managing them instead of them managing us. We can start knowing that just because something triggers us, we don't have to respond to it. We can start living alongside and not within our triggers, and when we do this, we can start living in the world as it is, not as we are in it.

Pain is an elegant player in the Cycle of Stuckness, for without it we would not know that we were stuck and where. We must learn to understand our pain and discomfort as a wonderful and intelligent feedback system that keeps us alive, relevant, and useful, and not something that needs to be gotten rid of, but rather worked through.

Lastly, life is painful and if we can't stand pain, we can't look at life. If, for example, we avoid watching the news on TV because it causes us pain, then we risk living in an unrealistic world. If we avoid seeing other people's pain because we don't know how to handle it, we can lose them on a personal level and more broadly on a political level. We can live in a bubble and land up voting idiots into power.

Neville, the non-launcher

I was the third therapist or coach in Cape Town that Neville's parents had sent him to. His mother, who made the appointment, indicated on the phone that he had not found his pathway in life, and needed help in this regard.

Neville arrived, sloping hippy shoulders and a messy posture. He sat in my chair; it is big and soft and low because I am short and comfort seeking. I apologised and asked him to move to the couch, and he flopped over to the couch.

I asked him why he was here, and he slowly elaborated that he was not sure what direction he should follow in life; right, left, up, down, sideways, etc. etc. His father called him a non-launcher behind his back, but he was a mean man who did not have a kind word to say about anyone, even his mother said so. Neville had tried university, college, and various jobs but nothing seemed to stick. He was just not sure where or how the next step lay.

The backstory on Neville is that he came from a middle-class family in a good suburb in town, and his mom was a stay-at-home mom, helping his dad, him, and his sister do their best. Mom was very helpful, even doing some of his school projects, and letting him stay at home when he was tired. His dad was a bit tougher, believing that success and grit was built through effort and challenge. Dad had tried the grit approach to getting Neville going, but it was just too tough for Neville, and Mom had made him back off. Mom understood that moving was painful for Neville, she had always been on his side.

I asked Neville to take me through his day, just to get a feel for how he was living life. He said he got up at about 8 am, once his father had left the house, and went down for breakfast. Mom usually whipped up something nice for him for breakfast, and he chatted to her for a while before he got on with his email. After this, he said that he would spend some time researching jobs online and send his CV in when something looked interesting. The rest of the day was spent smoking joints at the bottom of the garden and gaming. Mom turned a blind eye to the joints, and Dad somehow did not notice either.

I think that you can see that Neville's mother has a habit of taking responsibility for his life. She had helped him to believe that life was meant to be only easy and pleasant, and that pain could be avoided. Furthermore, that pain or anxiety is unnecessary and bad, and worse than that, that he cannot handle it. As a result of this assumption, Neville organised his life around avoiding feeling pain and because of this did not develop any stamina for it. And of course this meant that he avoided pain even more. Neville's strategy for avoiding pain was by getting stoned, blaming others, and avoiding taking responsibility for his life.

Did I mention that getting stoned makes things pleasant for Neville, AKA numbs him to pain? Not only that but the quantities he smokes sucks out any momentum he may build in his life. Every time he thinks he will act; he smokes a bong and boom, the activities are back to the planning stage. Pain intolerance is compounded by narcotisation which lowers the threshold for pain and action and the vicious circle ultimately lands up with Neville still lying in bed while the world gets on with itself outside.

Neville is stuck because he can't tolerate pain and has amputated it from his way of being. Avoiding pain has orchestrated his life and led to his current state of inertia and ennui. Whilst he was at first involuntarily trained into this role, he did in fact consolidate this learning him *self*, so much so, that he is now able to implement this strategy with very little supervision at all. Avoiding pain is his modus operandi, weed is his enabler. Neville does not have freedom of choice, he can only respond to the world in a way that avoids pain, and this means he must remain stuck outside life in video games.

My strategy for working with Neville was to build an understanding that his actions were not free, rather they were curtailed by the merest threat of discomfort. He was enslaved rather than emancipated by his relationship with pain. His safe cave of computer games and weed was not a home, but a jail.

Together we grew to understand discomfort and pain as the doorway to his new life, a doorway he had to go through to live the life he wanted. In fits and starts, he learned to be ok with using energy to meet new people, sticking with boring tasks, promoting himself to possible employers, and generally getting out into the world. Luckily his re-entrance into the world was lubricated by a chance meeting with Veronica who went on to be a great source of motivation for him to stay in the flow of life.

Taking our self less seriously

Sometimes we can get caught up with our own thoughts and feelings, needs, and wants, forgetting that the world exists outside us and does not circle around us or depend on our moods. As a remedy for this misperception, I love the idea of taking one's *self*, feelings, and thoughts less seriously. There are many components of this, and I have included some below, including being less entitled, giving up curating our *self*, avoiding believing and acting on all our feelings and thoughts, tempering our *self*-love, being more creative and playful, and laughing at our *self*.

Taking our *self* less seriously has so many benefits, it's an emotional superfood that liberates us in many ways. A primary benefit is to free us up to enjoy life, even when it is not as we want it to be. This way we can avoid disappointment because we don't always expect things to roll in our favour.

Work on our entitlement

Part of taking responsibility for our *self* is working on our levels of entitlement. Entitlement is in fact the opposite of taking responsibility for one's *self*; it is the belief that the world owes us money, love, a mansion, stardom, and a life deprived of queues without us having done anything to deserve it. We all have some level of entitlement, small though it may be, but we may not be aware of it.

Not all entitlement relates to wealth and status; we can also have entitlement around how we expect the world to treat us. This can include whether we have a partner and children, that we should always be treated with kindness, that *others* must listen to us carefully, or that all our needs always be respected and met.

Entitlement comes from many places, including feeling not good enough. We may become entitled as a way to compensate for past injuries, and needing to stamp an identity of being particular and special. It may be motivated by a need to have status, and/or a belief (conscious and unconscious) that the world will continue to prioritise us as our parents did.

Some level of entitlement can be good as it can help us get what we want. However, it is a problem when it starts to interfere in our relationships; we can saddle *others* and our environment with the burden of our expectations and demands. On a broader scale, entitlement can affect the way we create the socio-economic structures in countries, where some are entitled to more than *others*.

The Stoic philosophers offer many cures for the state of entitlement, including valuing what we have, and changing our attitude to what we don't have. They recommend valuing only what we can control, and getting comfortable and intimate with poverty so that when we experience more, we feel it.[8]

Curate our self less

I have coached many people who curate their *self* very carefully; how they dress, the language they use, how they present their work and children, etc. etc. We know what this looks like and may even do it ourself, most of us do to some extent. Of course, there are rational backstories for doing this, but the principle of taking one's *self* too seriously is at play here, and it's just exhausting and counterproductive. Curated images need upkeep and defence. Curated masks undermine relationships because *others* tend to wonder who they are really with. Curated people can also land up wondering if those who love them, really love their mask or their *self*.

Curating a *self* can cause stuckness because by its very nature it involves becoming bewitched, amputated, or dead. We lose our *self* behind a mask, and because a mask is likely to be stable and unchanging, it creates a less adaptive way of being. A curated *self* is a stuck *self*.

We won't fall apart if we stop curating ourself. We can use our curatorial skills selectively and with cynicism. The best way to build a *self* is from the inside, there will be some coherence and some irony and parts of you might argue, but this is the nature of authentic humans.

Don't believe everything you think

This tip is especially for those who may be entranced by their own thoughts. This is because our thoughts are not pure and objective, they include a lot of assumptions, hand-me-down notions, and historical data that may be inappropriate for the current context. Our thoughts are not always right and so we need to question them, and certainly not just act on them because we happen to have them. Part of getting more fluid is changing how we think, so not believing all our thoughts is a good start to doing this.

One of the more interesting coaching dilemmas I have explored with clients, is what happens to decision making when only heads are used. When feelings are not in play, heads can spiral into endless circles trying to make a rational decision around yes or no. This occurs because they don't have access to emotional and/or qualitative information to weigh or evaluate the importance of the data. To fix this spiralling, we need information from our gut or feelings to come in, weigh the data according to our needs and our *self*, and then we can decide. Thoughts on their own are weak and suitable only for some decisions, certainly not for existential crises and decisions involving *others*.

Ideological systems like capitalism and neoliberalism suggest that all we need is a brain to get ahead and that it is weak to have feelings. This can lead to decisions that damage people and nature but benefit the numbers. If we want to build a better world, we had better start from inside by being wary of our thoughts, they are not always the friends of our *self*, *others*, or the Earth.

You don't have to act on all your feelings

On the other side of the coin and across the street, is that idea that we don't have to believe or act on all our own feelings. They obviously have their place, especially when used in combination with our thoughts and our gut, but we don't need to take them seriously just because we have them. The road to becoming more fluid includes changing how we feel, so not believing all our feelings is a good start in doing this.

The problem with overusing our feelings is the same as with overusing our brains. Both are informed by all sorts of historical data, projections, and rationalisations that may not be appropriate for the current situation. Not only that, but humans often have trouble getting to grips with what their feelings are. Feelings can be unconscious or confusing. For example, we can believe we are motivated by one feeling but are actually motivated by another. Feelings can also be addictive, like having to always feel good, or in charge, or better than *others*, and this can lead us further astray. It tends to be a bit messy for humans when it comes to feelings.

This is the reason we need to work hard to know what our feelings are, what our habits of feeling are, and what is informing them. We need to be able to mediate our feelings with thoughts and sensations and together find a more balanced way to be in the world. We are much more than just our feelings, so let's not get too hooked on these alone.

And we do need to take in information provided by our feelings, especially the so-called negative ones like envy and anger. Anger and envy are really underappreciated in our world. The reason for this is that we often assume that they expose our inner badness or invite us to act in some bad or socially unacceptable way. This is not true at all; we can feel these feelings and not do anything about them. We can separate anger/envy and action.

A way to do this is to think about anger and envy as sources of information that we could consider, and then if we want to, we can get into action. Anger tells us when we feel that our own or other's boundaries have been violated, and when additional defensive action could be considered. When we act on anger in an unthinking way, we are in danger of doing something stupid or harmful. When we use it as a source of information, drive, and direction, then we have an opportunity to do something much more profound, responsive, and effective.

Envy tells us what we want, even when we don't think we know what we want. It is a curious expression of desire and as such a very useful emotion if we can figure out what we are actually envious of. The problem is that we can get really confused about what it is that we are envious about; is it the handbag or is it the prestige or is it access to finances that we want? It's confusing but doable and necessary if we want to start shaping our life to suit our *self*.

Knowing we are good and bad

Mature people can see and acknowledge their successes and failures more impartially. These don't define who they are but are simply added to their identity, alongside other things they have done. They don't require ululations of recognition by witnesses, nor commiserations for failures. We should learn how to take our successes and failures less seriously.

We can do this when we have a broader perspective, have worked with, and can hold their own pain better, and have a wider range of sources of *self*-esteem. As a result, failure in one area does not mean the total failure of one's *self*. My experience with people at later stages of maturity[9] is that they can smile and say quite humorously; 'it's a full-time job to keep up with my fuck-wittage'. They don't take their *self* too seriously, they don't expect to be perfect, and they are aware of how their *self* can get up to mischief behind their backs. This is a very useful attitude to hold, both for our *self* and the world, because it makes us humble and generous towards *others*.

Watching that self-love

Something else that bothers me about taking one's *self* too seriously is the epidemic of *self*-love we are currently experiencing. Now I know the idea behind it was really good; that is to help people accept and love themself, no matter how different we are. However, when the *self*-love idea hit, so did an epidemic of narcissism and individualism, and when these three joined in wedlock without the sobering presence of humility and reality, we began to see some very bad impacts. Some of these include brittle, reactive *selfs*, public grandstanding, aggrandisement, entitlement, and more. I know there are always backstories for why people do these things, but this does not undermine the necessity for always combining *self*-love with reality and humility.

A better version of *self*-love is to learn how to love all of oneself, even the unlovable parts. This does not mean these parts are not troublesome or may need changing. It's more that we must accept that we actually have unlovable or less constructive parts, and maybe work with them a little here and there. This is a much more humble and realistic way to love oneself.[10]

Laugh and play

Humans are very funny, with our dramas and *self*-importance, and belief that we are central to the world. We are funny, and cute, and so very naïve. Would it not be great if we could spend some time laughing at our *self*, instead of taking it so very seriously. We are mere specks on the dust of creation, and we think we are the centre of the universe, how curious and hilarious is that! It's funny that we think the world was set up to meet our needs, it's funny that we need to work so hard to be a thing in this world, and it's funny that we get so grumpy when things don't go our way.

To play and be creative we need to take our *self* less seriously. We need to be able to laugh and learn from failure rather than take it as an indictment of our value. Creativity is a most generative practice for humans because it truly values our inner worlds and births them into something solid. It also teaches us to value and enjoy difference because creativity is birthed through variance, it is by its very nature different from what already exists. This process is incredibly meaningful for humans and for many it is this process alone that makes life worth living. But to do this we need to take our *self* and what we produce less seriously.

A last and most important aspect of being a good companion to ourselves is find our *self* interesting. Play with, outwit, and explore our *self*. As Sartre said, if you are lonely while being alone, you are in bad company.[11] You are with your *self* for life so why not make the journey as pleasant and interesting as possible.

Catching up with Celia, the coconut cheese girl

Do you remember Celia, the coconut cheese girl? She is the black woman whose mother guided her into a white lifestyle and who later took up the role herself. She is the one who aspired to a white lifestyle because it had more opportunities and advantages than a black lifestyle. Adopting white behaviour enabled her to fit in better in a world owned by whites, enabling her to succeed at a white school and at a white job. She is also the same woman who worked so hard to build a flourishing career but struggled to have friends or find a significant other.

In our sessions, we had a number of conversations about identity; was she really in between two identities, or was she racially fluid, or was she in her own identity box that no one else could understand. These conversations would make her angry; angry at her oppression, and angry at not being properly included by white people or black people. She wondered if she should strengthen her connection to her blackness or maybe just leave the country and its madness, but where would she go?

She did in fact explore her black heritage and met up with some of her mother's family, but it was difficult to connect with them as they only spoke isiXhosa, were very rural and traditional, and asked her for money which she duly paid. Celia also consulted a sangoma (traditional healer) and asked to speak with her ancestors in the hope that maybe one of them would offer something useful. Her great-granny spoke to her through the bones, saying that she was the bleeding edge of the wound in South Africa and her job was to heal herself as a way to heal her family and country. Celia did not know what to make of this but agreed with the idea of healing herself.

Celia found some excellent material from millennial coconuts on TikTok. Their coconut positive, fluid, choice-based approach to identity was appealing to her and the clips made fun of their in-between status, while not hiding from the pain of this. One video raised the issue of speaking and thinking in vernac (vernacular) as opposed to English, and Celia realised that she had not lived in isiXhosa (the language) since she was a young girl. She then knew what her next steps would need to be.

So, Celia found someone to improve her vernac, and we carried on working with exploring who she was. We started investigating not what she had curated herself into, but that she curated at all. Yes, there was the learned inferiority of being black in a world that defiles blackness, but maybe there were additional reasons for her being open to wearing a mask in the first place.

I think we got to some of those issues, including growing up poor and without a father, not knowing who she was in the world and wanting to be something solid and successful. She started to remember parts of herself that she had forgotten, like her playfulness and love of stupid practical jokes which she had apparently inherited from her father. Her fashion sense broadened out from tailored suits to brighter coloured dresses, still clearly designer, but much freer than the suits.

Celia is still on this journey, down to her roots and up into her emerging self. She has a boyfriend now and a social life and no, he is not black, but they share many black friends only some of whom are coconuts. She is comfortable being in the company of black, brown, and white people, and although she still winces at being called a coconut, it's not quite as painful as before.

What is the impact of knowing and growing our *self*?

When we know who we are, and still remain open to who we are becoming, we have a greater capacity to direct our life in a way that is satisfying to us. We have a better understanding of where to place our *self* in life with regard to friends, partners, and work.

When we know our *self*, we have a better understanding of our impact on *others* and how we may want to shift this. We can learn to see our *self* and the world from inside our *self*, as well as from outside our *self*. This means that we can start to see the world as it is, rather than how we are in it.

When we know our *self*, we have a better chance of creating a less volatile and more supportive inner world. This will make our life easier and less exhausting, so we can spend more time and energy doing the things that bring us happiness and *meaning*.

When we grow *self*, we also grow our capacity for relationships and *meaning*.

How do coaches grow more *self*?

The quality of the coach is more important than the tools we use. We need to be working with our wounds, sense-making, and thinking patterns to be a quality coach. The ideas on growing *self* above are useful for coaches too.

One area that I would like to stress is that of taking one's *self* less seriously, including curating our *self* less. Because we are in the business of inner worlds, we can often take our own too seriously. We can believe that everything we think and feel is true for the client as well as for us. We can project our way of being onto client.

When we take our *self* too seriously, we can make interventions that are too strong, instead of making offerings that clients can use or lose. We need to have a humbleness about these and present them lightly in a way that the client can refuse, and where we can recover the relationship well and easily if the client says no. We don't want to land up in a situation that encourages the client to look after us, or rebel against us, we want them to be able to act freely and in their own interest. Humility helps with this.

As a coach, what is the impact of knowing and growing our *self*?

Our *self* is the most important instrument that we use. The success of any intervention is dependent on the inner world of the intervener, the *self*.[12] Of course there are other factors, including those related to the client, but if the coach's *self* is not in shape, then neither will the outcome be.

When we have access to many inner identities and ways of being, when we have allowed life to grow us, we can enable the client do the same. Holding a broader range of identities within us allows us to be agile in the world and our work because we have access to a broader range of tools and insights and ways of being. Multiple identities inside our *self* are also useful to mirror the many identities of the clients we sit with.

Everything we do is a portrait of our *self*, even coaching. When we know who our *self* is, we have a greater capacity to know what is ours and what belongs to our client. We can start seeing our clients more clearly, with fewer of our projections obscuring our sight. This is a great gift to the client, one that not every coach can offer. It allows us to work with the client more cleanly and more helpfully. It allows us to see the client as they are, and not as we are.

Questions to ask your *self*

- What is your greatest source of information about your *self*, your thoughts, feelings, or physical sensations? See if you can switch this around a bit.
- Have you ever been confused about what is your feeling and what feelings you may be feeling that belong to another person? Can you tell the difference between these two source of feelings?
- How good are you at being a good companion to your *self*? Are you caring and kind, too soft, or too hard on your *self*?

Notes

1 van Deurzen, E., et al. (2009). *Everyday mysteries: A handbook of existential psychotherapy* (2nd ed.). Routledge; Perrel, E. (2006). *Mating in captivity: Unlocking erotic intelligence.* Harper Collins; Spinelli, E. (1989). *The interpreted world: An introduction to phenomenological psychology.* Sage Publications, Inc.
2 Winnicott, D. W. (1957). *The child and the outside world.* Tavistock/Basic Books.
3 Just in case you are interested, the ABCEF included the following rationales for exploring feelings: 1. providing him with direction and motivation, 2. building connections with others, and 3. understanding others better to lead them better.
4 Aurelius, M. (2014). *Meditations* (M. Hammond, Ed.). Penguin Classics.
5 West, B. (2020). *The mountain is you: Transforming self-sabotage into self-mastery.* Thought Catalogue.
6 West, B. (2020). *The mountain is you: Transforming self-sabotage into self-mastery.* Thought Catalogue.
7 West, B. (2020). *The mountain is you: Transforming self-sabotage into self-mastery.* Thought Catalogue.
8 Durand, M., Shogry, S., & Baltzly, D., Stoicism. In *The Stanford encyclopedia of philosophy* (Spring 2023 ed.). Edward N. Zalta & Uri Nodelman (Eds.), https://plato.stanford.edu/archives/spr2023/entries/stoicism/.
9 In my other life, I am a researcher in adult maturation. I have been lucky to meet many people in later stages of maturity and it is from these conversations that I draw the data and conclusions I reach in this section.
10 Tillich, P. (2000). *The courage to be* (2nd ed.). Yale University Press.
11 Sartre, J. (1963). *Essays in aesthetics* (1963 ed.). Philosophical Library.
12 Scharmer, C. O. (2008). Uncovering the blind spot of leadership. *Leader to Leader, 2008*(47), 52–59.

Bibliography

Aurelius, M. (2014). *Meditations* (M. Hammond, Ed.). Penguin Classics.
Durand, M., Shogry, S., & Baltzly, D. (n.d.) Stoicism. In *The Stanford encyclopaedia of philosophy* (Spring 2023 ed.), Edward N. Zalta & Uri Nodelman (Eds.), https://plato.stanford.edu/archives/spr2023/entries/stoicism/.

Scharmer, C. O. (2008). Uncovering the blind spot of leadership. *Leader to Leader, 2008*(47), 52–59.

Perrel, E. (2006). *Mating in captivity: Unlocking erotic intelligence*. Harper Collins.

Spinelli, E. (1989). *The interpreted world: An introduction to phenomenological psychology*. Sage Publications, Inc.

Sartre, J. (1963). *Essays in aesthetics* (1963 ed.). Philosophical Library.

Taleb, N. N. (2012). *Antifragile: Things that gain from disorder*. Random House.

van Deurzen, E., et al. (2009). *Everyday mysteries: A handbook of existential psychotherapy* (2nd ed.). Routledge.

West, B. (2020) *The mountain is you: Transforming self-sabotage into self-mastery*. Thought Catalogue.

Winnicott, D. W. (1957). *The child and the outside world*. Tavistock/Basic Books.

Chapter 11

Growing relationships with *others*

This is the second stage of moving towards a more fluid existence. This stage can overlap with the previous or following stages because they have interdependencies and are iterative in nature. Building one area may build another as well. For example, at this stage we have built a stronger connection with our *self*, and this may create more connection with *others*.

Others: The with whom of life

In this chapter we get to learning about how to have engaged relationships. I want to offer some simple and common-sense things we could think about doing. These include understanding and working with our attachment style, letting people in, getting into *others*, balancing *others* with our *self*, and treating humans as humans.

Before we go there, it would be useful to recap why *others* are important, and how we can lose them.

We need *others* to define our *self*, we create our *self* in relationship to others, and connections with *others* enable our learning and growth. We also need *others* to humanise our *self*. This humanising force is critical to both our own survival and that of our species as a whole.

We can lose *others* in many ways; through our attachment style, by isolating our *self*, through death, trauma, and addiction, or by using *others* as tools or objects of utility.

Earlier, we explored the structural factors in our lives that can create and accelerate the loss of *others*. When this happens, we may not notice because everyone else seems to be doing this too. In a world that values getting ahead, autonomy, *self*-love, and *self*-help, we can forget the importance of *others*. This can happen slowly, like the boiling frog story, and one day we wake up and realise that we are not surrounded by friends and a community.

DOI: 10.4324/9781003536253-11

The journey of finding more relationship

The rest of this chapter is about how we build engaged relationships for our *self*. And once again, the ways are many and varied, so pick and choose what has relevance for you.

How to grieve the loss of relationships?

The process of building more engaged relationships needs to start with noticing their absence or limited presence in our lives. We may grieve this and the isolation we have experienced. We can acknowledge the structural factors in our lives which mitigate against engaged relationships like competitive workplaces, commuting, and individual living. We can also notice the loneliness of seeing client after client each day, and not having the time or energy to connect with our professional community, friends, or family. All of this we should grieve, because the grieving will give us energy and motivation to change the situation.

Grieving is better when it can be shared, and sharing builds relationships.

Completing wounds related to *others*

Most wounds tend to relate to *others* and we will automatically work on these when we rebuild our relationships. Much of the creation of our *self*, including the healing of historical wounds takes place in relationships. It is for this reason that our relationship with our clients is so very important as it supports their transformation.

Although all wounds benefit from gaining *self*, *others*, and *meaning*, we can also be more intentional and actively work on these directly. Once again it would include a process of surfacing these wounds, tracking their influence in our lives, grieving their impact, and working with shame. The next step is to create an enabling narrative that allows us to embed the new version in our being and, of course, finally allowing our new skills of relationship to manifest in our lives.

There are many and varied ways to do this work, ranging from talking therapies to bodywork to ritual.

Building a container for engaged relationships

The best way to go about this is to build our *self* a container that supports this, rather than going for targets like meeting like-minded people. Below are some ideas for you to use or lose. They include:

• Treating *others* as humans.
• Working on our attachment patterns.

- Balancing too little and too much of *others*.
- Letting *others* in.
- Getting into *others*.

Treating **others** **as** **humans**

We have already spent some time exploring what it means to treat *others* and be treated as an object or tool, but what does it mean to treat *others* as humans? An African philosophy of humanism, *Ubuntu*, offers us the idea that my humanity is dependent on our humanity, and both our humanities are necessary for us to survive and thrive.[1]

Perhaps a start would be to think about all humans as full people and not just someone who stands on the side of the road or does something for us. We should know that everyone has an inner world of feelings and thoughts, they are more than the role they are playing now, and they have the capacity to change and grow. Everyone has value and deserves the right to be treated with respect, just as we do. Humans have inherent dignity in their humanity. They are not replaceable, not as workers, partners, clients, or children. Each person brings value to the world based on their uniqueness.

Catching up with hatchet Harriet

Do you remember Harriet, the coach who was objectifying herself and her clients. The same one that was burned out and still taking on more clients than she could cope with.

My first objective was to get Harriet to treat herself more humanely, figure out how she could be safe in her inner world as a full human. Yes, this did require getting her to express her emotions and moreover value them as sources of direction. It also required her to work more actively with her self-talk. This was to listen to her own voice more fully and ignore the 'musts' and 'shoulds' she had built up around herself and her coaching practice.

I also worked with her in her language, how she described herself to herself, and the overuse of coachisms. These were not useful because they generalise and this mitigates against a more nuanced understanding of ourselves and others. When we use these too much we start generalising everyone out.

After some time on a very neutral coach vocabulary I was pleased to hear her say 'fuck' occasionally as she struggled to find correct words to explain her inner world. And slowly she moved into a more subtle vocabulary, one entirely suited to herself. As her linguistic liberation made space for her to be more herself, she started to bring her idiosyncrasies to coaching. And I could see how she got pleasure from this.

We explored whether there was anything unresolved from her past jobs or life that could still be influencing how she worked with her clients. It was then that she told me about being called Hatchet Harriet behind her back in her first director

*job, and that it had followed her to her second. With tears in her eyes, she told me
how hurtful this had been, she was just doing her job well, but people judged and
isolated her as a result. She was angry about this, feeling their blaming and shaming her was unjustified.*

*We wondered together if and how her work gave her meaning above financial
outcomes. She said that she was bored with her execs needing remediation, this
work was not meaningful. I offered the idea that maybe they did not need remediation, just some support in thinking through how they could express their freedom and individuality given their context.*

*She mentally chewed this over, and came back the next week with very different
ideas of how she could coach. She could be more contextual and more individual
and this might be a source of meaning to her. She could help people (and herself)
be more themselves, have more agency in their context, and take responsibility for
their lives. As she made space for her own individuality and personhood, she made
space for her in clients' fullness as well.*

You can see from this case study, the process was once again to grow *self*,
find *others* and *meaning*, and it was only through rebuilding these losses that
Harriet could find her clients.

Working on our attachment patterns

I hope you remember the earlier section on attachment patterns in the chapter
on losing *others*, the same chapter where I introduced you to Horace. I described
the four attachment patterns: secure, anxious-ambivalent, anxious-avoidant,
and disorganised.

It is very helpful to understand our attachment pattern because they describe
how we go into relationships, who we chose, how we feel in relationships, and
what we expect from them. There are many resources on the web, and I would
encourage you to use them to understand your specific attachment pattern. We
can change our attachment pattern and if you do wish to do so, it would be
useful to work with a therapist who understands this work.[2]

Let's catch up with Horace.

Catching up with Horace

*Now I think you remember Horace the horrible who had been sent to coaching
with me by his girlfriend. He was the scary guy who had difficulty feeling his vul-
nerabilities but who also was brave enough to face them. Horace was the guy with
the difficult attachment patterns, low levels of empathy for others, and a persis-
tent feeling of being a victim of the world.*

*Before I go ahead and tell you about the course of Horace's life changes, I want
to say that I used a mixed coaching and therapy approach. For many professionals, there are technical differences between these two methodologies, but I am less
concerned about this and more pragmatic in my approach. So, I will call what I*

did coaching but know also that I used many therapeutic techniques as well so that we could do a good job on surfacing and processing issues from Horace's past.

Well, the course of coaching was turbulent, but I am glad to say I was intrepid and resilient. Horace was not used to negative or even neutral feedback, or any restrictions, and reacted aggressively to both. Each time I highlighted an area of possible growth, even as just a question, he would attack me viciously. This included claiming I was no good at my job, or was jealous of him, or getting pleasure out of humiliating him. When Horace wanted special treatment including the right to change his appointments an hour before his session, I would refuse, and bill him when he did not attend. When he refused to pay my annual fee increase and spent many sessions arguing why he was right, I used this as material to explore his inner world and continued to bill increased fees.

This made Horace furious because he was not used to meeting the requirements of someone else, even in a professional partnership such as ours was. It was all quite maddening for Horace, but he kept going. It was not always clear to him why but maybe there was some value in it, or maybe he just needed the company.

Now I did not take the above approach because I was trying to hurt Horace, I was holding a tight coaching frame that would give him certainty and structure and enable him to work more equally with someone else, in a partnership. I managed to not take his hurtful words too seriously because I knew that in all likelihood, he was just repeating how his parents and others had behaved towards him. These 'conflicts' surfaced his view of relationships and invited him to decide whether this was useful to himself and others. My supervisor helped me stay out of the emotionality of it all so that I could be calm, present, and empathic even though he was quite scary from time to time.

To cut a long story short, Horace's coaching went on for years. Over time he softened, found, and experienced his pain, saw how his whole life was built on this pain and anger, and then began to make some behavioural changes.

His outer life responded well to his inner changes and Jennifer, the girlfriend who had sent him to coaching in the first place, stayed. Jennifer understood Horace's anxiety and fears around people, but did not tolerate any of his theatrics. Horace found this comforting, grounding, and reinforcing. Together they founded a sanctuary for abused animals where Horace worked until his death, tending to the needs of creatures with similar histories to his.

Now clearly Horace not only had a tricky attachment pattern, but there were also other things going on as well. This is the same for all humans. With us, things are always mixed up and layered. The big story here is that we can understand and adapt our attachment patterns so that we can have more engaged relationships and a life with greater *meaning*. Also, that when we have our *self*, *others*, and *meaning*, then life is so much more rewarding.

Balancing too little and too much of **others**

When we only meet our own needs, we risk losing *others*, and when we only meet *others'* needs, we risk losing our *self*.[3] This means we have to juggle things continuously. Sometimes we may veer towards one pole or another, for example, with our new baby. However, we have to return to some level of homeostatic balance, or we will get stuck.

The balance between being-for-oneself and being-for-*others*[4] varies from person to person; it's something we must figure out for ourself. The measure of this balance might be in how we are feeling but, as we know, feelings are not always the perfect measurement.

One way to go about this is to review our history and context. What were the assumptions we learned as a child about how much *others* we should have in our life? What did our family of origin teach us about looking after our *self*, was it considered selfish or *self*-care? This data will provide our baseline and if we go above or below this we might experience guilt or discomfort.

Intimate relationships are often overloaded with demands; our partners need to be our confidante, lover, best friend, shared parent, co-adventure seeker, sexual performer, sports partner, and more. Historically, this was not always the case, we used to spread our relationship needs across a variety of people like lovers, friends, colleagues, etc. However, due to many factors, we have tended to locate these demands in one person.[5] Perhaps we need to spread the load a little, and thereby broaden our capacity for being touched and influenced by many *others*.

Growing relationships by letting **others** *in*

I guess I need to be a bit more specific here about what is meant by letting people in. This refers to how much of our *self* we share with *others*, how much we allow people to see our inner world. We all have habits around this, some of us overshare, and some under share, but we have to figure out what is right for us and those around us.

Family habits around sharing one's inner worlds, worries about making one's *self* vulnerable, the fear of being hurt, may motivate us to not share our inner world. We may also not know how to share our innermost thoughts and feelings, or feel that sharing may be a burden on the other person. However, when people do not open up appropriately, it can feel like they are not present in the conversation, a bit snooty, or even rejecting.

Oversharing can happen when we get nervous, when we are lobbying for attention, when we can't regulate our emotions, or when we lack appropriate boundaries. We can also overshare our worlds in the hope that this will build connection and intimacy. However, when we overshare, it can feel overwhelming or frightening to the listener or that someone else's world is dominating the conversation.

What we need to learn is how to share appropriately and of course there are many variables involved, including the context, social norms, the relationship type, our *self*, and the personality of the listener.

Let's catch up with Gertie who grows by letting *others* in.

Gertie, who could not stop grieving

Gertie came to see me three years after the death of her beloved husband Siya; she said she could not stop grieving. When she was not crying, she had a runny nose, and when she did not have a runny nose, she was crying. Water poured out of Gertie constantly and scientist that she was, she even upped her water intake to accommodate these excessive outflows. Gertie was not used to dealing with herself in this state, she was not used to the overwhelming emotions, and felt trapped and panicked by them. Three years went by in watery misery and Gertie started wondering if this was to be her permanent state.

So now we find Gertie after the crash, grieving, crying, working too hard, and avoiding the home and garden she had shared with Siya. Gertie was stuck in her grief and was struggling to find a way back into life. She was grieving Siya and also the loss of her own life.

We spoke at length about emotions and their tendency to work on different schedules and paradigms to their owners. We wondered what they were expressing and how they filled in for Siya in his absence. We wondered too what would happen if the absence remained empty, would this be disloyal, would this nullify the beauty and meaning of the relationship, or would this void allow something valuable in?

Gertie did not reach any conclusions with regard to these questions but became gentler and more easygoing with her feelings. She started to enjoy using her feelings as sources of information and direction without becoming too lost in them. She started to like combining her thoughts and feelings and getting a better picture of what was going on inside herself.

One of the things we explored was home, what home meant now that Siya had left. Siya's cave was still intact. According to Gertie, the house was a bit messy as she had ignored it for three years. Gertie needed some help to clear the house and so we hired a house organiser who specialised in this kind of work. I was curious and said I would go along too.

When the house organiser and I arrived, it became clear that not just Siya's cave but the whole house needed significant clearing and cleaning. Gertie had become rather a hoarder, mainly of items that she intended to recycle or reuse, but never got around to doing. She had filled the house with empty bottles, plastic cartons, and folded cardboard, she must have thrown very little away in the last three years.

Clearing the house and Siya's cave took a month and was very traumatic for Gertie who took to hiding objects in her car and lab to avoid them being thrown away. Once the house was clear(ish), a gardener was brought in to cut back the now overgrown indigenous garden. Space opened in the house and garden, and also in Gertie.

To both Gertie's and my surprise, she joined the indigenous bulb society. She liked the way in which bulbs were dormant for most of the year, bloomed once, and then went back to their hidden state. According to Gertie, they felt a bit like her own life.

She joined the bulb rescue wing of the society and was often seen spade in hand marching across public land with like-minded peers, many of whom were kind and gentle and introverted. She liked them, their quiet companionship, and their purposefulness. They rescued bulbs that needed safe housing, so many of which found their way back to Gertie's garden. This of course meant that many of her bulb rescue colleagues did as well, including Paul who loved cycads.

I think you can already tell that Paul is going to be the new love interest and bring Gertie more fully back into the world. I am not going to bother you with the details because I think you have sufficient imagination to fill those in yourself. As you can see it was time; she had found her *self*, found *others*, and *meaning*.

Getting into others

We read *others* with different glasses to the ones with which we read our *self*. We tend to read *others* objectively, and our *self* subjectively.[6] What this means is that we tend to understand our *self* from the inside – how it feels to be me, and we understand *others* from the outside – how it looks to be them. This can lead us to judge *others* by their impact (on us) while at the same time we judge our *self* on our intention, no matter what our impact was. Perhaps we should try to switch this around and attempt to read *others* subjectively and from inside themselves.[7] Maybe we could also try to look at our *self* from the outside as well. To do this we need to be able to get into other's inner worlds.

We get into *others'* worlds in many ways; a touristic sort of way where we venture in for a day, or a collegial way where we journey in within certain contexts for longer periods of time (like learning how to work with a colleague). We can also do it in a deeper way where we allow *others'* inner worlds to start changing our own. We need all three strategies otherwise we may land up with too little *others*, and of course this will depend on our own attachment patterns and needs.

Below are some tips for getting into other people's lives. They include understanding our impact on *others*, and how to be interesting and useful to *others*. There are clearly many more things that we can do that have not been included here, like building our communication skills.

Earlier on, I spoke about the difference between intention and impact. We judge our *self* on our intention and *others* on their impact. If we want to bring *others* into our world, we need to understand how they experience us. To do this, we should look at how they respond to us, their verbal, physical, and psychic cues. We could also ask them directly and be prepared for an answer that we may not like. We need to watch for differences between how we are experiencing our *self* and how *others* experience us, for example, we may think we are being funny, but *others* might not. We don't have to change our *self* to suit *others*, but it is important that we understand the impact we're having on them. We can have vastly different views and still get on as friends.

Being interesting to *others* is a curious topic to which we don't always pay attention. We talk to *others* about our own stuff, things we enjoy, not always remembering that this may not be interesting to them. We also just say things because we have a need to say them, not because *others* need to hear them. We offer advice and opinions when they are not requested, or clarification and repetition, where they are not needed. There are naught so annoying as those who unnecessarily insert their *self* into conversations.

Let us try to not be so needy in conversation or to flatter *others* into submission. Give people space to be, let them feel peaceful and good enough in the conversation. If we are not interesting to *others* they won't hang around.

We often assume that we can't listen or help *others* if we are in pain. We can believe that what is going on in our inner world is too painful and pressing for us to focus on someone else. This is not true: we can be very skilful about this, we can hold our pain, and we can focus on *others*. Or, at a more sophisticated level, we can feel ours and *others'* pain fully and together, and see what happens. How amazing we humans can be.

The trouble with enjoying variety in humans is difference. We humans have a tricky relationship with difference. When we are less mature, we can experience difference as criticism, and we all know how this can make us respond (withdraw, deny, attack *self*, and attack *others*). We tend to want to make one side win, preferably our own.

When we are more mature, we can let differences exist between our *self* and *others* without having to resolve them. We can use difference to grow and build our *self*. When we don't have this capacity, we can find our *self* in constant reaction to difference, and this will undermine relationships.

The best way to develop skills around difference is to work with our own differences within. For example, instead of saying that I must decide whether I like or don't like something, maybe say, 'I like it and I don't like it'. The idea is to let both sides of the binary hold hands but never quite merge inside us. If we can learn to live with differences within, then we have a much better chance of living with differences without.

What is the impact of growing relationships with others?

We need others to humanise our *self* as well as define our *self*; *others* pull us out of our narrow *self*-interest, and individual sense-making. This enables us to adapt and grow, create a broader *self*, and a more satisfying life.

It is easy to see how dehumanised relationships get us stuck in the world; we have no access to our *self* or *others* under these conditions. This means we get stuck in old and less useful patterns of relationship and being in the world.

When we rebuild relationships with *others*, we can regain our *self* and when we do this the possibility of finding *meaning* occurs. These factors together build a more fluid life.

How do coaches grow their connection to *others*?

Earlier I spoke about the importance of holding effective relationships with clients. To do this well we need to build our connections to them. This of course means not treating them as objects as did Harriet.

Building our professional community enables our learning and may indeed build our business. The tricky bit is which communities we want to associate with.

There are coach accreditation organisations which are seeking to professionalise the sector by creating quality standards, which is helpful. However, we must find one that speaks to our context and orientation towards coaching. Coaching bodies that assume we all operate in the same context may not be useful here. This is because they could invite the homogenisation of approach, right across the world. We don't want this; we want the coaching profession to flower in many different and contextual ways that appreciate difference.

How much should coaches share of their lives in coaching?

This is an interesting question and the general answer is very little. We want to avoid inserting our life into the flow of coaching, and keep our clients focussing on their *self*, not ours. When we share too much of our *self*, clients can get caught up in pleasing or rebelling against us. We don't want to encourage clients to try to be our friends because our relationship is a working one with a specific focus. As a result the general answer to this question is that we should not tell them too much about our *self*.

However, as we have discussed we are not *tabular rasas*, and our humanity plays an important role in us being effective as a coach. If we are authentic, then this encourages the client to be so as well, and being authentic builds trust. Lastly, we may have a few experiences from our lives that would be useful to share. I say a few because we are not our clients, and our experiences are not often relevant to them.

Once again it is a situation of polarities that need balancing. We must find an appropriate balance between staying cleanly out of the client's coaching and being authentic as a human. If we are wondering which side to err on, it would be to stay out.

What is the impact of coaches broadening their relationships

When we deepen our coaching relationships, we build their capacity to support our clients. When we broaden our relationships, we learn skills for being in different types of relationships and this can only enhance our coaching relationships. When we build our professional community, we have a chance to learn and share and grow.

Questions to ask your *self*

- How diverse are the people with whom you have engaged relationships? Do their inner worlds and life experience mimic yours or do they bring new perspectives to you, ones that may even challenge your assumptions about life?
- Do you know your homeostatic orientation between being-for-yourself and being-for-*others*? Would you be prepared to hold a little discomfort and change this? Would this change be useful in your life?
- How do you feel about the Harriet case study, have you ever done anything similar and if so, do you know why?

Notes

1　Gade, C. B. N. (2012). What is *Ubuntu?* Different Interpretations among South Africans of African Descent. *South African Journal of Philosophy*, *31*(3), 484–503; Mbembe, A., & Dubois, L. (2017). *Critique of black reason*. Duke University Press.
2　The Attachment Project. (2024). https://www.attachmentproject.com (Accessed: 5 March 2024).
3　Heidegger, M. (2008). *Being and time*. Harper Collins.
　Polt, R. (1999) *Heidegger: An introduction*. Cornell University Press.
4　Heidegger, M. (2008). *Being and time*; Polt, R. (1999) *Heidegger: An introduction*.
5　Perrel, E. (2006) *Mating in captivity: Unlocking erotic intelligence*. Harper Collins.
6　Heidegger, M. (2008). *Being and time*. Polt, R. (1999) *Heidegger: An introduction*; Garvey Berger, J. (2019). *Unlocking leadership mindtraps: How to thrive in complexity* (1st ed.). Stanford University Press.
7　van Deurzen, E., et al. (2009). *Everyday mysteries: A handbook of existential psychotherapy* (2nd ed.). Routledge.

Bibliography

Gade, C. B. N. (2012). What is *Ubuntu?* Different interpretations among South Africans of African descent. *South African Journal of Philosophy*, *31*(3), 484–503.

Garvey Berger, J. (2019). *Unlocking leadership mindtraps: How to thrive in complexity* (1st ed.). Stanford University Press.

Mbembe, A., & Dubois, L. (2017). *Critique of black reason*. Duke University Press.

Heidegger, M. (2008). *Being and time*. Harper Collins.
Perrel, E. (2006). *Mating in captivity: Unlocking erotic intelligence*. Harper Collins.
Polt, R. (1999). *Heidegger: An introduction*. Cornell University Press.
The Attachment Project. (2024). https://www.attachmentproject.com (Accessed: 5 March 2024)
van Deurzen, E., et al. (2009). *Everyday mysteries: A handbook of existential psychotherapy* (2nd ed.). Routledge.

Chaper 12

Growing *meaning*

This is the third stage in moving towards a more fluid existence. This stage can overlap with the previous stages because they have interdependencies and are iterative in nature. We can also find *meaning* in growing our *self* and building engaged relationships.

Meaning: the why of life

Meaning creates the why of life, if we don't have *meaning*, it can be hard to understand why we should keep grappling with life. *Meaning* gives us energy, direction, and purpose. It creates an inner coherence, a values and purpose structure for our life that guides us, soothes us, and helps us get through times of despair and confusion. It can even help us transcend death. Without *meaning*, we can bob around on the Earth directionless like plastic bottles in the ocean. *Meaning* is the measure we use to understand how valuable we have been to our *self* and the Earth during our time here.

Earlier we learned that there are many ways to lose *meaning*. However, just to recap, these include not actively *meaning*, making the wrong kind of *meaning*, not having *meaning* in all the right places, and through death, trauma, and addiction. Furthermore, as we have discovered, we can lose *meaning* and not notice it.

The journey of finding more *meaning*

The rest of this chapter describes how we can create more *meaning* for our *self* and our clients. And once again, the ways are many and varied, so pick and choose what has salience for you. We start again with grieving the loss of *meaning*.

How to grieve the loss of *meaning*?

When we notice that our life or work or partnerships have no *meaning*, it can feel like we have no rudder and have entered an existential void. In this state it

DOI: 10.4324/9781003536253-12

is very hard to see a future or direct a life towards something. We need to notice and grieve the state we are in so that we can build energy and flexibility for strengthening the *meaning* of our life and work.

Completing wounds related to *meaning*

Wounding around meaning is more prevalent than we would expect, sometimes even revolving around the *meaning* of the wounding. We seek to understand why me for this experience, what is the *meaning* of this in my life, and what does this mean for my future *self*, relationships, and more. Much of this healing will come through the process of rebuilding *meaning*.

We can frame our meaningless as a learning opportunity, a pause for incubation, or as absurdity in action. Sometimes, absurdity is the best option as a way to accept the loss of *meaning* in our lives during our time of being stuck. It takes a lot of courage to choose absurdity because humans in general want to fit their lives within a *meaning* framework. We want to believe our lives have *meaning* and are progressing towards something transcendent, so it takes a lot of courage to say something was meaningless.

Ritual is an excellent way of working with *meaning*. This is because ritual is the physical manifestation of *meaning*, we can use it to generate and narrate *meaning*.

Building a container for *meaning*

Once again, it's more useful for us to build a container for a meaningful life than focus on targets such as finding meaningful work, although these can be useful too. Below are some ideas for this:

* Knowing where to find and create *meaning*.
* Creating our own *meaning*.
* Being less special.
* Adapting to our life stage.
* Getting comfortable with absurdity and no *meaning*.

Knowing where to find and create meaning?

We can find and create *meaning* in many places, I want to provide lots of options so that you can find one or two that work for you.

Before I start, I just want to remind us that not all *meaning* is equal, some *meaning* is more meaningful. We need to be careful how and what we choose is meaningful.

There are some things in life that are intrinsically meaningful, like rearing children well. However, most of the time we need to consciously make *meaning*. Making *meaning* is difficult because it requires us to find a naturally forming metanarrative or big story that can hold our lives together and create direction and energy. If I wanted to confuse us, I would say we are looking for an archaeological and teleological narrative that makes our lives coherent. This means a big story about our past and future that contains the idea of our purpose, what we are passionate about, and explains most of what we've been up to. For *meaning* to be meaningful, it must speak to our growth as a person as well as to something transcendent like serving *others*.

Spiritual schools of thought suggest *meaning* can be found in God, growing in our religion/spirituality, helping *others*, and doing good in the world. Communicating with God through prayer and meditation can make one feel less alone, and in connection with the universal patterns of life.[1] Gratitude has a similar effect.

Transpersonal versions of *meaning* can be found in how we serve the greater good: how we contribute to the service of *others* and our world. Environmental activism and supporting other's wellbeing are examples of these.

We can also find *meaning* in life by learning to love our *self* and having the courage to be our *self* more fully.[2] Growing our *self*, building a rich inner world in which to live, learning new skills, and taking pleasure in our *self*, our bodies, and our environment, are all acts of *meaning*. Experiencing beauty can also be a way of finding *meaning*. And lastly, when we can't find or create *meaning*, then we can derive *meaning* from the attitude we bring to the meaninglessness of a situation.[3]

Meaning is amplified through commitment and adversity. The energy we expend on getting something can enhance the *meaning* of our achievement even if the achievement is as seemingly purposeless as owning a designer handbag.

Meaning tends to be multi-layered and sometimes paradoxical. It changes over the course of our lives, but for most people there is some consistency in what is meaningful to us.

Creating our own meaning

I think that we understand intuitively what is meant by creating our own *meaning*. *Meaning* is about our purpose and direction in life, what we need to have the courage to live even while we suffer. Your *meaning* is about you.

We need to create our own *meaning* and it has to come from our own life, background, and hopes for the future. We cannot buy *meaning* in a store or even online, we have to dig it up for our *self*. If we borrow *meaning* from someone else it may be useful in the short term, but ultimately it won't give us the sense of place, purpose, and pathway that our own *meaning* can give us. This is not always clear in life, especially in the early stages.

Being less special

The Western world values individualism, and we are schooled to demonstrate this by expressing our opinions, our use of language, the intensity of emotions we feel, and even what we eat (can I have x without the y and done on rye with deep-fried anchovies).

We can make *meaning* of this specialness and build an identity around it, and this is not necessarily wrong. However, we must not forget that we are humans with common things, and that these common things are not common in the bad sense of the word, they are just things we share as part of the human race. *Meaning* is one of these. This is because useful, empowering, and directional *meaning* for everyone, comes from growing as a person, helping *others*, and accomplishing something transcendent in life. When we get caught up in being special rather than building deeper *meaning*, we are orientating towards our *self*, and not towards *meaning*.

Now, I know that you are thinking how I can now suggest that we be more common in *meaning* just after the section where I talk about growing our own *meaning*. Well, it's one of those existential paradoxes again; we only find our common *meaning* if we go into our individual *meaning*. We have to go into our *self* to find our commonality because that is where our transpersonal knowledge lurks. Let's catch up with Cas and see how she does it.

Catching up with Cas, the curator

Do you remember Cas, the social media doyen who had multiple unrelated identities online. She was the same person who had lost herself in all her curated identities. She was looking for some kind of meaning and purpose to integrate all the parts of herself that she had uncovered.

Cas had many curated identities and not an ugly pic amongst them all. She wore many disguises most fairly stereotypical in a Madonna kind of way. We spoke at length about who she was and how these images may represent aspects of her, or aspects of how she would like to be viewed. My focus here was on how she created meaning in her life.

The meaning question came out of the blue for Cas; she had read a lot about purpose online and its importance in life but had not really figured out what the meaning of her presence in the world meant. Cas had seen how people had helped others by talking about this eating disorder or that neurodiversity online, but she could not figure out what the meaning and purpose was around her posts. She was not sure what she was saying with them, or what they were in fact doing in the public space at all.

We spent a long time on this question, and Cas became worried about other people wondering what the use of these posts was. She felt that some of her followers did not need something meaningful and coherent – make-up, scenery, and some drama was enough. However, there might be others who would consider her flighty in the wrong way. She became worried that she did not have a disability to promote, or minority cause to support, or even a make-up range to endorse. This really became an existential crisis of meaning.

And then she got it, her job was to provoke meaning by not being meaningful, by being superficial. She decided to post shots of herself in various disguises counterpointed with strap lines like 'Genocide in Gaza and I am living my Best Life with Moet'. She wanted to force her followers to explore the meaning of superficial pursuits in a world that was in crisis.

The first few posts received a confusing response – some of her followers loved it but the majority were irritated and posted rude remarks on her social media. And then her posts were picked up by a different audience, one who appreciated the social commentary she seemed to offer.

Her likes and followers increased, and she was interviewed on a podcast about the way in which social media could be used to get people to think more deeply and empathically about the world. No make-up brand came in to sponsor her, but she was asked by a global NGO to help them think through their social media strategy, and then this of course led to more work for her.

Cas went on to complete a master's degree in media studies, and discovered she had a knack for academia. You will find her today up at the university completing her doctorate on social media and political activism.

Adapting to our life stage

Meaning changes as we change, what is meaningful today is not always meaningful tomorrow. This is due to many factors, including our life stage. We can understand this well when we look at our own cupboard with dormant objects and outfits from a previous life. These are the trappings from a previous set of *meaning*-making protocols. Let's look at Mohammed making *meaning* in his retirement.

Catching up with Mohammed making meaning

I think you must remember Mohammed who was struggling with creating a mean-ingful retirement for himself. He had realised that helping others was meaningful to him but was struggling to find others to help. His kids had left home, and his wife was getting on with her life and did not want to be the target of his relentless service.

In our sessions we discussed Mohammed's options: old people, young people, unemployed people, animals, and so on. None of these seemed satisfying so he went home to think about it.

There was a mosque close to Mohammed's house and next door was an empty field where residents such as Mohammed walked their dogs. The dog walkers were very social, and Mohammed had got to know many of them, including two nuns, Sister Marie and Sister May. They often chatted while throwing sticks for their dogs, and the dogs themselves got on very well.

During one of these conversations the question of maintaining the empty *field popped up. The Sisters wanted the dog walkers to organise and get the council to develop a garden that could be used by local residents. They also wanted the mosque to be involved and were not sure who to approach in this regard, would it be the Imam or was there someone else who was responsible for more practical matters? Mohammed offered to make the right introductions.*

Mohammed, the Imam, and some additional elders met Sister Marie and Sister May on the open field. It was a convivial meeting and they all agreed that the land was worth developing for public use. The Imam indicated that they would be interested in using the space for their youth activities, and the nuns thought that was a good idea and perhaps they could also do so.

They agreed to set up a committee and Mohammed was elected to be the point of contact with the council. This was an ideal job for him because he had a lot of experience getting reluctant stakeholders to go along with him.

Getting council commitment took over a year, but Mohammed was intrepid and got them to agree to invest in and maintain the public space. By the time this happened, people from both religious groups as well as some local residents had already started laying out a park and putting in some plants.

There had been some dispute about the name of the park, but they finally settled on Union Park, a park where people from various backgrounds could come together. A park where youths from different religions could join and maybe find each other.

Once the park had been opened by the mayor, the Sisters, and the Imam, things got into full swing and the venue became well frequented by people of all religious orientations. Over the years there were a number of minor religious conflicts in the park, a few homeless people were evicted, and teenagers prevented from making out in the bushes, all of which could be expected. On the whole, Union Park was a place of union and peace and over the years becoming more beautiful as the trees grew and lawns became more verdant.

During this time Mohammed stopped coming to me, he was too busy, and was not feeling depressed about his life, he had *meaning*. When he died, there was an article in the local newspaper describing how he had brought communities together, and there were deep and loving condolences from both Christian and Muslim users of the park.

Growing meaning by having it in all the right places

To have a satisfying life, we need to have *meaning* in more than one place, we need enough *meaning* to stretch into the cold and desolate places where we are cogs in machines, or are lonely and in pain. This was Jane's problem; she had a doughnut life, all the *meaning* was around the outside, with nothing going on inside. Let's see how she changed that.

Catching up with Jane, the justice fighter

If you remember Jane, you will recall that she was a super crime fighter with a donut dilemma. As we chatted through this, I became aware that she was burned out. Now, although meaning is a good antidote to burnout, she was probably too tired to make changes in her life. Her first step would thus be one of recovery and building her energy.

Recovery from burnout can be hard and time-consuming, some say that if burnout has gone on too long then the chances of a full recovery are scarce. Recovery is not about lying around doing nothing, it is about doing less work and more pleasurable and meaningful activities. We explored what she could do, activities that were not energy sapping but energy-creating. Jane said in the past, she had not taken up hobbies or other pursuits because they were always interrupted by work calls.

I wondered if there was a way to avoid some of these calls and Jane responded no, her department was under-resourced, people were not as skilled as they needed to be, and so things would always land on her desk. I asked if she could deputise the work some of the time, find someone to take a turn on emergency calls. Maybe there was someone ambitious enough to be grateful for the extra responsibility. She said she would think about it, but there probably was no one who wanted extra work.

It turned out that Jane was wrong and there was someone who had their eye on her job and wanted the opportunity to prove that they could do it. Without going into details, Jane managed to start delegating weekend work a bit more and this opened some space for her.

We spoke about a range of energy-creating activities from exercising, meditation, clearing, and fixing up her house, cleaning up her diet, doing artsy or craftsy things, getting back to playing the piano and much more. She chose yoga because she liked being in the warrior pose, and also the child pose. Yoga was good to her, and she managed to start inserting sessions into her week as well as on the weekends.

The next job was to strengthen her friend network, to maybe see if there was a special person out there for her. She could not do this online because of her high profile but she could reconnect with old friends, and hope that they introduced her to other people. She could have them around and see what happened. Her old friends were happy to reconnect with her and she soon found herself back within a fun social network.

Jane had a sister Lulu, who had three kids. She began to spend more time with Lulu, often chatting about their childhood and their parents. Her sister reminded her of parts of herself that had laid dormant for years, like her rebellious nature or the time she was arrested. They laughed at Jane's first brush with the law.

Jane started helping Lulu with lift clubs and through this met Charlene, who was the granny of one of the kids at Lulu's kids' school. Charlene lived with her son and his wife and was very involved in their kid's logistics. Over time, Jane and Charlene started attending the kid's hockey matches together and sharing a bottle of wine when either was collecting kids.

One thing led to another, and suddenly they were a couple. This surprised themselves and indeed everyone around them, neither having identified as lesbians before. Despite the surprise element, the relationship felt positive and easy, and people got used to them being together.

So, over the course of six months, Jane rebuilt her familial and social network, strengthened her body, improved her cooking, and found love, wow. She was feeling alive and great, and she started delegating more and more work to her colleague as well as talking about him as her successor. Our next step was to think through her exit strategy, understand and consolidate her legacy at work, and choose her timing well for a gracious departure.

As the meaning of her life outside work grew, she began to feel less depressed and anxious about retirement. As her work legacy became more apparent to her and her successor's skills grew, the more comfortable she became with taking her hands off the wheel and moving towards retirement. It was then that we stopped our sessions and said goodbye. A year later I saw in the press that she had retired.

Getting comfortable with absurdity and no meaning

Perhaps it's a hangover from the Enlightenment or an unrepentant neural pathway baked in by scientific rationalism, but we as humans are always trying to locate cause and effect in a linear kind of way, a+b=c. Sometimes this will serve us, and often not. Sometimes it will lead us down all sorts of alleyways that waste our time and take us nowhere.

In some cases things just are, and there is no rational explanation for their existence, nor does there need to be. In these instances, perhaps we should spend our emotional energy on accepting things rather than trying to explain them. An idea to play with is that there is no *meaning*, life is just absurd.[4] Perhaps this can help us live in the present and enjoy each minute of our lives.

What is the impact of growing *meaning*?

When we have *meaning*, we have direction and purpose and we have the energy and motivation for change. The process of making *meaning* can drive us to find our *self* and *others* more fully, and together these factors can enable us to live a more fluid life.

As we would expect, the more *meaning* we find, the more we find our *self* and *others*. *Meaning* gives us a direction for the development of our *self*. Furthermore, because *meaning* allows us to transcend our *self*, we can build our connection to *others*.

How do coaches grow *meaning*?

When coaches lose the *meaning* of their work, they struggle to commit to clients and to work through difficult problems. We need to keep building the *meaning* of our coaching practice so that we can retain our interest and motivation to do good work.

We can do this by continuing to learn, by working ethically, and by orientating our work towards something we are passionate about. Sharing our learning in the community or taking pleasure in supporting clients to grow are also rich sources of meaning. We can also use the other strategies mentioned in this chapter to locate and build *meaning* in our work.

As a coach, what is the impact of building *meaning* in our work?

When we understand the role of *meaning* in our work and lives, we are able to support clients to create this for themselves. We can strengthen clients to unearth and create their own *meaning* and help them avoid *meaning* that is not meaningful. But we can't do this until we deeply understand *meaning* and how it energises and directs lives.

Questions to ask your *self*

- How has your sense of *meaning* changed over the years?
- Have you ever worked actively to build *meaning* in your life, and if so how?
- When has your work been less meaningful to you and how did you change this if you did?

Notes

1 Buber, M. (2010). *I and thou*. Martino Publishing; Tillich, P. (2000). *The courage to be* (2nd ed.). Yale University Press; van Deurzen, E., & Iacovou, S. (2013). *Existential perspectives on relationship therapy*. London; van Deurzen, E., Craig, E., Laengle, K., Schneider, K., Tantam, D., & du Plock, S. (2019). *The Wiley world handbook of existential therapy* (1st ed.). E. Craig et al. (Eds.) Wiley Blackwell; van Deurzen, E., et al. (2009). *Everyday mysteries: A handbook of existential psychotherapy* (2nd ed.). Routledge; Van Deurzen, E. (2012). *Reasons for living: Existential therapy and spirituality*. Available at: https://www.researchgate.net/publication/307967655_Reasons_to_Live (Accessed: 8 October 2020).
2 Tillich, P. (2000). *The courage to be* (2nd ed.). Yale University Press.
3 Frankl, V. E. (2006). *Man's search for meaning*. Beacon Press.
4 van Deurzen, E., et al. (2009). *Everyday mysteries: A handbook of existential psychotherapy* (2nd ed.). Routledge; Camus, A. (2012). *The myth of Sisyphus and other essays*. Knopf Doubleday Publishing Group; Blomme, R. (2014). The absurd organization: The insights of Albert Camus translated into management practices. In Blomme, & Van Hoof, B. (Eds.), *Another state of mind: Perspectives from wisdom traditions on management and business* (pp. 161–174). Palgrave Macmillan.

Bibliography

Blomme, R. (2014). The absurd organization: The insights of Albert Camus translated into management practices. In Blomme, & Van Hoof, B. (Eds.), *Another state of mind: Perspectives from wisdom traditions on management and business* (pp. 161–174). Palgrave Macmillan.

Buber, M. (2010). *I and thou*. Martino Publishing.

Camus, A. (2012). *The myth of Sisyphus and other essays*. Knopf Doubleday Publishing Group.

Frankl, V. E. (2006). *Man's search for meaning*. Beacon Press.

Tillich, P. (2000). *The courage to be* (2nd ed.). Yale University Press.

van Deurzen, E., & Iacovou, S. (2013). *Existential perspectives on relationship therapy*. London.

van Deurzen, E., Craig, E., Laengle, K., Schneider, K., Tantam, D., & du Plock, S. (2019a) *The Wiley world handbook of existential therapy* (1st ed.). Edited by E. Craig et al. Wiley Blackwell.

van Deurzen, E., et al. (2009a). *Everyday mysteries: A handbook of existential psychotherapy* (2nd ed.). Routledge.

van Deurzen, E. (2012). *Reasons for living: Existential therapy and spirituality*. Available at: https://www.researchgate.net/publication/307967655_Reasons_to_Live (Accessed: 8 October 2020).

van Deurzen, E., et al. (2009c). *Everyday mysteries: A handbook of existential psychotherapy* (2nd ed.). Routledge.

van Deurzen, E., Craig, E., Laengle, K., Schneider, K., Tantam, D., & du Plock, S. (2019b). *The Wiley world handbook of existential therapy* (1st ed.). E. Craig et al. (Eds.) Wiley Blackwell.

Chapter 13

Experiencing fluidity

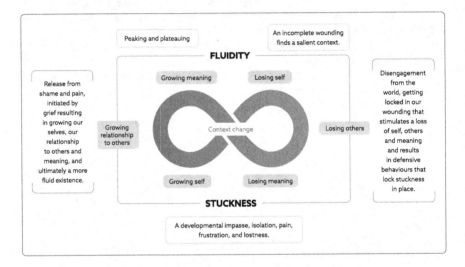

Here we are at the end of a full rotation in the Cycle of Stuckness. We have found our *self* more deeply, we have found *others*, and we have found *meaning* and are entering a patch of fluidity. Yeehaa – celebrations erupting, champagne-popping noises, fingers clicking, and jazz hands jazzing.

What does it mean to be fluid?

Being fluid is more than being not being stuck. It's also not about being able to avoid adversity. Being fluid means taking in the world as it is and rolling with it in a useful way. When we can do this, we become alchemists transforming suffering into meaningful and connected lives. When we do this we, are able to keep learning and growing in response to the world. Our sense of self enlarges, our connection to *others* deepens, and we have a sense of delivering beauty and value to the world.

DOI: 10.4324/9781003536253-13

What is the experience of fluidity?

For most people the experience of noticing fluidity builds over time. We may not believe the first indications of fluidity and need stronger signals to be able to acknowledge that things have indeed changed. Some of us have difficulty noticing when we are fluid because we are more experienced, skilled, and comfortable, at living out difficult lives. We are indeed a strange species.

Experiencing fluidity can be a joy if we let it in and flow with it; yes, we have to flow with our fluidity. Some of the experiences of being fluid are below, including feeling connected to our *self*, the world, good enough, clocking up achievements, and feeling gratitude without trying.

When we are fluid, we feel connected to our *self*, we chat to our inner worlds nicely, and we respond to their needs. Automatically, we build a container for staying connected to our feelings, exercising our bodies, embracing our hearts, and feeling a sense of spiritual connection.

For many of us, our inner world stabilises on the upside of *self*-esteem. When we are fluid, our actions have traction, and we feel competent and good enough. We can survey our impact and reflect with wonder and admiration at what we have achieved. We have come through a patch of learning that has brought us increased satisfaction with our *self* and *others*, and a sharper vision for our lives.

When we are in a state of fluidity, we feel connected to the world as if we are dancing in a partnership with the world. The dance may change but we remain embraced and intertwined, and in sync. This is more than having a nice dance. This means living in a strong current of life, understanding the patterns and flows of it, and using these to become more fully our *self*, connected to *others*, and offering a meaningful contribution to the world. This is about creating our own slipstream and then riding it.

When we are connected to our *self* and the world, we know where the rapids are, where the leg-ups and leg-downs reside, and where the 'on' switches hide behind the curtains. When we are moving fluidly, synchronicities and opportunities flourish, and we notice how enabling the world can be. We are able to take risks and leaps and our lives begin to take the shape we want.

When we are fluid, we don't need a discipled gratitude journal to remind us of how lucky and gifted we are. Our life and all its facets are tangible evidence of our brilliance and we automatically and frequently feel blessed. And, when we feel grateful, we easily find energy to help *others* and the world.

What does a fluid person look like?

From the outside, a person living fluidly looks like someone who is getting on with their life, accomplishing things, having engaged relationships, and doing something meaningful with their time. They can look happy or at the very least satisfied with their lives. When we are not fluid we may even feel envy when we look at them.

The burdens and benefits of fluidity

There are some perils with being in a state of fluidity, they include trying to stay permanently fluid, and getting puffed up about being so brilliant (hubris).

When we try to stay perpetually fluid, we are in fact aiming at getting stuck in a permanent state of fluidity. Life needs to flow in a cycle with things changing, then stabilising, then stagnating, and then changing again. We need to flow with this cycle. When we are always fluid, we may not be able to consolidate and manifest the changes we have made. We may also risk losing our *self* by not knowing who we are in our rapidly changing identities.

The success of this stage can cause one to become arrogant or puffed up with hubris. It is always best to remember that this is just a time in our life and not our whole life, we will become stuck again and we will fail. Furthermore, we are likely to get even more stuck if we fixate on holding on to the us that is fluid now, rather than being with the us that we are becoming.

When we are fluid, we are adaptive and responsive to the world and, as we know, this does not last forever. So, while we are fluid and buoyant, we need to actually make any additional changes we may want, even if they are scary. This is our moment of opportunity when we must seize the day, enjoy life, and keep growing. The longer we can retain this fluidity by keeping connected to our *self*, *others*, and *meaning*, the more we can build a satisfying life.

Building a container for fluidity

Although I have provided quite a few tips on building fluidity in the previous chapters, there are also other things that we can do that can create and sustain fluidity. These include ideas about:

- Building a fluid approach to stuckness and fluidity.
- Holding paradoxes.
- Figuring out our context.
- Working with our body.
- Psychological, medical, meditation, and other approaches to support fluidity.
- Rituals to enable and support fluidity.

Building a fluid approach to being stuck and fluid?

The objective of building and retaining a fluid approach to stuckness and fluidity is to enable the Cycle of Stuckness to complete its revolutions of fluidity, consolidation, stagnation, stuckness, and then change. Furthermore, to enable these cycles to complete in an easy, and comfortable way for us, each part of the cycle is critical for us to grow; we cannot miss out any part.

By now we know the signs of emerging stuckness, and we may panic if we see our *self* living these out. Getting stuck is painful, but stuckness is necessary, so we should not panic and use up energy unnecessarily. We need to let things take their natural course. The trick here is to rest and look around, and figure out what is going on. Go chat to someone, build your *self*, and take a look at where you are getting *meaning* from. And conversely when you are fluid, don't get overexcited and alert the media, this too will pass. Notice and celebrate both stuckness and fluidity as signs of our ongoing growth and vitality.

Holding paradoxes

Paradoxes have appeared all over this book. When we experience these we should not try to solve them by throwing our *self* into one side of the binary. Paradoxes are meant to be managed and not solved, we need both sides. The trick here is to find out what is the right balance for you in the paradox. When we do this we get the value from both sides, and maybe even an integrated solution at some later date.

In the world of stuckness, the most important paradoxes that we need to hold include:

- Having a stable yet emergent inner world.
- Growing upwards (transcending our *self*) and downwards (being our human *self*).
- Being for our *self* and being for *others*.
- Creating *meaning* while knowing life is absurd and meaningless.
- Allocating shame to the past while taking responsibility for our future.
- Knowing we create our own narratives and trying to read the world as it is.
- Seeing the world as we are in it, and seeing the world as it is.

Figuring out our relationship to our context

By now we have realised that stuckness is a particular type of relationship with one's context. We can understand it as relating to a previous context, however, the relationship is still one of not taking in cues from the world in which we are participating. So, an important part of staying fluid is about the relationship we have with our context, even as it is changing.

We don't have to rush out and embrace the world, we just have to notice how big and interesting our context is, and maybe broaden this, even just a little. This can be as small as trying new foods, or as large as changing jobs. We are in control of our relationship with our context; decide how you want to engage but remember that full lives need full contexts to make them so.

We can decide that we have had enough of the world and reduce all the ways in which it can touch us, and this can be healthy sometimes. But know that we need the world to make life worth living and avoid becoming bored and stuck with our *self* in a small world where we stop growing.

Stuckness tends to bleed into a stuck person's wardrobe and home. Clearing out cupboards, moving pictures, shifting the furniture around, weeding the garden, throwing out clothes, and trying new looks are all excellent ways of supporting a more fluid life.

Working with our bodies

I have mentioned somatic work throughout this text, but want to reiterate its importance here. Somatic techniques can allow access to information that our heads may deny us. We can use a fluid and flexible body to build the ground for a fluid and flexible *self*.

Lastly, we need to build a safe relationship with our body. This means accepting it, not controlling it within an inch of its life, exercising it well but not too much, feeding it properly but not in a fascist kind of way, and responding to its needs for connection, rest, and excitement appropriately. And if we are not in a collegial relationship with our body, then find out why and do something about it.

Psychological, medical, meditation, and other approaches to support fluidity

A second head and pair of ears is always useful when we are stuck, and I would recommend getting a professional set for when we are stuck. However, friends and colleagues can also offer support and we will get the added bonus of getting closer to another.

We may need medical and psychiatric help as well. My only caution is that we need to feel to get out of stuckness and sometimes medicines can be narcotising. When we don't feel the pain, we may not be motivated to do something about it. However, if the pain is too much we may become frozen, it's a tricky balance. We have to learn to use medicines in the right way. Medicines alone cannot get us out of stuckness, we have to do the work our *self*.

Meditation and mindfulness are often seen as panaceas for a multitude of ills. Used well, they can help us feel our pain, process things, and motivate us to change. Used badly they can narcotise us into staying the same. This is of course a huge generalisation, but something to watch out for, nevertheless. This advice goes for plant medicines and hallucinogens such as MDMA. And don't do anything without the right safety, support, and flow through into life.[1]

Rituals to enable and support fluidity

Sometimes, non-psychological ways of healing and growing are the best approach to being more fluid. This is the reason that all cultures have rituals of some sort, although more traditional cultures often have better access to these tools. Rituals are useful for reflection, connection, commitment, and devotion. We can use them for purification and forgiveness, as well as for closures and grieving. They help define and create beginnings, strengthen us to act, and of course create vision and purpose.[2] Rituals also have incredible power in terms of reducing shame. These tools all support the rebuilding of our *self*, *others*, and *meaning*.

Supporting our fluidity as a coach

I have spoken at length about projections, connecting to our *self*, *others*, and *meaning* and how these can support or undermine our fluidity as a coach. Furthermore, how a contextual approach to coaching is always more effective than a completely intrapsychic one. Aside from giving an empathic view on how behaviours are created and sustained, it reduces shame by placing at least some blame outside the client, with its rightful owner – another context.

An important way to stay fluid as a coach is to join a learning community. Many coaches operate as sole practitioners and miss out on the learning and mutuality gained from interacting with other coaches.

Fluidity is enhanced when we as coaches take risks and are creative in session. Creativity allows us to tailor interventions to our client. It does, however, require humility so that we can easily accept the client's decision as to the relevance of our offerings or not.

Lastly, we as coaches need to be realistic about what we can achieve, after all our client spent a lifetime in creating the *self* they have now. We cannot expect them to move beyond this in three sessions.

How do coaches look and feel when they are fluid?

Fluid coaches roll with the client even as they sit with their own *self*. When we are fluid we can parallel process, think and feel about our client, and our response to the client at the same time. We can be in the world as we see it and also as it is. We can parallel process.

When we are fluid, we do less in sessions, we are more comfortable with silence and uncertainty, we allow our clients to unravel their own lives without jumping ahead of them and trying to look clever or helpful.[3] When we are fluid we don't star in our clients' lives.

Questions to ask your *self*

- What is your relationship to getting stuck, do you panic and flail around, or can you settle into the opportunity it presents?
- What rituals do you have in your life and how can you use them more effectively for your growth?
- Look at the people around you, how contextual are they? What relationship do you want to have with your context?

Notes

1 Safety: MDMA-Assisted Therapy 101 – MDMA Podcast # 18. (2024).
2 Thank you, Lucille Greeff, for sharing your experience and perspectives around rituals.
3 Kaufman, W. (1974). *Nietzsche: Philosopher, psychologist, antichrist* (REV-Revised). Princeton University Press; van Deurzen, E., et al. (2009). *Everyday mysteries: A handbook of existential psychotherapy* (2nd ed.). Routledge.

Bibliography

Kaufman, W. (1974). *Nietzsche: Philosopher, psychologist, antichrist* (REV-Revised). Princeton University Press.

Safety: MDMA-Assisted Therapy 101 - MDMA Podcast # 18. (2024).

van Deurzen, E., et al. (2009). *Everyday mysteries: A handbook of existential psychotherapy* (2nd ed.). Routledge.

Chapter 14

Growing in spite of our *self*

Are you tired yet? It has been a long and sometimes dense journey. I hope that as you read you drifted in and out of the theory, your life, and your clients' lives. My wish is that you were able to bring your whole world into the experience of reading this, and that this was useful to you. It's time to end now, and maybe your dopamine is waiting to kick in to reward you for completing this journey. However, closing is always slower and more important than we expect, so let us just review where we have been and how we can end this relationship well.

Summarising our journey as humans towards inner freedom

An existential approach

This book provides a largely existential approach that draws on a wide range of existential philosophers. Key thinkers informing this book include Heidegger, Sartre, Camus, Biko, Yalom, van Deurzen, and Spinelli. Existential philosophy helps us to live better given the circumstances we live in, and tells us about the nature of human existence. We are beset by slavery of all kinds, made anxious by death, bereft through isolation, and despairing through meaninglessness. Moreover, we are energised by freedom, inspired by death, universal and transcendent through *others*, and *meaning*.

For existential philosophy, the defining quality of a human is our ability to grow and learn and adapt. Objects cannot do this, and when we lose our capacity for adaptation we become like an object. The theme of becoming objects and objectivising *others* is threaded throughout this book.

The journey to fluidity is the journey of inner freedom. Freedom refers to the very real freedom that exists for us to do what we want to with our lives, but with this freedom we have the responsibility and anxiety of uncertainty, not knowing, and choice. This kind of freedom is frightening because it implies that there is no innate structure to our world, that we have to create it, and to do this, we need to make choices because even no choice is choice.

DOI: 10.4324/9781003536253-14

The value of stuckness in our lives

Stuckness is an impasse, caused by the presentation of an incomplete wound and the loss of *self*, *others*, and *meaning*. It is held in place by defensive behaviours that lock us into being stuck. When we experience the losses and our lack of traction in the world, we feel pain and this forces us to look inwards. When we do this well, we have a chance to process incomplete wounds, grow our *self*, our relationships with *others*, and *meaning*. Through this we can incubate a new future, one that is more satisfying to us and one that is more contextually appropriate. As such, stuckness is the engine of our growth and learning, and the creator of our future *self*. The existential purpose of stuckness is to make sure we adapt to life and are therefore able to survive and thrive.

The cycle of stuckness

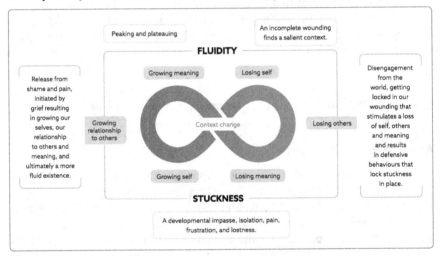

We are always in the Cycle of Stuckness. We grow into a context, we find our *self* effective in that context and our growth plateaus. Our behaviours then sediment, and we stop adapting to our changing context. This continues until the pain of stuckness wakes us up, and thrusts us back again into a cycle of growth and change.

Stuckness is always a stuck relationship with a context, be it an environment or other people. Contexts are forever changing and becoming more volatile. There are structural factors that enhance our chances of getting stuck and they include neoliberal sense-making, ubiquitous trauma, loss of community and humanity, inequality, and climate change.

If we are not able to adapt, then we risk becoming stuck. We may also make our worlds smaller so as to manage our anxiety. Arthur and Avril of the small world is the case study used to describe this.

The Cycle of Stuckness begins when an incomplete wound becomes present to us as we enter a salient context. This context reminds us, either consciously or unconsciously, of the pattern and nature of the incomplete wounding. Incomplete wounds are wounds that need our attention, they want to heal, discharge stuck energy, and through this help us create a more satisfying life. Incomplete wounds are ambitious and want more than just healing, they want to be integrated into our lives, and validated for what they can bring. For intergenerational types of wounding, they want to halt the progression of wounding with us.

To be able to take this freedom, we need to take responsibility for healing our wounding, even if we did not create it. It is the nature of the world that those who are hurt must take responsibility for their own healing. The wounders, be they people, systems, or events are less motivated to solve things. It is also the nature of the world that wounded people may in fact wound, and this includes us too.

When we re-enter the wounding, we re-enter the milieu of the original wounding, and this results in three losses, that of our *self*, *others*, and *meaning*. We also develop a host of defensive behaviours that keep us stuck.

When we lose our *self*, we lose our capacity to adapt and we become one-trick ponies, good for a coalmine or a circus, but never both. We lose our *self* by becoming bewitched, amputated, or dead. Case studies for these processes include those of Ashwin, Celia, and Angelique. There are also structural factors that increase our chances of losing our *self*, including oppression, trauma, and objectification.

When we lose *others*, we lose their humanising influence and the way in which they help define and grow our *self*. We do this by staying in less than useful attachment styles, by living in a castle, through trauma and addiction, and by treating *others* as objects. The stories of Horace, Alice, Solomon, and Harriet illustrate these processes. I also note structural factors that undermine engaged relationships, such as structural isolation, neoliberalism, and technology.

When we lose *meaning*, we lose our purpose and direction in life. We do this by not knowing how to make *meaning*, by making *meaning* that is not meaningful, by not having *meaning* in all the right places, and through trauma and addiction. Mohammed, Cas, Jane, and Li are the case studies for this. Capitalist Life Syndrome and trauma are cited as structural factors enabling this loss.

Our incomplete wounding, the three losses, and the resulting defensive behaviours mean that we do not have the capacity to adapt to the ongoing contextual change. We are now in a holding pattern that gets us nowhere, and this can go on for a long time. The experience of stuckness is one of frustration, confusion, anger, and *self*-criticism. We have an unstable and wobbly inner world that starts to dominate our thinking, rather than let us engage in our contexts.

To become more fluid in our relationship with our context, we must regain our *self*, *others*, and *meaning*. To regain our *self* more fully, we need to learn how to be a good companion to our *self*, build our capacity for discomfort and pain, and take our *self* less seriously. Ashwin, Celia, and Neville are examples of how this could work.

We rebuild our *self* through working on our *self* as well as deepening our connection to *others*; they help us to know and define who we are. We can regain *others* by understanding and working with our attachment styles, balancing too much and too little of *others*, letting *others* in, and by getting into *others*. Lastly, we regain *others* by treating *others* as humans. Horace, Gertie, and Harriet are the case studies for these processes.

Meaning can be developed by creating one's own *meaning*, by being less individualistic, by viewing *meaning* through the lens of life stages, and by ensuring that we have *meaning* in all the right places. Our case studies for this are Jane and Mohammed.

When we become more fluid, we grow and learn easily and continuously, and feel effective in the world. We notice where opportunities and synchronicities live, and are able to use these to our advantage. There are, however, a few cautions around being in this state. These relate to getting stuck in fluidity, or becoming puffed up with hubris at our own success because, as we know, fluidity never lasts.

Chapter 13 deals with how to be more fluid around stuckness and fluidity, so that the troughs and peaks are not so high. To build a container for a fluid life, we must take a relaxed attitude to stuckness, learn to hold and not solve paradoxes, figure out our relationship to our context, and create a safe inner world. We can use multidisciplinary approaches to do this, including rituals, and we must figure out how we want to relate to our context.

Pain, shame, and grief

When working with stuckness, we cannot avoid working with pain, shame, and grief. Pain is a valuable and elegant companion on the Cycle of Stuckness. It motivates us to change. If we narcotise or deny pain, we risk losing out on this valuable source of inspiration and action.

Shame is the feeling that we are defective and bad, it is different to guilt where we feel guilty about something we have done. Shame is not always useful in the Cycle of Stuckness because it reconnects us with our original wounding, and does not allow us to move beyond and around it. We have to find a way to move through or live around shame to grow into our future *self*.

Grief plays a critical role in the cycle. It allows us to mourn our stuckness and the unlived lives created by it. When we do this, our rigidity can melt and this allows us to reconnect with our *self, others,* and *meaning*. Grief can also be a cause of stuckness.

Summarising our journey as coaches towards fluidity

Being an existential coach

Chapter Two explores what an existential coach is, including some key interests for us. These are a focus on individuality, freedom, responsibility, and agency. We respect the roles death and endings play in life, and encourage authenticity even as we understand that *our* self emerges and changes. Despite these commonalities, existential coaches make idiosyncratic choices about the specific approach they follow. We prefer to build our own approaches and not take them shrink-wrapped off the shelf.

The value of stuckness for coaches

All coaches get stuck, in life and in their profession. It matters less how often and how deep we get stuck. What matters more is that we use our stuckness as a growth point and not a dead end. We should use it to kickstart our learning and growth, get us out of bad habits, and enable better outcomes for clients. Stuckness brings the gift of more life and *meaning* to our work. This is something we all want.

The cycle of stuckness for coaches

We can become stuck in coaching for many reasons, including a good old-fashioned personality mismatch. We get stuck when we don't bring our *self* into coaching instead offering a *tabular rasa* or airbrushed version of our *self*. When we do this, we could seduce our clients into doing the same. We also miss out on the humanising impact of our own humanity.

The coaching relationship can be magical, with capacity for all sorts of transformation. Our first duty is to sustain this bridge between our *self* and our client. When our work as a coach is not meaningful, this can impact on our commitment and courage to be with the client. We can also be tempted into using our clients as objects of revenue, like Harriet did.

The journey towards fluidity for coaches is the same as that of humans. There are, however, additional aspects that I have emphasised over the course of this book. These relate to knowing our *self* deeply, working with our woundings and our projections, keeping our *self* contextual, and making sure our work is meaningful. In this way we can have a better chance of seeing our clients as they are, not as we are.

When we become stuck, we are less effective at coaching, and can begin to doubt our skills, feel less satisfied with engagements, and even wonder if this really was the career for us. When we are fluid in coaching, we work less hard, are more comfortable with silence, and allow the client to set the pace. We do not jump in ahead of clients, but walk alongside them.

Working with stuck clients

The entire book provides guidance on how to work with stuck clients. I have also described how to identify physical, linguistic, and psychological behaviours that point to stuckness.

There is, however, one case study on Shawn and Sara that speaks directly to working with stuck clients. This case study warns us to stay out of the gravitational pull of stuck people, to stay on the bank and think clearly. This is very hard to do and we need regular supervision to enable this.

Working with contexts in coaching

Working with stuckness is always working with a context. This is because stuckness is a relationship issue, it is not just intrapsychic.

We are always working in and with a context. This includes the historical contexts embedded within our *self* and clients that created our way of being. When we are contextual in this way, we can reduce shame and *self*-criticism because we can allocate these emotions appropriately to an external context. Shame holds stuckness in place and any intervention that can reduce this is useful. We must, however, not do this at the cost of the client avoiding responsibility.

The contexts for our work can be supportive or undermining of our clients. They can also be bad faith contexts where coaching is purchased as a performative step. In these instances, we as coaches need to be creative and find ways to support clients to take their freedom. Fanon advises that we should not enable clients to adapt to an oppressive situation, but rather to enable them to choose their freedom within it. This is an important distinction to make.

It is important for coaches to manage the context for coaching. This means paying attention to the coaching frame and how the client responds to this. It also means building a structured process for ending the engagement.

Contexts create behaviours, and if we keep this in mind, we can use them to support our clients' growth. We can suggest that clients change contexts because this can prompt a change in thinking and behaving.

Lastly, we as coaches can use our clients as salient contexts for working with our own wounding. However, when we do this, we run the risk of confusing our own story with that of the client. We need to understand our *self*, including our own projections and narratives, to be an effective coach.

Working with paradoxes in coaching

When we work with client paradoxes, we should not attempt to resolve them to one side of the polarity. We should help clients value and get the best out of both sides. This is a more appropriate response to polarities, and may in fact create an integrating solution at a later date.

The most critical polarities we should seek to manage in coaching include:

- Supporting our client to have a stable yet emergent inner world.
- Guiding clients towards growing upwards (transcending our *self*) and downwards (being our human embodied *self*).
- Thinking through with clients their approach to being for them *selves* and being for *others*.

- Helping clients create *meaning* even while knowing life is absurd and meaningless.
- Allocating shame to the past while taking responsibility for our future.
- Knowing we create our own narratives and trying to read the world as it is.
- Helping our *selves* and our clients to see the world as we/they are in it, and as it is.

Death, trauma, and addiction

You will notice death, trauma, and addiction recurring throughout this text. These are leading causes of wounding and loss of *self, others*, and *meaning*. Stuckness related to these factors can require very specific interventions, ones that may be outside the remit of a coach. We can, however, work alongside a specialist therapist.

The duty of self-care for coaches

I have already spoken to the need for us to know our *self*, just in case it decides to behave mischievously in a session and project onto a client. I want to reiterate this and mention again that all coaches need to have therapy and supervision. A significant majority of coaches do not do this and this severely undermines their capacity to be effective.

We also need to keep growing and learning, and can use professional bodies to enable us. These bodies should be relevant to the context in which we work, and not lead to the homogenisation of coaching. A diversity in methodologies and approaches enables coaches to be more contextual.

Burnout is a very real possibility for coaches because our work can be emotionally and mentally exhausting. We should therefore include *self*-care as part of and not separate from our professional activities.

You will grow in spite of your *self*

And one last shot across your departing bows, a gift perhaps?

I know I have said a lot in this book about what we can do to have a more fluid relationship with stuckness and fluidity. What I am going to say now does not undermine this, instead it can support the actions we take in this regard.

The comment I want to make is that the process of regeneration is built into our DNA and soul. We and our clients will, in most cases, eventually, get out of stuckness. Furthermore, we may do this despite our stuck *self*. We humans are built for growth and this will kick in when our survival and thrival is threatened. We sometimes just need to back off and let intrinsic ambitions towards a better life take over. I think you may have noticed in the case studies that when people stepped into their lives, the world responded supportively with synchronicities and opportunities.

Ending our conversation

My not-so-secret objectives for this book were to encourage you and me to be our *self*, connect with *others*, and live meaningful lives. Trauma, shame, and grief are not good enough reasons to foreclose on our birthright of being our *self*. Living beyond trauma and grief are entirely possible, and it's never too late to grow around and beyond our historical and current lives. We are an ambitious and resilient species after all.

I would also like to remind you that our relationship to our *self* is the source of our relationship to all humanity. When we have a safe, supportive, and fluid inner world, we can offer this to *others*. The source of my humanity is the source of your humanity, I cannot be human without you being human too.

Index

Please note that page numbers in *italics* represent a figure.

abandonment 66–67, 88, 102
absurdity 137, 143; life 35
abuse 33, 66–67, 89, 108–109, 128;
  see also neglect
accommodation 41, 102
adaptive capacity 15, 44, 62, 93
addictions 3, 11, 15–16, 70–72, 86–88, 98,
  109, 111, 124, 136, 155, 158–159; cycle
  17; meaning of 88; programmes for
  16; shopping 86–88
agency 2, 12, 73–74, 127, 156; loss of
  28, 49
alienation 49
amputation 9, 39, 42, 44, 46–47, 54–55,
  102, 110, 115–116, 155; bewitchment
  and 47; losing and 47, 59; types of
  49–50
anxiety 2, 9, 13, 28–29, 43, 52, 58–59, 83,
  86, 94, 98, 108, 111, 114, 128,
  153–154; death 9, 153
anxious-ambivalent behaviours 67, 76, 127
anxious-avoidant behaviours 67, 76, 127
anxious-disorganised behaviours 67
assimilation 41, 102
attachment: patterns 67–68, 75–76, 125,
  127–128, 131; styles 33, 65, 67, 155
attention deficit disorder (ADD) 5
attribution error 25
Aurelius, M. 111
authenticity 2, 39, 65, 75, 81, 84, 156

becoming stuck 3–4, 9, 53, 61, 71, 148,
  153, 157
behaviours 1, 25, 30, 34, 41–43, 60,
  73–74, 76, 154; changes 128; context

and 25, 158; creating 61, 151;
  defensive 15, 93, 154–155; fixation 75;
  human 20; monitoring of 26; old 34,
  103, 108; other people's 25; patterns
  of 34, 41; psychological 157–158;
  racially oriented 119; repeating 34, 98;
  stuck 7, 33, 104; survivalist 39;
  sustenance of 151; unproductive 2
Berger, J.G. 6
bewitchment 9, 39, 42, 44–47, 53–55, 62,
  102, 106, 116, 155; amputation and
  47; losing and 44, 47
Biko, S. 1, 49, 153
blame 11, 19, 28, 42, 61, 65, 69, 94–95,
  109, 127, 151; internalising 81; others
  108, 114; self 94, 104, 106, 109
body, human 12
boredom 59, 81, 83, 89
bullying 11, 16, 29, 37, 65–66, 90–91
burnout 91, 142, 159

Camus, A. 80, 153
Capitalist Life Syndrome 81, 84
childhood 29, 34, 42, 66–68, 71, 84, 87,
  103, 112, 142; painful 66
choice 8–9, 13, 17, 21, 31, 34, 50, 75, 81,
  103, 105, 115, 120, 153, 157;
  avoidance of making 21; freedom and
  115, 158
climate change 29–30
coaches 98–99; context and 30–31, 60;
  existential 12–13; self, loss of 55;
  self-care for 159; stuckness and 156;
  types of 13
colonialism 53, 72

community 11, 28, 45, 53, 58, 62–63, 70, 72, 81–82, 124–125, 133–134, 144, 151, 154; loss of 154
companionship 9, 48, 62, 85–86, 131
compulsions 1, 18, 34
context 24–25, 57; bad faith 31; behaviours and 158; changes 57, 60, 158; childhood 42; coaches and 30–31; genetics and 40; salient 14–15, 34, 36, 61, 93, 155, 158
continuity 2
courage 13, 36, 42, 74, 79–80, 89–90, 102, 107, 113, 137–138, 157
curation of self 116
Cycle of Stuckness 4, 18–19, 24, 34, 36–37, 57, 62, 74, 113, 146, 148, 154–157

death 9–10, 12, 25, 46, 52, 60, 71–72, 81, 86, 94, 124, 128, 130, 159; anxiety of 9, 153; confronting 11; engaging with 37; experiencing 88; grief and 11; philosophy and 109; premature 64; relationships, influence on 76; role in life 156; transcending 79, 136
defeat, self 1
dehumanisation 63, 72
digestion 3, 34
dignity, humanity, in 126
disconnection 3, 43, 61
disorientation 59, 93–94, 110
distraction 1, 37, 69, 83, 88, 98, 112–113

early life 33, 42, 45
education 13, 27–28, 50–52, 56, 64, 81
ego 39
emergence 8, 98
empathy 25, 71, 73, 98, 127; fluidity and 25
Enneagram 6
ennui 11, 25, 115
entitlement 113, 115–116, 118; relationships and 116
epigenetics 40
existential: coach 12–13; orientation 2

fallibility 10, 68
Fanon, F. 2, 31, 158
fear 9, 52, 58–59, 67–68, 93–94, 97, 105, 113; death, of 9; hurt, of 129; isolation, of 9; people, of 128; self, of 109
feedback 15, 17, 75, 102–103, 113, 128

financial success 45–46, 74
fluidity 4, 5, 16, 43, 98, 105, 107–108, 146–148; empathy and 25; enhancement of 151; freedom and 153; moving towards 3–4, 157; supporting 151; stuckness and 2–3, 7, 156, 159
frailty 10, 58, 102–103
Frankl, V.E. 80
freedom 2, 9, 127, 153–154, 156, 158; choice, of 115, 158; ingredients for 9; fluidity and 153; types of 2
Freud, S. 18, 34, 55, 111
frustration 3, 4, 15–16, 20, 30, 93, 155

gaslighting 54
genocide 72, 140
gestalt 6
globalisation 26, 28, 64
grief 2, 10–11, 54, 71, 89, 95, 98–99, 104, 130, 156, 159; death and 11; pain and 10, 16; pattern 12; stuckness and 11–12, 93, 156; unresolved 34
grieving 3, 16, 33, 71–72, 88, 93, 99, 103–104, 125, 130, 136, 151
growth 4–5, 8, 19–20, 27, 63, 76, 83, 99, 105, 113, 124, 128, 138, 149, 151, 154, 158–159; capacity for 27; economic 28; humanity and 21; individual 62; non-psychological 150; post-traumatic 29; spiritual 47; stuckness and 19, 156
guilt 11, 14, 94, 98, 129, 156; see also shame

healing 4, 10, 12–13, 18, 33–35, 61, 80, 103, 113, 120, 125, 137, 155; non-psychological 150
Heidegger, M. 34, 153
hermeneutic circle 18, 34
holding pattern 1–2, 155
hope 36–37, 138
hopelessness 16, 90, 109
human body 12
humanity 2, 5, 9–10, 13, 27, 55, 63, 74–75, 103–104, 126, 133; dignity in 126; growth and 21; loss of 26, 28–29, 154, 157, 160; self and 102
humility 10, 25, 75, 118–119, 121, 151

identity 6, 40, 44–45, 49–50, 53–55, 59, 64–65, 73–74, 97, 103, 107, 116, 118–120, 139; inner 121; multiple 84
imperfection 42, 65, 108

individualism 28, 62, 64, 118, 139
individuality 2, 6, 13, 62, 74, 127, 156
inequality 28; social 26–27
integrity 75
intimacy 9, 129
isolation 9–10, 12, 37, 67–68, 71, 74, 85,
    87–88, 125, 153; fear of 9; losing and
    74; pain of 69; social 64; structural 64,
    155; wounding from 34; *see also*
    loneliness

judgement 19, 25, 49, 65, 84; shame
    and 25
Jung, C. 18

Kierkegaard 1

learned inferiority 120
life: doing 9; early 33, 42, 45; loss of 130;
    meaning of 3
loneliness 10, 29, 47, 62, 64, 94, 125, 141;
    see also isolation
losing: amputation and 47, 59;
    bewitchment and 44, 47; inner world,
    connection with 43; isolation and 74;
    meaning 4, 20, 74, 81, 83–84, 86, 89;
    others 4, 20, 62, 68, 70, 72, 74, 127;
    pain and 93; place 49, 59; self 4, 20,
    27, 42–43, 50, 54–55, 57, 84, 102, 129,
    147, 155; stuckness and 57
loss 4, 11–12, 15–17, 54, 80, 88, 99,
    103–104, 154–155, 159–160; agency
    28, 49; community 154; confidence 99;
    grieving 103–104; humanity 26, 28–29,
    154, 157, 160; life 130; meaning 33,
    80, 83, 88; others 33, 63, 124;
    relationships 125; respect 28; self 33,
    42–44, 49–50, 73–74, 88, 93; stuckness
    and 93; weight 46
lost, feeling 3, 52, 71, 82, 89–90, 93;
    see also loss

making sense of: life 39; psyche 27;
    world, the 26, 61, 88, 108
material success 11, 46
materialism 28
Mbembe, A. 1
meaning 10, 91, 144; addiction, of 88;
    creating 137–138; distribution of 86;
    experiencing 80; finding 131; life,
    of 3, 79; loss of 33, 80, 83, 88,
    136–137; making 39, 41; why of life,
    the 79

meaninglessness 9–10, 12, 37, 95,
    138, 153
meditation 35, 47, 138, 142, 148, 150
mental health 5, 27–29, 81
misogyny 52
Murthy, General 64

neglect 33, 55; *see also* abuse
neoliberalism 26–28, 46, 64, 72, 86, 117,
    154–155
Nietzsche, F. 13, 95

objectification 53, 64–65, 72–74, 155
oppression 46, 50, 53, 108, 120, 155;
    inner 49; racial 31
orientation 6–7, 31; Camus 80; coaching
    13, 133; dis- 110; existential 1–2;
    Freudian 34; homeostatic 134;
    religious 141; Winnicott 18

pain 3, *4*, 9–11, 15–16, 20, 36, 43, 47, 54,
    66–67, 80–81, 86, 97–98, 111–115,
    118, 128, 132, 141, 150, 155–156;
    capacity for 104–105; grief and 10, 16;
    hiding from 120; isolation and 69, 74;
    life, of 101; loss and 93; management
    112; processing 54; relationships and
    89; shame, of 94; stuckness and 94,
    148, 154
peaking *4*, 17–18
perfectionism 11, 35, 65
perspective 8, 42, 94, 118, 134; coach 8;
    human 8, 24
philosophy 6, 13, 39, 53, 80, 110, 126;
    death and 109; existential 153; goal of
    9
Piaget, J. 41
plateauing 1, 17–18, 20, 154
play 119, 126
pleasure 10, 28, 43, 87, 107, 109, 126,
    128, 138, 144
positivism 13
post-traumatic growth (PTG) 29
post-traumatic stress disorder (PTSD)
    29, 71, 85
poverty 25, 28–30, 33, 44, 46–47, 116
prayer 35, 104, 138
predisposition 46
psyche 27

racism 15, 17, 25, 29, 31, 49
redemption 3, 11
reflection 18, 103, 150; self 8–9, 41–42, 53

relationships 3, 9, 17–18, 52, 64;
    accountability 74; chaotic 67; closing
    of 75; container for 125; context and
    24; death and 76; engaged 63–64, 71;
    entitlement and 116; neediness in 75;
    self 101; skills 44–46; stressed 28–29;
    stuckness as an issue 18, 157; trauma
    and 29
religious hatred 53
remediation 30, 127
repetition compulsion 18, 34
respect 30, 44, 49, 63, 91, 116, 126, 156;
    loss of 28, 125
responsibility 2, 9, 17, 19, 26–28, 61, 81,
    91, 104–109, 114–115, 127, 142, 149,
    153–154, 156, 158; avoiding 158
righteousness 11
rupture and repair 18, 35

sacred dance 35
salient context 14–15, 34, 36, 61, 93,
    155, 158
scapegoating 74, 94; wounding from 34
self: care 35, 91, 129, 159; criticism 109;
    curation 116; defeat 1; fear of 109;
    humanity and 102; loss of 4, 33,
    42–44, 49–50, 73–74, 88, 93; reflection
    8–9, 41–42, 53; relationship with 101;
    sense of 9; shame 102
sense of self 9
sexism 15, 31
sexuality 26, 50
shame 3, 10–11, 16, 28, 35, 46, 54, 61, 74,
    94, 102, 104, 106, 108–109, 149–151,
    156–159; healthy 11; judgement and
    25; physical 94; self 102; stuckness
    and 11; toxic 53, 109; working with
    125; see also guilt
shopping addiction 86–88
social inequality 26–27
social media 64–65, 72, 83–84, 139–140
somatic: coaching 6; intervention 12;
    work 35, 47, 104, 150
Spinelli 1, 153
spiritual growth 47
spirituality 35, 39, 47, 80–81, 89, 138
stereotyping 53, 69, 74, 113

stuck: becoming 3–5, 16, 18–19, 97,
    147–148, 151, 153, 156; behaviours 7,
    33, 104
stuckness 1–2; advantages of 3; causes of
    3; climate change and 29–30; Cycle of
    4, 18–19, 24, 34, 36–37, 57, 62, 74,
    113, 146, 148, 154–157; fluidity and
    2–3, 7, 156, 159; grief and 11–12, 93,
    156; growth and 19, 156; losing and
    57; loss and 93; pain and 94, 148, 154;
    peaks and troughs of 5; relationships
    and 18; shame and 11
submission 132
suicide 9, 11
supervision 19, 55, 60, 73, 99, 115,
    157, 159
survival 62, 80, 124, 159; behaviour 39;
    mechanism 62, 98; species, as a 5
survive and thrive 18, 25, 48, 126,
    154, 159

tabular rasa 55, 133, 157
technology 26, 28, 63–65, 155
transcendent function 18
transformation 5, 8, 74, 76, 108, 125, 157
trauma 12–15, 26, 28–29, 33–34, 50,
    53–54, 64–65, 70–71, 80, 86, 88, 98,
    104, 124, 136, 154–155, 158–159

uncertainty 9, 26, 29, 59, 112, 151, 153
urbanisation 64

van Deurzen, E. 1, 13, 153
van Deurzen-Smith, S. 13
violence 11, 29, 70, 72
vision 3, 147, 150
void, the 10, 89–90, 94–95, 136
Vos, J. 1, 80–81

weight loss 46
Winnicott, D.W. 18, 104
wounding 2, 4, 4, 14–18, 33–35, 37,
    92–93, 98, 104, 113, 137, 154–158;
    incomplete 33–34; isolation and 34;
    scapegoating and 34

Yalom, I.D. 1, 153

Printed in the United States
by Baker & Taylor Publisher Services